USING AN INCLUSIVE APPROACH TO REDUCE SCHOOL EXCLUSION

Clear and accessible, *Using an Inclusive Approach to Reduce School Exclusion* supports an inclusive approach to teaching and learning to help schools find ways to reduce exclusion and plan alternative approaches to managing the pathways of learners at risk.

Offering a summary of the contemporary context of DfE and school policy in England, this book considers:

- Statistics and perspectives from Ofsted

- The literature of exclusion and recent research into effective provision for learners with SEN

- The key factors underlying school exclusion

- Case studies and practical approaches alongside theory and research

- The impact of exclusion on learners at risk

Written by experienced practitioners, *Using an Inclusive Approach to Reduce School Exclusion* encourages a proactive approach to reducing exclusion through relatable scenarios and case studies. An essential toolkit to support the development of inclusive practice and reduce exclusion, this book is an invaluable resource for SENCOs, middle and senior leaders.

Tristan Middleton is Senior Lecturer in Education and Joint Course Leader for the MA Education suite at the University of Gloucestershire. Tristan is an experienced primary school class teacher, Senior Leader, Special Educational Needs Coordinator and designated teacher for both safeguarding and looked-after children. He also ran a nurture group for seven years. Tristan is Chair of Directors of Leading Learning for SEND CiC which oversees the work of the National SENCO Award Provider Partnership and also a member of NurtureUK's Research, Evidence & Ethics Trustee Sub-Group.

Lynda Kay is Senior Lecturer in Inclusion/SEN and Joint Academic Course Leader for the MA Education suite and the PG Cert NASENCO at the University of Gloucestershire. Lynda is an experienced primary school teacher, SENCO, designated teacher for safeguarding, Senior Leader and local authority specialist SEN advisory teacher. Lynda is Vice Chair of Directors of Leading Learning for SEND CiC which oversees the work of the National SENCO Award Provider Partnership Working Group. Lynda is studying for a PhD – her research is focused upon exploring effective pedagogy for children with speech, language and communication needs who present with challenging behaviour in primary schools in England.

Other titles published in association with the National Association for Special Educational Needs (nasen):

Using an Inclusive Approach to Reduce School Exclusion: A Practitioner's Handbook
Tristan Middleton and Lynda Kay
2019/pb: 978-1-138-31691-1

Supporting SLCN in Children with ASD in the Early Years: A Practical Resource for Professionals
Jennifer Warwick
2019/pb: 978-1-138-36950-4

How to be a Brilliant SENCO: Practical Strategies for Developing and Leading Inclusive Provision
Helen Curran
2019/pb: 978-1-138-48966-0

Successfully Teaching and Managing Children with ADHD: A Resource for SENCOs and teachers, 2ed
Fintan O'Regan
2018/pb: 978-0-367-11010-9

Brain Development and School: Practical Classroom Strategies to Help Pupils Develop Executive Function
Pat Guy
2019/pb: 978-1-138-49491-6

Essential Tips for the Inclusive Secondary Classroom
Pippa Whittaker and Rachael Hayes
2018/pb: 978-1-138-06501-7

For a full list of titles see: www.routledge.com/nasen-spotlight/book-series/FULNASEN

USING AN INCLUSIVE APPROACH TO REDUCE SCHOOL EXCLUSION

A PRACTITIONER'S HANDBOOK

Tristan Middleton
and Lynda Kay

Routledge
Taylor & Francis Group

LONDON AND NEW YORK

First published 2020

by Routledge

2 Park Square, Milton Park, Abingdon, Oxon, OX14 4RN

and by Routledge

52 Vanderbilt Avenue, New York, NY 10017

Routledge is an imprint of the Taylor & Francis Group, an informa business

British Library Cataloguing-in-Publication Data
A catalogue record for this book is available from the British Library

Library of Congress Cataloging-in-Publication Data
Names: Middleton, Tristan, author. | Kay, Lynda, 1963– author.
Title: Using an inclusive approach to reduce school exclusion: a practitioner's handbook/Tristan Middleton and Lynda Kay.
Description: Abingdon, Oxon; New York, NY: Routledge, 2020. | Includes bibliographical references and index.
Identifiers: LCCN 2019018998 | ISBN 9781138316898 (hardback) | ISBN 9781138316911 (pbk.) | ISBN 9780429455407 (ebook)
Subjects: LCSH: Inclusive education – Great Britain. | Children with disabilities – Great Britain. | School improvement programs – Great Britain. | Education and state – Great Britain.
Classification: LCC LC1203.G7 M53 2020 | DDC 371.9/0460941—dc23
LC record available at https://lccn.loc.gov/2019018998

ISBN: 978-1-138-31689-8 (hbk)
ISBN: 978-1-138-31691-1 (pbk)
ISBN: 978-0-429-45540-7 (ebk)

Typeset in DIN Pro
by Apex CoVantage, LLC

Printed and bound in Great Britain by
TJ International Ltd, Padstow, Cornwall

CONTENTS

Contents

ACKNOWLEDGEMENTS

Lynda and Tristan would like to thank those colleagues, students and additional contacts who have shared their experiences and stories with us, to support the development of this book. We would also like to thank our colleagues at the University of Gloucestershire for their support and encouragement and in particular Hazel Bryan for her facilitation and positiveness towards this project. Thank you also to Liz Ramshaw, Adam Boddison and Tina Rae for their valuable feedback on our first draft.

Tristan would also like to thank his friend Lesley Newman for her inspiring approach to education and all she taught him about inclusion over the 16 years they worked together. He would like to thank Lynda for providing him with the opportunities to join her on a range of projects and for being a valuable writing partner. Finally, he would like to thank his family for their ongoing support, both practical and emotional, and enabling him to follow his passions.

Lynda would like to thank Chris Taylor and Richard Gasser for their encouragement and faith which started her on this journey. She would also like to thank Sally O'Hare and Julie Brooks for their inspirational and ethical perspectives on inclusion, and for all they taught her in the time they worked together. In addition, Lynda would like to thank Tristan for his unfailing patience, listening ear, positivity and for being an invaluable and incisive partner, in this and other projects. Finally, Lynda would like to thank her family for their encouragement, love and for their understanding over the long hours she spends hunched over texts and the computer.

FOREWORD

Exclusion from school – either informal or formal, temporary or permanent, can and does have negative effects upon children and young people and their families, reinforcing vulnerabilities and difference – particularly for those with additional learning, social or mental health needs and, ultimately, reduces their life chances.

This is a timely and much needed book given the increase in exclusions as a means of managing behaviour in schools. The challenge for practitioners is to see the issues from a 'different lens'. Whilst this may initially appear to be a somewhat daunting task, the authors ensure that the solution focused approach they advocate is accompanied by reflective questions and prompts. This is underpinned by a collegiate approach underpinned by the values of social justice alongside a range of evidence-based resources and activities to achieve better outcomes for all children and young people.

The authors initially encourage a reflection upon relevant policy and the impact upon the classroom. This is vital. As practitioners, we need, more than ever, to critically reflect how we do/do not adopt policies which influence what we do in schools – notwithstanding the constraints of time and financial pressures. I would argue further that given such constraints, it remains more important than ever before that we only adopt policy and practice that really works for all and increases the life chances of all our young people. Understanding the historical and political perspectives and agenda is critical to the development of the thinking teacher who needs to identify 'best practice' and how the policy will impact upon the delivery of the curriculum, behaviour and performance in the learning context. The authors rightly challenge the reader to consider key reflection questions posed and this is a powerful and safe means of generating debate and clarifying personal and shared perspectives and understandings. They also explore some of the challenges to leading on such inclusive practice, presenting their own theoretical framework of the six dimensions of inclusion: Learning and difference, social justice, human rights, empowerment, creativity, humanism and praxis. The need for us all to adopt such a principled approach – particularly in the current challenging political and economic climate resonates throughout.

However, the authors do not leave us without the necessary resources to deliver on such a key agenda. This is another real strength of the book – the wealth of targeted and individual strategies and programmes and the unique approach to guiding the practitioner with a framework of questions to use when gaining an understanding of such interventions and how to implement them in the school context. The framework for practitioners to support their reflections is a particular strength.

This is an accessible, user friendly and beautifully written book underpinned by thoughtful and systematic research. The clever combination of theory and practice and the challenging of practitioners to engage in the process of reflection whilst also presenting a wealth of creative ways to promote the learning and wellbeing of all children and young people makes this a unique publication. It is also, in my view, essential reading for all staff in schools and those who really care about 'real' inclusion.

Dr Tina Rae
BA (Hons) PGCE MA(Ed) MSc
RSADipSpLD ALCM DipPsych Doc App Ch Ed Psy

FOREWORD

Inclusion and exclusion are complex concepts that continue to have a significant influence on school education. As part of my role as Chief Executive of nasen (National Association for Special Educational Needs), I am fortunate to have the opportunity to visit schools regularly and to learn more about their particular approaches to inclusion. In some schools, inclusion and exclusion are referred to as opposite ends of the same spectrum, but increasingly the inter-relationship between these concepts is expressed as being dynamic and contextual.

When Tristan and Lynda asked me to write this foreword, I was immediately struck by the relevance and timing of a book to support practitioners to reduce exclusions by using an inclusive approach. With a portfolio spanning research, teaching and professional development, Tristan and Lynda are well placed to bring this important area of our education system to life.

I often make the comment that professionals working in schools are generally working in this sector because they want to make a positive difference to all learners. They don't typically wake up in the morning with the intention of being non-inclusive or excluding learners from our education system. However, the many competing demands, pressures and tensions mean that non-inclusive practice and school exclusions happen too often.

Tristan and Lynda have taken great care in this book to present the concepts of inclusion and exclusion from a broad range of perspectives and to position them with a wider historical and political context. This is important because the current views about inclusion and exclusion do not exist in a vacuum and have been developed both over time and across the sector.

I sometimes describe nasen as a champion, friend and protector of the SEND community and so a key part of our role is to support wider activity that is aligned to these aims. In the latter part of this book, Tristan and Lynda have been proactive in exploring strategies that could reduce school exclusions and so I would actively encourage you to think about how you can use this book as a force for good in your own school.

Dr Adam Boddison
Chief Executive – nasen
Chair – Whole School SEND

POEM

Difference

Being independent
Doesn't mean doing everything
Alone. If only they taught that
In school, between missed spellings
And late papers.
If only they let us breathe, open our hearts
Like night-capped flowers
To the moon, the first great singular
Lady, who learned from the tides
That difference
Means freedom, means flowing back and forth
To parallel rhythm not
Marked in red ink against the black faced lie
Of normal.
If only the difference in our souls and
Minds and hearts
Beat their little unformed patterns
Like baby waves on the shore
Of adolescence,
Unbridled by the terror of falling
Some unspoken
Unwritten rule
Of co-dependence to the tides of masses.

This poem was commissioned from Beth Calverley of The Poetry Machine at the Womad Festival, Charlton Park, Wiltshire in July 2018. It was written immediately following a short discussion about inclusion in education.

HOW TO USE THIS BOOK

This book has been created to act as a resource for a range of practitioners, as well as those interested in an academic perspective of the issues of educational inclusion and school exclusion.

There are five distinct parts to this book and depending on the reader's role, interests and needs, it can be read from start to finish or parts and chapters may be selectively read in any order. To help readers navigate their reading of the book, the content and purpose of each part is laid out in the next sections.

Part I

This provides the current context of school exclusion in England, providing information about policy and practice which is relevant to the topic of exclusion, clarifies definitions pertinent to the topic and explores the impact which school exclusion can have on children and young people, families and schools, with a particular focus on Special Educational Needs and Disability. This part will be useful to practitioners and students who are interested in developing their thinking about, and understanding of, the topic of exclusion.

Part II

This part focuses on the topic of educational inclusion. It explores current literature about inclusion and explores a range of ideas and definitions of inclusion in education. The authors present their own theoretical framework through which to understand and evaluate inclusive practice, before moving on to explore the practical implications of implementing an inclusive approach in schools. This part will be useful for practitioners and students who are interested in developing their thinking about, and understanding of, the topic of inclusive education.

Part III

This part provides practitioners with ideas and explanations about a range of programmes and approaches which could be used within a framework of inclusive practice in order to support schools to reduce exclusion. In order to support the reader's understanding of these approaches, we have included explanations of the theoretical underpinning of these approaches and programmes, as well as further reading and resources which can be explored. Practitioners may wish to use this part as a resource to inform their thinking about ways to develop practice in their settings.

Part IV

This part is intended as a resource for practitioners to use either as individuals, in practitioner groups, or as whole schools. It provides a range of questions, linked to the authors' framework for an inclusive approach, which will support practitioners to reflect on their practice and consider the developments they can make in moving towards a more inclusive approach.

Part V

This concluding section provides the reader with further ways to develop and widen thinking about inclusion and exclusion in schools. It looks beyond inclusion and SEND, reflecting upon the current education landscape in England. This section will be of interest to practitioners and students who are interested in exploring how practitioners might find effective ways to navigate the challenges they encounter when seeking to take an inclusive approach.

INTRODUCTION

Exclusion is a topic which has received much attention within news reports, social media and other forums in recent times. Much of the dialogue has debated the negative impacts of exclusion upon children and young people who are excluded from school, their families and the wider community. Whilst, exclusion is a sanction which may be used by schools, government statistics, news reports and anecdotal evidence suggests that exclusion is being used with greater frequency by schools within their toolbox of behaviour management strategies. Statutory guidance (DfE, 2017a, p. 6) advocates that permanent exclusion is a sanction to be utilised in circumstances in which significant issues around health and safety issues and behaviour have been identified. Permanent exclusion is at the most severe end of the range of strategies under the exclusion spectrum; a spectrum which includes temporary exclusion and less formal measures, such as internal exclusion. Whichever format exclusion is employed within, it may be argued that this conveys that for children and young people with special educational needs (SEN) their needs have not been met. Additionally, it is of huge concern that recent data from the Department for Education (DfE) identifies that exclusion for children and young people with SEN 'had the highest permanent exclusion rate and were almost 7 times more likely to receive a permanent exclusion than pupils with no SEN' (DfE, 2017b, p. 6).

Further concerns arise from the acknowledgement that exclusion, whether permanent or temporary, impacts negatively upon the learner, their families and wider society. This may be in relation to one or more of the dimensions of social relationships, emotional wellbeing and mental health, progress and achievement, attitudes towards school and education, economic factors and behaviour and criminality. Thus, it is vital to work to develop inclusive practice within the setting so that each learner's needs are met and the use of an exclusion measure is significantly reduced or eradicated.

This book examines the wider context of exclusion and the negative impact exclusion has over a range of dimensions for the learner, their families and wider society. It explores a range of perceptions of how the notion of inclusion may be defined and operationalised. The authors draw upon the construct of 'spaces' proposed by Dyson, Gallannaugh and Millward (2003, p. 238) which they suggest are 'occupied by (relatively) inclusive values and approaches'.

We contend that inclusive practice is about finding those spaces and working to develop and make the most of those spaces in order to design pedagogical approaches to meet the diverse needs of learners. These are not physical spaces, rather the notion of spaces which we are presenting relates to practitioners working collaboratively to find opportunities for reflective thinking and debate to inform developing practice. The spaces may be elicited from creative approaches to reframe circumstances which may initially appear insurmountable. One approach to facilitating this is through the formulation of questions to support practitioners with looking at the issue from another standpoint or through a different lens. This will be supported by operating the space as a safe place in which practitioners can engage in critical reflection and dialogue in order to challenge their own and other people's thinking. This enables approaches and solutions to be identified which may not have previously been considered. The scenarios in the following paragraphs seek to illuminate this notion of spaces further; we present some scenarios to stimulate reflection upon how this may be enacted within schools or settings.

The contrasting rhetoric surrounding the drive to increase standards, inclusion and accountability within schools may appear to open a great chasm between what appear to be disparate policies. However, intertwining the dialogue within these policies facilitates finding a space underpinned by values of social justice in which practitioners can work together to adapt pedagogical approaches to support all children and young people to develop skills to become independent adults.

Many of our children and young people with SEN needs, and their parents and carers, experience difficulties with articulating their views about their experiences, needs and aspirations. The use of creative approaches to support people who are not using their voice to make their voices heard, such as changing the venue for meetings with parents and carers or using visual strategies with children and young people, creates spaces in which parents, carers, children and young people are empowered. In this way, learners and their families are included within assessing (gathering information), planning decision-making and reviewing to support learning, progress and positive outcomes.

In this book we use the term 'SEN' to describe children and young people experiencing specific barriers to their learning and 'SEND' to describe the area of policy related to SEN. This choice of terminology was made in order to reflect the current approach in policy and guidance documents, for example, the SEND Code of Practice (DfE, 2015), which uses the terms 'SEN' and 'SENCO'.

Sometimes, the nature of the metrics and assessment tasks used to judge learners' attainment and progress (and indeed the performance school or setting) appears an unsurmountable mountain for children and young people with SEN to be able to showcase their knowledge and skills. Adopting a broader view in which different types of achievement are valued and celebrated and a range of modes of assessment are employed embodies spaces in which difference is valued. Additionally, this is supportive of developing a broad and balanced curriculum for all children and young people.

Introduction

The challenges from the economic climate have influenced changes in the availability and access to support services. One perspective which has been frequently articulated is this has set up challenges for schools and settings that are experiencing difficulties with meeting needs of children and young people with SEN. Whilst there are plenty of reports and anecdotal evidence of experiences which are supportive of this perspective within the educational landscape, there are alternative stories which have been shared with us by practitioners. In some places, the economic climate has stimulated creativity and entrepreneurship for schools to join together to share expertise, resources to collaboratively solve problems. In this way, space is created and used for joint thinking to support inclusion.

There have been many policies introduced in education that schools and settings are required to implement. The operationalisation of policy offers opportunities for the creation of spaces for inclusive values to be the lens through which policy is interpreted and incorporated into practice. The professional development school teams engage in to support their understanding and implementation of a focused policy, facilitates the formulation of spaces for dialogue in which to relate inclusive approaches to social justice and values. This has the purpose of influencing senior leaders' attitudes and actions.

Schools sit within their wider community. It may appear that schools are a reflection of the wider and local society's views in relation to community and mutual support and acceptance. Through the activities schools engage in with (or to reach out to) their communities, the opportunity is created for spaces in which schools can be at the vanguard of developing values and to make a difference. This may be through actions, dialogue, modelling positive attitudes and adopting empathetic approaches towards members of the community.

This notion of spaces and the solutions that are facilitated through the spaces in their various formulations offer hope that we are able to find inclusive values-based approaches to meeting diverse needs and reduce exclusions.

In this book, we present our theoretical framework for inclusion which underpins the practical strategies presented. Practical strategies are set out for headteachers, SENCOs, teachers and teaching assistants to support and inform planning and enactment of pedagogy to meet the learner's needs. This is also accompanied by reflective questions and prompts to support practitioners with analysis of their practice and issues within their own settings, together with signposting to further sources of support. The aspiration is that in working together collaboratively within these spaces for inclusion, we can achieve better outcomes for all children and young people.

References

Department for Education (DfE). (2015) *Special Educational Needs and Disability Code of Practice: 0 to 25 Years. Statutory Guidance for Organisations Which Work With and Support Children and Young People Who Have Special Educational Needs or Disabilities. DFE-00205–2013*. London: DfES. Available at: www.gov.uk/government/publications/send-code-of-practice-0-to-25 (accessed 24 February 2015).

Department for Education (DfE). (2017a) *Exclusion From Maintained Schools, Academies and Pupil Referral Units in England: Statutory Guidance for Those With Legal Responsibilities in Relation to Exclusion*. Available at: www.gov.uk/government/uploads/system/uploads/attachment_data/file/641418/20170831_Exclusion_Stat_guidance_Web_version.pdf (accessed 18 December 2017).

Department for Education (DfE). (2017b) *Permanent and Fixed Period Exclusions in England: 2015 to 2016*. Available at: www.gov.uk/government/statistics/permanent-and-fixed-period-exclusions-in-england-2015-to-2016 (accessed 18 December 2017).

Dyson, A., Gallannaugh, F. and Millward, A. (2003) 'Making space in the standards agenda: Developing inclusive practices in schools'. *European Educational Research Journal*, 2(2), pp. 228–244.

PART I

Within the busy life of a school it is difficult to find the time to reflect upon education policy and legislation and debate the impact this has upon the classroom. The focus is more often upon mediating the policy within the everyday life of the school. This section of the book presents a distillation of policy and legislation in relation to inclusion and exclusion and aims to create the space for you to reflect upon how policy and legislation influence and frame practice in schools.

Chapter one
BACKGROUND CONTEXT TO EXCLUSION

Defining exclusion

Exclusion is the severest punishment that schools may implement and is frequently associated with disruptive or challenging behaviour (Kane, 2011; Munn, Lloyd and Cullen, 2000; Pomeroy, 2000). The Department for Education's (DfE, 2017) statutory guidance uses the phrase "barred from school" within its explanation of exclusion (DfE, 2017, p. 56).

Thus, exclusion may be understood to be an enforced banishment from school (Kane, 2005; Cooper *et al.*, 2000). Interestingly, Hodkinson (2012, p. 678) describes exclusion as a "forced absence of children from their classrooms" during which they are not perceived to be the responsibility of the teacher.

We were interested to note that in many discussions of exclusion within literature an explanation of how this term might be defined was not offered, hence the reader's understanding of the concept appeared to be assumed.

Our definition of exclusion

Exclusion is a sanction which may be employed by schools, within the remit of school leaders and governors. Exclusion means that learners are banished from attending school or from learning or social activities with their peers within the school environment.

Schools may implement the sanction of exclusion as a fixed-period exclusion, in which a length of time for which the pupil is excluded is set out, or a permanent exclusion from the school's roll. Within the sanction of fixed-period exclusion, schools may also exclude children and young people for a period of the day, such as for lunchtimes over an identified period of time. Statutory guidance for exclusion is provided by the DfE (2017). The term exclusion is used within sanctions of formal, informal and internal exclusion. Informal and internal exclusion will be explored within Chapter 2.

It should be noted that the sanction of exclusion is included within earlier legislation. Changes made to legislation over time included amendments made to terminology and the tariffs for fixed-period exclusions together with prohibiting indefinite exclusion. Legislation also placed a requirement upon schools to inform parents of exclusion together with the rationale for the decision and the right of appeal together with the appeal procedures was introduced. The tariff of 45 days across the school year was set out by the 1996 Education Act.

The information within the next section does not present a comprehensive review of the legislative framework. The focus of this flowchart is to present information pertinent to inclusion and exclusion.

The legislative framework influencing exclusion (1997–2018)

1997 UK Government affirmation of the Salamanca statement

In 1994 a world conference was held in Salamanca in Spain; the focus was upon special educational needs (CSIE, 2018). There were 92 governments and 25 international agencies represented at the conference, the conference set out a statement, The Salamanca Conference Salamanca Statement (UNESCO, 1994), and a Framework for Action. The framework sought to work for the inclusion of children and young people with disabilities and diverse and disadvantaged backgrounds. This promoted the notion that education is a basic right for all children and young people and that pedagogical approaches to meet diverse needs should be enacted within educational settings (CSIE, 2018; Rix and Simmons, 2005). The statement advocated that mainstream schools using inclusive practices provide effectual education for most children and young people and facilitate constructing communities in which all people are accepted and valued (Rix and Simmons, 2005). The affirmation from the UK government to the Salamanca Statement was evidenced within policy, such as Excellence in Schools (DfEE, 1997; Glazzard, 2013).

This is pertinent to exclusion in light of the DfE's statutory guidance for exclusion which identifies that challenging behaviour may be a communication of a learner's needs not being fully met (DfE, 2017, p. 6).

1998 School Standards and Framework Act	The 1998 act introduced measures related to class sizes within infant classes, discipline and targets relating to school attendance and rates of exclusion. This act also set out arrangements for school admissions and related appeals, including for children and young people with statements of SEN. The act also included home-school agreements. This act was followed by initiatives seeking to raise standards and improve outcomes for children and young people. These included National Childcare Strategy (1998), Sure Start programme (1999), Excellence in Cities (1999), reductions made to the statutory National Curriculum (1999) and the National Literacy and Numeracy Strategies (1998). These two national strategies set out programmes of study, pedagogical approaches and expected standards of attainment for specific age groups. In 2000, Curriculum Guidance for the Foundation stage set out guidance for teaching and learning linked to the early learning goals which had been published in 1999 (Ball, 2013).
2001 Special Educational Needs and Disability Act (SENDA) and SEN Code of Practice 2001	This act sought to encourage and develop inclusion. It outlawed discrimination to pupils with SEND within a school's admission policy (Tomlinson, 2005). A revision of the SEN Code of Practice was introduced which included advice for practice and guidance on processes for educational professionals across schools and other settings and for local authorities (Forrester and Garratt, 2016; Tomlinson, 2005). This was supplemented in 2004 with the introduction of the Inclusion Development Programme (IDP) which provided professional development and resources for educational practitioners to support inclusive practice (Forrester and Garratt, 2016). In relation to exclusion, this act and IDP were aimed at supporting schools to meet diverse needs (including challenging behaviour).

2002 Education Act

The 2002 Education Act was informed from the 2001 White Paper: Schools – achieving success. Schools were allowed to be innovative in teaching approaches if this would have a positive impact upon standards (Tomlinson, 2005). This act set out the terms under which schools could employ fixed-period or permanent exclusion and required alternative education to be provided from the sixth day by the school in the case of fixed term exclusion and the local authority with respect of permanent exclusion in addition to requiring governing bodies to review the headteacher's decision and setting out processes for appeal (Parkes, 2012). The Foundation Stage was brought within the National Curriculum. This act also placed an obligation on schools to seek pupils' views (Ball, 2013).

2006 Education and Inspection Act

A code of practice for school admissions was also introduced by the Education and Inspection Act 2006 in order to constrain selection of pupils by schools. This act also extended the range of schools available in order to increase the availability of schools classified as good for those from areas of disadvantage (Ball, 2013). The 2006 act placed a requirement upon local authorities to offer support to parents and carers to help with choosing a school for their child.

In relation to exclusion, the act extended parent–school agreements to increase parental obligations to ensure their child's positive behaviour in school (Ball, 2013). Parents were held responsible for excluded children and young people and could be fined if their child was found in a public place when excluded or if they should have been attending schools. The act set out circumstances under which an application could be made to the magistrates for a parenting order (DfES, 2006, sections 97, 98 and 99).

2010 Equality Act

The 2010 Equality act prohibits all educational institutions from discriminating between pupils on the grounds of disability, race, sex, gender reassignment, pregnancy and maternity and religion or belief. This relates to admissions, pupils enrolled including those on fixed-period exclusions and any pupils who are no longer enrolled but have a continuing relationship with the setting. The law sets out how direct and indirect discrimination may be identified and reaffirms the duty for reasonable adjustments to be made (including auxiliary aids and services) for disabled current and prospective pupils. The act also defines harassment and victimisation. (CSIE, 2018)

2010 Academies Act and 2011 Education Act

These acts continued the drive to expand academies, through initially enabling outstanding schools were to apply for Academy status and introduced new school provisions of studio schools, University Technical Colleges (UTCs) and Free Schools (Forrester and Garratt, 2016).This was driven by the continued belief that academies facilitated improved standards for all pupils, including vulnerable and disadvantaged learners. Although Academies are given the sanctions to be able to control their own budgets, their curriculum and employment of unqualified staff, Forrester and Garratt (2016) suggest that these sanctions are held in check by the measures used to ensure accountability to which all schools are subject. The 2011 act gave powers to headteachers and senior leaders in pupil referral units for fixed-period or permanent exclusion and set out processes for appeals panels.

2012 The School Discipline (Pupil Exclusions and Reviews) Regulations

This guidance set out the legal obligations for all those who may exclude children and young people from maintained schools, academies and pupil referral units in England. This gave power to headteachers/Senior Leaders to exclude and set out processes for appeals with an independent panel. The statutory guidance brought in new regulations to ensure that students with SEN and other vulnerable groups are handled fairly. Children and young people were to be facilitated to take part in all of the processes of exclusion. Appeals panels were to have an SEN expert to advise them. In addition, there were financial penalties for the school to be paid to the local authority in the case where an independent review panel recommends that the decision be reconsidered (DfE, 2012). The 2012 regulations remain unchanged – the role of the school's governors gained greater emphasis within the 2017 guidance; this guidance seeks to clarify areas of potential confusion and Annex C was provided to provide advice for parents and carers.

2014 Children and Families Act & 2015 SEND Code of Practice

The 2014 Children and Families Act made changes to safeguarding and child protection, adoption, services for children and young people and families including childcare for children and young people with SEN. Statements of SEN were replaced with a single assessment process and the introduction of an Education, Health and Care (EHC) Plan with the extension of age range to 0–25 years. This act places parents/carers and children and young people at the centre of planning as they are to be included in discussion and decision-making. In addition, information about local services have to be communicated clearly in a local offer and made available to parents/carers. Services for children and young people are to be commissioned jointly by health services and local authorities. The right to request a personal budget is also identified. The changes introduced by this act were focused upon enhancing parental confidence in the systems and improving long-term outcomes for children and young people.

The SEND Code of Practice (CoP) (DfE 2015) sets out guidance for procedures for assessment and planning of provision for children and young people with SEN for educational settings and local authorities and places emphasis on the class/subject teacher's responsibility for learners with SEN. SENCOs are required to have qualified teacher status (QTS) and to have successfully completed their new qualified teacher induction. Within three years of appointment they must gain mandatory NASENCO Award (DfE, 2014). This is a postgraduate (level 7) qualification for SENCOs. There were two editions of the SEND Code of Practice (CoP); the initial CoP implemented in 2014 was updated in 2015, the main changes were related to arrangements for children and young people with SEN detained within the Youth Justice system.

2015 Mental Health Code of Practice

This is pertinent to exclusion in relation to actions that schools may apply within the process of internal exclusion. In the Mental Health Act Code of Practice the use of seclusion is identified as being potentially traumatic and having, 'adverse implications for the emotional development of a child or young person' (Department of Health, 2015, pp. 26, 57). This guidance goes on to outline that such 'restrictive interventions' should only be used as part of a positive behaviour support plan where there has been input from the child or young person and their family (Department of Health, 2015, pp. 26, 53).

2015 & 2017 Statutory Guidance on the exclusion of pupils	Guidance was issued in 2015 and 2017 on the implementation of the regulations set out in the 2012 act. The guidance sets out the legal obligations for all those who may exclude pupils from maintained schools, academies and pupil referral units in England. Headteachers are required to avoid permanently excluding pupils with EHC Plan or looked after children (children in care) (DfE, 2017, section 23, p. 13). Headteachers are also required to immediately notify parents of the reasons and provided written information about the exclusion and the process of appeal. This information is to include that during the time before alternative arrangements for education are started the pupil is not to be 'present in public place any time during school hours' (DfE, 2017, section 29, p. 15). Alternative arrangements for education during the fixed-period of exclusion or permanent exclusion must be made to start at least from the sixth day. As before, financial penalties are set for the school to be paid to the local authority in the case where an independent review panel recommends that the decision be reconsidered and the pupil is not reinstated (DfE, 2017, p. 41).

Education Policy in England 1997–2018: contextual influences upon inclusion and exclusion in schools

Policy is never monolithic but the tension between two aspects of policy – inclusion and exclusion – seem particularly stark.

(Kane, 2011, p. 16)

Education policy is subject to frequent change and the development of policy is influenced by a range of interacting influences drawn from components such as culture, social, political, economic, technological factors and religion. Forrester and Garratt (2016) and Ball (2013) propose that policy should be considered in terms of being a manifestation of the process of these interacting components rather than a fixed artefact, such as a policy document. It is important to note that education policy is inevitably closely related to the philosophy or beliefs of the proposers of the specific policy. Thus, in examining education policies which have been introduced over time, it is possible to identify a range of influencing beliefs, attitudes and values which influenced the development of those policies (Forrester and Garratt, 2016; Slee, 2011). It is also important to note that there may be variance in the discourse between the initial articulation of a policy and the enactment of that policy (Ball, 2013). There may be further changes observed as the policy is implemented, owing to the varying ways in which the policy is interpreted. Thus, the operationalisation of policy may not be the same as the purpose informing the initial policy (Forrester and Garratt, 2016; Ball, 2013; Slee, 2011).

So why are we including information and analysis of policy in this book about inclusion and exclusion?

This is because the wider policy context has an influence upon inclusion and exclusion through the changes which impact upon schools directly and the broader environment in which they operate (Brodie, 2001). Thus, many aspects of classroom practice are directly affected by local and national policies which have been influenced and developed by a range of factors as discussed in the previous paragraph.

Since at least the Second World War, the political discourse from all major parties has embodied the notion of a key purpose of schools being to educate children and young people for their future roles thus ensuring a strong competitive economy for the country (Waugh, 2015; Munn, Lloyd and Cullen, 2000). This suggests that academic standards have been held at the centre of political discourse in relation to education over a long period of time (Hayden, 1997). From 1997 onwards there have been frequent changes and reforms within education. Indeed, education policy remains at the forefront of policy within the UK and internationally owing to the link made between economic output and success within global markets. While many of the policies which have been implemented in England have been emulated in other countries, there have been influences from other countries upon English education policy (Ball, 2013). This includes the US (e.g. the notion of charter schools) and Sweden (e.g. free schools). Other influences have come from organisations such as the World Bank, Organisation of Economic Co-operation and Development (OECD) and the European Union (EU) through the inclusion of policies such as quasi-markets, quality assurance and the notion of education providing a business opportunity (Ball, 2013).

Knowledge economy

The link made within policy between education and economic output can be observed through the increasing use of the term 'knowledge economy' within discourse about education. Ball (2013) proposes that this term refers to the importance of the positive influence of knowledge upon learning, skills and organisation within invention and creativity and thus upon manufacturing. Ball suggests that the World Bank's support for education within developing countries in order to develop a well-trained workforce to facilitate economic success exemplifies this notion of the link between knowledge and improved economic output being enacted in education policy. Education is thus being examined through the lens of economic enhancement. This is important to reflect upon in light of the policies which have sought to direct different aspects of schooling, such as curricula, standards and accountability.

Policy related to inclusion

Inclusive schooling is a social movement against educational exclusion.

(*Slee and Allan, 2005, p. 15*)

The term 'inclusion' arose from the social model of disability and was put forward by the disability movement (Hodkinson, 2012). The models of disability will be further discussed in Part II, Chapter 1. Inclusion plays a central role in government policy and is based on the principles of fairness, equality and human rights (Cowne, 2003; Alisauskas *et al.*, 2011). This is a substantive area; lots of national and government policies have influenced the way inclusion has been shaped. We present here a short distillation of policy related to inclusion and SEND from 1997 onwards.

There were policies and legislation prior to 1997 which did ensure that local authorities assessed the needs of children and young people with SEN, provided mainstream support and offered parents and carers of these children and young people choices in where they were educated. However, it is interesting to note that within the 1981 Education Act local authorities were offered what may be considered to be an opportunity to continue segregation, owing to the inclusion of the requirement that integration should make efficient use of government resources and that it should not damage the progression of other children and young people (Denziloe and Dickens, 2004). This presents an interesting conceptual qualification in that neuro-typical children and young people's needs could be seen as being prioritised over those with SEN.

This propensity was challenged within the 1994 UNESCO Salamanca Statement with the declaration of the rights of the child to be included in mainstream society and education. This is significant because it moved the discourse away from a dialogue of integration and placement of children and young people with SEN away from mainstream schools, and placed an emphasis upon challenging mainstream settings in relation to their acceptance, accommodation and participation of children and young people with SEN (Slee, 2011). Other elements which influenced the changes in government policy at this time include the civil rights movement which demanded equality for people with disabilities and challenged attitudes and processes within society, which were prejudicial together with changes within professional perceptions of the impact of segregation for children and young people with SEN (Forrester and Garratt, 2016; Hodkinson, 2016). International impetus for change was provided not only through the Salamanca Statement but also though other actions, such as an earlier convention, the United Nations Convention on the Rights of the Child (UNCRC) (1989) and the goals set within the Education for All programme (2000) (Forrester and Garratt, 2016).

From 1997, the reforms of education throughout the last decade of the twentieth century sought to widen inclusion within mainstream schools and increase the capacity of mainstream schools to meet the needs of children and young people with SEN (Hodkinson, 2016). The New Labour government policies were formulated within a social inclusion agenda based on the values of community, inclusion, fairness and social justice (Forrester and Garratt, 2016). The principles from the Salamanca Statement were embedded in law in the 2001 SEN and Disability Act (SENDA) (Smith *et al.*, *2014*). This policy remains the dominant legal policy around SEN; there have been adjustments to this in further legislation over time. It made illegal discrimination (active or accidental) which disadvantaged disabled people and required that reasonable adjustments be made in order to enable their fullest participation to the fullest degree possible. The dual system of mainstream and specialist provision continued within a discourse advocating wider inclusive practices (Forrester and Garratt, 2016). This has been argued to place limits upon inclusion and continue segregation (Hodkinson, 2016).

Concerns raised by Ofsted (2004) increased the focus upon the differences in the quality of provision for SEN in mainstream schools and influenced further policy developments which linked with the Every Child Matters (DfES, 2004) agenda to advocate closer collaboration between agencies to remove barriers to achievement for vulnerable groups of children and young people (Forrester and Garratt, 2016). This included a focus upon intervening early and professional development for teachers. A national programme, Inclusion Development Programme (IDP), which aimed to increase knowledge and expertise within schools for meeting needs of learners with SEN was developed by the Department for Education.

The debates about inclusion and SEN are wider than explorations of the function of education. The debates also reflect upon the disconnections and reconnections between specific groups and their communities over time. These changes are influenced by the prevailing perceptions of SEN and practice in education, health and care. It is interesting to observe that the debates surrounding inclusion and SEN are more than just questions of the function of education. These perceptions may include a medical model in which the focus is upon the within-person deficits or a social model in which the focus is upon adjustments made to the environment and within societal attitudes and actions. For practitioners, this frames a question regarding whether the influences of inclinations towards segregation or integration might still be underlying inclusive dialogues and practice.

The National Curriculum introduced by the government, which has been subject to revision, is aimed at meeting needs and ensuring all children and young people have a broad curriculum. It gave the appearance of government being dedicated to the notion and ideology of inclusion. However, whilst the rhetoric is supportive of inclusion and indicated that it is a strong value within education, the implementation of the national curriculum in practice was hindered by problematic definitions and conceptions of inclusion.

The education workforce has been subject to restructuring since the early 2000s to support the aspirations for inclusion and standards (Forrester and Garratt, 2016). One aspect of this was the introduction of teaching assistants (TAs) who have had a variety of job titles and professional roles within the classroom. The number of TAs has increased substantially over time (Webster, Russell and Blatchford, 2016). One of the key roles assigned to TAs has been supporting children and young people with SEN, with both academic and social aspects of school. A number of research studies have identified concerns about the quality of deployment of teaching assistants, isolation of children and young people with SEN from their class or subject teacher and their peers and the quality of pedagogical approaches for these learners (Webster, Russell and Blatchford, 2016). This sets up issues regarding whether all learners have high and appropriate expectations set for them within their learning environment.

Government policy post-2010 has sought to encourage the development of diversity with the education market place in order to offer wider choice to parents and meet the diverse needs of learners (Forrester and Garratt, 2016). This has led to an increase in the number of academies and other schools (such as free schools) which are not under the control of a local authority (Chitty, 2014). These schools are, however, obligated to adhere to legislation related to SEND and equality.

The 2014 Children and Families Act placed children and young people with SEN and their parents or carers centrally within planning for the child or young person, aiming to change the existing culture within schools, settings and local authorities (SEND CoP, DfE, 2015, 6:52). This policy was informed from research (such as Lamb Enquiry [2009] and Ofsted report [2010]) (Tutt and Williams, 2015), which identified parental frustrations and lack of confidence in the existing system, conflations of SEN and poor progress, and low expectations of learners with SEN (Glazzard *et al.*, 2015). Within the changes introduced the SENCO is presented as holding a strategic leadership role for SEN within schools and settings and the recommendation was made that SENCOs should be part of the senior leadership team. The implementation of this recommendation has been varied, possibly influenced by the priorities held by school leaders and possibly linked to there being no legal requirement to include SENCOs within senior leadership. Schools and settings are required to follow a graduated approach to meet needs related to SEN, with the key responsibility for the individual child or young person's progress being held by the class or subject teacher (Tutt, 2016). The statutory assessment timeline was reduced. Statements of SEN were replaced by education, health and care plans. The definitions of SEN and SEN provision remained unchanged and the categories of SEN needs was adjusted with the replacement of Behaviour, Emotional and Social Difficulties (BESD) to Social, Emotional and Mental Health (SEMH) needs in recognition of the necessity to examine needs which underlie presenting behaviour. Some analysts have expressed the view that the new CoP and legislation place a renewed emphasis on individual difference (or dialogue of deficit) rather than adaptations of the environment in which learning takes place (Forrester and Garratt, 2016). Trussler and Robinson (2015, p. 39) note that for children and young people with SEN, the 'right to a mainstream education was neither reduced nor strengthened'. Perhaps this may be a reflection of the finding within the Ofsted (2010) report which stated that no specific model of setting was more effective than other models. Tutt (2016) contends that there is a need to clarify the language and terminology related to inclusion, SEN and disability and the new legislation provided the chance to do this, but was unfortunately missed.

Inclusion has become defined and controlled by the government's agenda of accountability, performativity and standards; it has been argued that this accountability has pushed an emphasis upon narrow concepts of attainment and performance (Dyson, Gallannaugh and Millward, 2003).

In this chapter, we discuss the impact of the themes in Figure 1.1 within education policy on approaches to inclusion and exclusion.

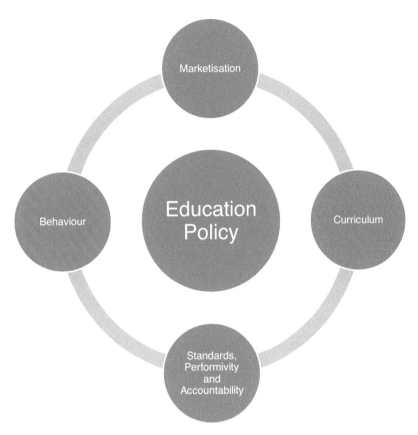

Figure 1.1 Four themes within education policy

Education as a market place

Prior to 1997, during the 1980s and 1990s the focus of social and public policy changed from social-democracy to neo-liberal philosophies; neo-liberalism advocates the utilisation of market forces for the supply of services and resources (Forrester and Garratt, 2016; Adams, 2014). This is predicated upon the belief that those who provide services are influenced by the market – their success is reliant upon meeting expectations of their consumers in an efficient (cost-effective) way. Thus, those service providers who do not operate efficiently or meet consumer requirements will have to close their business. The belief that this mechanism enhances efficiency and quality of services, together with the notion that individuals have responsibility for their own wellbeing, underpins the idea that the free market enhances allocation of resources (Adams, 2014). This neo-liberal approach was combined with neo-conservative beliefs with different weightings accorded to each of these two philosophies within policy at different times.

Neo-conservatism

Neo-conservatism seeks to rejuvenate a strong state and authority together with traditional moral values through the medium of government intercession (Forrester and Garratt, 2016). This focus upon tradition aligns with a belief that those teaching methods which may be considered progressive lead to a reduction in standards within education.

During the 1990s government policies were developed to reduce the role of the state within education and introduce market forces within the education sector. This development brought closer alignment between the education department and policy changes within other departments; this was a significant move from previous policy approaches which had accorded education a degree of independence from other areas (Ball, 2006; Brodie, 2001). Brodie (2001) notes that this alignment of policy across departments was maintained by the Labour governments which followed.

Quasi-market

Market forces within education have at their foundation the conceptualisation of schools and settings as individual businesses, rather than being part of a cohesive whole. This encapsulates the components of competition, choice and movement, success and failure and reducing centralised controls over admissions (Ball, 2013). The marketisation introduced within the education sector is described as being a 'quasi-market' owing to the fact that state schools provide education free of charge and are not-for-profit organisations (Hayden, 1997).

Supporters of the quasi-market focus upon the notion of competition positively influencing effectiveness, independence and efficiency of schools (Ball, 2006, 2013). Ball (2006, 2013) argues that the effects of implementing the quasi-markets within education have led to decisions being underpinned or informed from self-interest for both educational settings and parents and carers/learners making choices. Thus parents and carers making choices of schools for their children are influenced to behave as consumers which may change their approach to selecting and interacting with the school. This philosophy perceives parents and carers as being a homogenous group who all have an interest in their child's education and the social capital to make an informed choice of school, in addition to there being a feasible range of options of schools available (Forrester and Garratt, 2016). In our professional experience this is not always the case, and choosing schools is often a complex process which may be fraught with anxiety for parents and carers. Choice may be thus played out in a variety of ways for different families, influenced by economic and geographical factors (CSJ, 2016; Wright, Weekes and McGlaughlin, 2000).

Social capital

The OECD defines social capital as 'networks together with shared norms, values and understandings that facilitate co-operation within or among groups' (Scrivens and Smith, 2013, p. 41).

Scrivens and Smith (2013, p. 9) identified four focus areas within the concept of social capital:

- Personal relationships (networks of people known to the individual and the nature of the social interactions between them).

- Social network support (resources available to the individual through their social network; this may include emotional, material, practical, financial, intellectual or professional factors).

- Civic engagement (the activities people engage into support civic and community life; this may include activities such as volunteering, political participation and group membership).

- Trust and cooperation (this refers to a variety of forms of trust including trust in other people and in institutions in addition to the shared values which underlie the operation of society).

Ball (2013) draws upon several research studies and identifies that market forces may influence the values of the schools, such as understating their inclusive practice in order to ensure that students with potential to achieve good attainments are attracted to the school.

Likewise, this may influence schools to deter potential children and young people who may negatively influence the way in which the school is perceived publicly, such as those who are less likely to attain well or present with complex needs including challenging behaviours (Pomeroy, 2000). The notion of choice of schools for children and young people from disadvantaged backgrounds and/or with SEN is thus subject to further complexity.

Ball (2006) suggests that one potential outcome of introducing market forces and thus competition within the education sector has led to the reduction of mutual support between settings. Whilst this aspect of competition makes cooperative working less apparent, postgraduate students who are headteachers, SENCOs, teachers and other practitioners have reported to us that the more recent challenging economic environment, which has led to cuts in support services, is engendering a more cooperative spirit between schools. An example of this is a cluster of schools working to support one another with developing areas of skill or expertise. It may be argued that this could be another outcome of market economy as the schools trade services in skills ('we can support this if you do X for us').

Curriculum

Prior to 1997, greater central control over the curriculum commenced through the introduction of a National Curriculum for all state schools in England and Wales by the 1988 Education Act (Waugh, 2015). This presents a contrast in approach to the reduction of central control for schools with the introduction of market forces. The National Curriculum set out core and foundation subjects with identified programmes of study and expected levels of attainments for knowledge, understanding and skills within each subject, to be assessed by teacher assessment and external assessment. These are commonly referred to as Standardised Assessment Tasks or Tests (SATs), however, recent government publications appear to be moving away from this terminology towards "National Curriculum tests" (STA, 2018). Alongside the National Curriculum, there were subjects including health education, environmental education and economic awareness to be taught through cross-curricular themes. Each subject's programme of study was constructed by a committee to ensure breadth and depth. However, critiques of the curriculum argued that there had not been sufficient consultation with teachers and that the associated bureaucracy and assessment procedures and the amount of content were disproportionate (Waugh, 2015). Many teachers teaching at this time will remember the numerous folders containing the programmes of study and other information for each subject sent to schools for each teacher. Initially teaching methods were not prescribed, but this was set to change.

From 1997 onwards tighter controls from government were implemented (Forrester and Garratt, 2016). The Labour government elected in 1997 maintained the National Curriculum and introduced further direction through the National Literacy Strategy (NLS) and the National Numeracy Strategy (NNS). These strategies set out not only programmes of study and attainment targets but also aimed to guide pedagogical approaches through the imposition of the structure of literacy and numeracy hours with elements such as the amount of time allocated to each section of the lesson and whole-class and small group teaching approaches. The Independent Review of Early Reading (the Rose Review) was set up and the recommendations of the review were adopted and implemented by the government. These were implemented into the Teacher Standards 2012 and into teacher training programmes and checked through Ofsted inspections (Forrester and Garratt, 2016; Waugh, 2015)

The Cambridge Primary Review examined the quality of the primary curriculum, publishing their findings at the same time as the Rose Review. The Cambridge Primary Review criticised government policy and identified that the curriculum was overloaded; the review recommended that the curriculum should be restructured (Adams, 2014). Whilst these recommendations were not implemented by the government, the labour government did end the National Strategies in 2010 and proposed that the National Curriculum be revised (Waugh, 2015).

The 1987 Green Paper which proposed the National Curriculum only included a brief reference to SEN; this was amended within the Education Act to make allowances for the curriculum to be modified or adapted for some learners to be disapplied from this curriculum. Munn, Lloyd and Cullen (2000) propose that there was little guidance with regard to modifying or reducing the curriculum for children and young people with SEN provided for teachers. They contend that often greater focus is placed on the potential for learners to be at a disadvantage if they have reduced access to parts of the curriculum, and that anxiety about external judgements on this matter influences decision-making with regard to this in schools.

Performance and accountability

Economic discourses are appropriated and transformed into 'pedagogic discourse'.

Ball (2006, p. 132)

Ball (2006) contends that the relationship between the state and education has changed so that the focus of the state changes its mode from purely supplying education to that of regulation. In this respect the state sets out market conditions in which settings operate and appraises their achievements. This can be observed within the increased centralisation and control enacted by successive governments.

Over time, there has been an increased focus from the government on factors which can be measured and then appraised and this has become embedded within policy. These are all devices used to steer reforms within education (Ball, 2013). Ball (2006) contends that this suggests a change in ethical thinking around education in that focus is placed upon effectiveness, efficiency and public image at the expense of beliefs and values.

Performativity is a culture or a system of 'terror'.

(Ball, 2013, p. 57)

Ball (2013) presents the philosophy of performativity as being immersed within metrics and setting of goals to inform judgements about performance and what is valued or deemed to demonstrate quality. The actions which are employed within the processes of reviewing performance may be argued to be directed at managing performance. These processes impact upon the amounts of time being used to gather or produce the evidence and potentially upon the nature of the pressure and relationships experienced by all involved. In respect of the consideration of inclusion and exclusion, this focus upon performance and accountability may lead to feelings of there being differences in key values or priorities between leadership and classroom practitioners (Ball, 2013). An example of this might be the leadership appearing to be most concerned with influences upon the school budget and the public perception of the school, whereas the classroom practitioner appearing to feel their priorities lie with planning teaching and learning activities, meeting diverse needs of their learners and related administrative tasks.

The increasing focus placed on attainment to inform judgements including teacher appraisal has been argued to be encouraging practitioners to focus on deficit models of diverse needs (within learner deficits), rather than reflecting upon how to make adjustments in their approaches/learning environment (Glazzard, 2011; Hall et al., 2004). Additionally, within the changes introduced in response to policies aimed at raising standards, the value placed on social relationships becomes considerably reduced as measurable attainments become highly valued (Ball, 2006). Ball (2006) notes that within a performative culture investment is most likely to be directed towards those areas which will lead to improved outcomes against the metrics used to evaluate school effectiveness. This, he suggests, means that SEN is less likely to be considered for significant investment owing to the likely poor or limited return. Indeed as the expected attainments set out age-related expectations for all children and young people, which may be inappropriate for some learners with SEN, this has the potential to effectively marginalise this group of learners (O'Brien, 2016). As practitioners we need to challenge these notions – all children and young people are worthy of investment and best practice.

In 1992, league tables of school performance were published with one unintended outcome of a huge rise in the number of children and young people being permanently excluded from school (Ball, 2013). Interestingly, the league tables did not include records of numbers of exclusions. This was accompanied by the setting up of Pupil Referral Units (PRUs) and of targets aimed at reducing exclusions. The rate of exclusion did fall over the next few academic years and in 2002 targets were abandoned which the government claimed was because exclusion rates had reduced (Ball, 2013). An exploration of policy in relation to behaviour and exclusion follows in the next section.

Behaviour

During the late 1980s and 1990s the previous perception of exclusion as focusing upon the individual (medical or deficit model) began to change towards being regarded as a concern for wider societal contexts, thus needing political intervention and systemic changes (Brodie, 2001). Policy related to behaviour in schools is underpinned by notions of causes for disaffected or challenging behaviour held by the policy makers. Explanations for challenging behaviour predominantly fall within one of two rationales: internal (biological) factors or external (environmental, e.g. school, wider societal factors) (Munn, Lloyd and Cullen, 2000). Munn, Lloyd and Cullen (2000) propose that policy and legislation upon exclusion from school exposes the tensions between these two rationales. This encompasses the focus upon the individual (hence the need for intervention, therapy or punitive sanctions) and upon systems (national, local and school based).

The school improvement agenda has been a part of the wider discourse on reducing social exclusion owing to the recognition of the relationship between social class and academic and employment outcomes. Kane (2011, p. 19) suggests that 'It provides a way of challenging poor educational attainment without the need for wealth distribution'. Kane cites Mortimore (1999) who notes that much research examining school effectiveness has been underpinned with an incorrect assumption that all children and young people have a desire to achieve well at school, which thus then sets up potential failure in the implementation of strategies.

Exclusion relates both to organisational and cultural factors within school and society (Slee and Allan, 2005). New Labour policies perceived that exclusion from school evidenced, and aggravated, social exclusion (Kane, 2011). Thus working to reduce schools' utilisation of the exclusion sanction was a vehicle to support measures to promote social inclusion (McCluskey *et al.*, 2016). This contrasted with policies being introduced around school discipline in which the sanction of exclusion was included. Kane (2011) contends that as the children and young people most likely to be excluded had a dual vulnerability in that they were also at risk of social exclusion, the tension between these two policies was exacerbated for this group of learners.

Social exclusion

Social exclusion is a term which has been frequently used within discourse about policy within the UK and in Europe. Kane (2011, p. 17) identifies these dimensions are included within an explanation of social exclusion:

- Long-term or repeated occurrences of unemployment

- Social isolation

- Family breakdown

- Reduction in community and wider support networks

- The links to the causes and effects of poverty

- Discrimination by others

- Disadvantage

Kane (2011, p. 17) notes that there is discord between the definitions offered for social inclusion. These include notions of including the excluded to social systems and networks and the critiques of 'power relations' which lead to social exclusion. The latter offers a challenge to the current social systems which exclude disadvantaged groups and argues that working to include those disadvantaged groups will require a change to those systems. Kane cites Tomlinson (2005) who contended that the pre-eminence of marketisation within policies has led to a reduction in the post-war pledges of developing and maintaining a welfare state. Furthermore the notion of welfare has become stigmatised, rather than being about supporting the decrease of inequality; thus moving further away from the central philosophy of working to increase equality.

Following the 1986 Education Act, there was a substantial increase in the frequency of exclusion reported by the National Exclusion Reporting System (NERS) (Brodie, 2001). The DfE (1992) discussion paper and the Ofsted (1993) response paper on the issues surrounding exclusion critiqued indefinite exclusions owing the risk to outcomes for children and young people having no educational provision for indeterminate periods of time. Following the 1986 Act teaching unions raised the issues of LEA decision for reinstatement of children and young people following an appeal being made owing to the negative impact upon the confidence of staff with managing the learner's behaviour and the learner's responses to the strategies implemented. Brodie (2001) notes that the Elton Report (1989) acknowledged that this argument provided a convincing rationale for removing the LEA right to reinstate excluded children and young people but highlighted the positive role for LEAs as an independent reviewer within this process. Brodie (2001) contends that the issue of reinstatement remains contentious.

The Labour Government (1998) introduced policy aimed at tackling wider issue of social exclusion, this included procedures designed to combat the increasing numbers of exclusions from school:

- National targets to decrease fixed-term and permanent exclusions by one-third by 2002.

- Arrangements made for children and young people excluded for a period longer than three weeks to be provided with 'alternative full-time and appropriate education informed by an individual learning plan which includes a target date for reintegration into mainstream schooling' (p. 35).

- Local authorities had to set staged targets for reduction of both fixed term (1999) and permanent exclusions (2000).

- Data to be published by the Government on performance on exclusions from school. This data to include details of school phase and ethnicity.

- Exclusion for minor misdemeanours was outlawed.

- Algorithms used for performance tables were to be adjusted so that exclusion could not be employed as a method to change the performance table.

- Ofsted to implement inspections at schools with high levels of exclusion.

- Schools who agree to enrol a child or young person excluded from another school to receive support package to support successful transition and thus reduce risk of exclusion.

(Munn, Lloyd and Cullen, 2000, p. 35).

A further Government response to the increasing trend of permanent exclusions was the introduction of widely publicised programmes aimed at changing this trend (Brodie, 2001). Brodie (2001) notes that the data gathered in both 1997–1998 (12,300) and 1998–1999 (10,400) showed reductions in numbers which suggests that these programmes may have had a positive impact.

Brodie (2001) cites a number of research studies (e.g. Ofsted, 1993, 1996; DfE, 1995, 1992; Imich, 1994) which have identified huge disparities in the number of exclusions between local authorities and also between schools. She notes that these findings led to the development of focus and pressure upon improving the quality of teaching including behaviour management of children and young people. Other influencing factors upon the lead up to the decision to exclude a pupil arise from the structure and systems within the school environment. An example of this may be a comparatively minor infringement of rules being rapidly accelerated to being dealt with by senior leadership with the resulting confrontation between pupil and SLT precipitating an exclusion sanction. One of the most prevalent rationales for exclusion is behaviour which interferes with the learning of others, often classified as persistent disruptive behaviour. This suggests that perceptions around what may be considered to be positive and negative behaviours is an important area to explore.

It may also be valuable to explore differences in tolerance, for example some teachers will accept quiet conversations whereas others will expect total silence. They may give children and young people time and opportunity to change behaviour or expect instant change when negative behaviours are pointed out to them or public or private/quieter rebukes or praise are made.

Summary

A key point to note is that education policy is closely related to economic policy and the demands arising from competition within the global market (Ball, 2013). The focus upon equality for all within policy had two key drivers: raising standards and widening inclusion (Forrester and Garratt, 2016). The disharmony arising from the two policies, in combination with the focus upon education meeting the needs of the economy, led to tensions felt deeply by practitioners and learners and noted by the Education Select Committee (2006) (Glazzard, 2013).

The certification function of education has been fashioned over the time of both Labour and Conservative governments through policies related to accountability and standards: the implementation of National Curricula, national assessment policy and legislation setting out rules for regulating the functioning of school governors and the reports to be given to parents and carers (Brodie, 2001). Furthermore, the establishment of Ofsted has increased accountability of schools for standards and information reported to parents and carers. This has afforded restrictions in the curriculum which may be argued to place difficulties and stresses upon modifying or adapting the curriculum to meet diverse needs and reduced the opportunities provided to foster personal, social and emotional competences (Brodie, 2001). There are arguments which frame this in an alternative light. These arguments contend that the dissonance between the standards agenda and real life demands (such as meeting diverse needs) creates 'spaces' which triggers practitioners to engage in actions which are both inclusive and achievable to meet needs regarding the underachievement of learners (Dyson and Gallannaugh, 2007; Dyson, Gallannaugh and Millward, 2003, p. 242). This book aims to support practitioners with creating these spaces for debate, actions and problem-solving to meet needs.

The certification function of education relates to one of the roles of assessment within education. 'Assessment of learning . . . involves making judgements about students' summative achievements for the purposes of selection and certification' (Bloxham and Boyd, 2007, p. 15). Examples of this are formal tests and exams, such as SATs and GCSEs. This also serves a function within accountability of settings.

Discipline has also been subject to regulation (Brodie, 2001). While communications from teacher unions have argued that the regulation around exclusion restricts schools' abilities to develop positive behaviours, there is evidence from a range of research studies (e.g. Ofsted, 1999; Ostler, 1997) which have identified that schools with low rates of exclusion have behaviour policies and inclusive practice that are effectual (Brodie, 2001). Brodie (2001) notes that the relationship between the quality of teaching and learning and the prevalence of exclusions has not been communicated clearly within media reports. The combination of less central control over aspects of education, such as school governance and budgets, with increased central control over other aspects, such as standards, curricula and pedagogical approaches, creates tensions for schools and practitioners in meeting diverse needs and maintaining a positive public image of their institution. Within this pressure, there is a dichotomy in the discourse around exclusion between the notions of it being weak and positive practice.

Before we move on to explore the statistics related to exclusion, please take some time to read and reflect upon this quotation

> *Policy emphasises inclusion, participation, the importance of education and skills, and yet each year thousands of vulnerable young people are excluded from school.*
>
> *(Kane, 2011, p. 12)*

Statistics

These statistics have been taken from the Department for Education's (DfE) data for schools in England, published on 19 July 2018. At the time of writing, this is the most recent published data from the DfE and was accessed from the DfE website: www.gov.uk/government/statistics/permanent-and-fixed-period-exclusions-in-england-2016-to-2017

Permanent and fixed-period exclusions in schools in England

Table 1.1 (DfE, 2018, Table 1.1) evidences an upward trend in the number of permanent and fixed-term exclusions across the academic years 2012/2013 to 2016/2017. It should be noted that between 2015/2016 and 2016/2017, the rate of permanent exclusion did reduce in special schools.

Table 1.1 Exclusion by type of school (DfE, 2018, Table 1.1.1)

Permanent and fixed period exclusions by type of school State-funded primary, state-funded secondary and special schools (DfE, 2018, Table 1.1.1)						
2012/13 to 2016/17						
England						
		2012/13	2013/14	2014/15	2015/16	2016/17
State-funded primary, state-funded secondary and special schools						
	Number of schools [1]	21,157	21,193	21,234	21,245	21,319
	Number of pupils [2]	7,616,870	7,698,310	7,799,005	7,916,225	8,025,075
	Number of permanent exclusions	4,630	4,950	5,795	6,685	7,720
	Permanent exclusion rate [3]	0.06	0.06	0.07	0.08	0.10
	Number of fixed period exclusions	267,520	269,475	302,975	339,360	381,865
	Fixed period exclusion rate [4]	3.51	3.50	3.88	4.29	4.76
	Number of pupil enrolments with one or more fixed period exclusion	146,070	142,845	154,060	167,125	183,475
	One or more fixed period exclusion rate [5]	1.92	1.86	1.98	2.11	2.29
State-funded primary schools						
	Number of schools [1]	16,836	16,831	16,799	16,804	16,837
	Number of pupils [2]	4,309,580	4,416,710	4,510,310	4,615,170	4,689,660
	Number of permanent exclusions	665	870	915	1,145	1,255
	Permanent exclusion rate [3]	0.02	0.02	0.02	0.02	0.03
	Number of fixed period exclusions	37,865	45,005	49,655	55,740	64,340
	Fixed period exclusion rate [4]	0.88	1.02	1.10	1.21	1.37
	Number of pupil enrolments with one or more fixed period exclusion	19,385	21,650	23,630	25,765	28,940
	One or more fixed period exclusion rate [5]	0.45	0.49	0.52	0.56	0.62

Permanent and fixed period exclusions by type of school State-funded primary, state-funded secondary and special schools (DfE, 2018, Table 1.1.1)						
2012/13 to 2016/17						
England						
		2012/13	**2013/14**	**2014/15**	**2015/16**	**2016/17**
State-funded secondary schools						
	Number of schools [1]	3,302	3,339	3,404	3,409	3,451
	Number of pupils [2]	3,210,120	3,181,360	3,184,730	3,193,420	3,223,090
	Number of permanent exclusions	3,905	4,005	4,785	5,445	6,385
	Permanent exclusion rate [3]	0.12	0.13	0.15	0.17	0.20
	Number of fixed period exclusions	215,560	210,580	239,240	270,135	302,890
	Fixed period exclusion rate [4]	6.72	6.62	7.51	8.46	9.40
	Number of pupil enrolments with one or more fixed period exclusion	121,055	115,675	124,995	135,925	148,820
	One or more fixed period exclusion rate [5]	3.77	3.64	3.92	4.26	4.62
Special schools						
	Number of schools [1]	1,019	1,023	1,031	1,032	1,031
	Number of pupils [2]	97,170	100,240	103,970	107,635	112,325
	Number of permanent exclusions	65	75	90	90	80
	Permanent exclusion rate [3]	0.07	0.07	0.09	0.08	0.07
	Number of fixed period exclusions	14,095	13,890	14,080	13,485	14,635
	Fixed period exclusion rate [4]	14.51	13.86	13.54	12.53	13.03
	Number of pupil enrolments with one or more fixed period exclusion	5,630	5,520	5,435	5,440	5,715
	One or more fixed period exclusion rate [5]	5.80	5.51	5.23	5.05	5.09

Source: School Census

(1) The number of schools as of January each year plus the number of schools which opened after January and reported exclusions.

(2) Includes pupils who are sole or dual main registrations. Includes boarding pupils.

(3) The number of permanent exclusions expressed as a percentage of the number of pupils in January each year.

(4) The number of fixed period exclusions expressed as a percentage of the number of pupils in January each year.

(5) The number of pupil enrolments receiving one or more fixed period exclusion expressed as a percentage of the number of pupils in January each year.

Table 1.2 Rate of population of children and young people who received fixed-period exclusions (DfE, 2018, p. 4, section 3)

Rate of pupils with fixed-term exclusion, excluded once in 2016/2017	Rate of pupils with fixed-term exclusion, excluded 10 or more times in 2016/2017	Rates of pupils with fixed-term exclusion, who were later excluded permanently in 2016/2017
59.1%	1.5%	3.5%

In their analysis of longer-term trends, the DfE reports that, 'Looking at longer-term trends, the rate of permanent exclusions across all state-funded primary, secondary and special schools followed a generally downward trend from 2006/07 when the rate was 0.12 per cent until 2012/13, and has been rising again since then, although rates are still lower now than in 2006/07'. While it is positive that rates of exclusion are less in 2016/2017, than 10 years earlier, the upward trend in the rates since 2012/2013 is cause for concern. There are an increasing number of children and young people who are experiencing an interruption to their schooling and for some of those, the need to find a new setting for their education. The DfE (2018) notes that there was a small reduction in the length of fixed-period exclusions in 2016–2017, with the majority of these being for the period of one day; however, the frequency of number of longer fixed-period exclusions was higher in secondary schools than primary schools. Table 1.1.2 shows the rate of the population of children and young people who received the fixed-period exclusion who had been excluded for one day, longer periods or later permanently excluded and was informed from data published by DfE (2018, p. 4, section 3).

Reasons for exclusion

DfE (2018) identifies that the most prevalent rationale identified for both permanent and fixed-period exclusion was persistent disruptive behaviour. The greatest rise in number of permanent exclusions were for these three reasons: persistent disruptive behaviour, physical assault against a pupil and other reasons. This was replicated for fixed-period exclusion except physical assault against a pupil (DfE, 2018). Figures 1.2 and 1.3 are from the DfE's published data for 2015/2016 and 2016/2017 (2018, pp. 5–6) and show the numbers of children and young people excluded for each of the identified reasons:

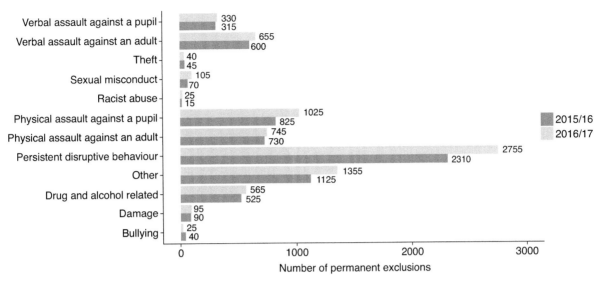

Figure 1.2 Reasons for permanent exclusion

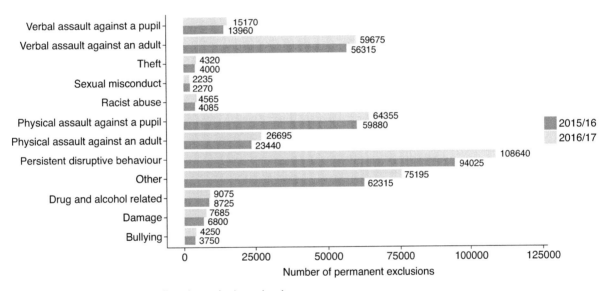

Figure 1.3 Reasons for fixed-period exclusion

Exclusion: patterns of exclusion for characteristics of learners

Table 1.3 was informed from the DfE (2018, p. 6, section 5) published statistics of the patterns observed from their examination of the exclusion data gathered in relation to characteristics of learners.

29

Table 1.3 Exclusions examined in relation to characteristics of learners

Characteristics of learners	Pattern observed by DfE (2018)
Age	25% of permanent exclusions were given to children and young people aged 14 years. Additionally, this group of children and young people had the greatest proportion of one or more fixed-period exclusions.
National Curriculum year group	Children and young people in year 9 or above had the greatest proportion of permanent (57.2%) and fixed-period exclusion (52.6%).
Gender	There was a higher proportion of boys than girls being permanently excluded and receiving a fixed-period exclusion.

gender	permanent	Fixed-period
girls	0.04%	2.53%
boys	0.15%	6.91%

Pupils eligible for free school meals (FSM)		

Proportion	permanent	Fixed-period
Percentage of all exclusions	40%	36.7%
Percentage of pupils eligible for FSM	0.28%	12.54%
Percentage of pupils NOT eligible for FSM	0.07%	3.5%

Pupils with special educational needs		

Proportion	permanent	Fixed-period
Percentage of all exclusions	46%	44.9%
Percentage of pupils with SEN	0.35%	14.76%
Percentage of pupils with ECH Plan	15.93%	15.93%
Percentage of pupils with NO SEN	0.06%	3.06%

| Ethnic group | The children and young people who had the lowest rates of exclusion were Asian Ethnic groups whereas the proportion of Black Caribbean children and young people who received the sanction of permanent exclusion was almost three times greater than the overall school population.

The DfE (2018) reports that the greatest number of exclusion sanctions (both permanent and fixed-period were for children and young people of Gypsy/Roma and Traveller of Irish heritage ethnic groups. They offer a caveat that as the population of these children and young people is small, a cautionary approach should be adopted towards figures for this group. |
|---|---|

Table 1.4 Exclusion by type of SEN need (DfE, 2018, Table 6)

	Number of pupils	Permanent exclusions		Fixed period exclusions		Pupil enrolments with one or more fixed period exclusion	
		Number	Rate[2]	Number	Rate[2]	Number	Rate[2]
Specific learning difficulty	146,875	295	0.20	15,070	10.26	7,055	4.80
Moderate learning difficulty	259,715	465	0.18	27,210	10.48	11,695	4.50
Severe learning difficulty	32,340	15	0.05	825	2.54	375	1.17
Profound and multiple learning difficulty	10,980	5	0.04	105	0.97	50	0.45
Social, emotional and mental health	186,795	2,030	1.09	86,560	46.34	32,605	17.46
Speech, language and communications needs	234,075	200	0.08	12,070	5.16	5,470	2.34
Hearing impairment	21,165	25	0.11	1,155	5.46	590	2.80
Visual impairment	11,890	15	0.13	635	5.33	305	2.56
Multi- sensory impairment	2,720	x	x	90	3.27	50	1.88
Physical disability	33,685	15	0.04	915	2.71	485	1.43
Autistic spectrum disorder	108,405	125	0.12	10,365	9.56	4,840	4.46
Other difficulty/disability	54,340	130	0.24	6,075	11.18	2,775	5.11
Total SEN with recorded primary need[1]	**1,102,980**	**3,325**	**0.30**	**161,070**	**14.60**	**66,300**	**6.01**

Source: School Census

(1) Figures are presented for pupils with a Statement of SEN, Education, Health and Care plan or SEN support and recorded primary need. This excludes those with SEN support who are yet to be assessed for a type of need and those with school action provision. SEN status is as recorded at the time of exclusion. For enrolments the SEN status at the time of the most recent exclusion is used.

(2) The number of exclusions (or the number of pupil enrolments receiving one or more fixed period exclusion) expressed as a percentage of the number of pupils (including sole or dual main registrations and boarding pupils) with the same SEN type at January 2017.

Exclusion: children and young people with SEN

Table 1.4 is taken from the DfE (2018, Table 6) and sets out the data regarding the use of sanction of exclusion with children and young people who have identified SEN needs in the academic year 2016/2017. This table is included to draw attention to the different types or areas of need and the differing rate of exclusions between the needs.

The highest proportion of exclusions were employed for children and young people with social, emotional and mental health needs. Indeed, there is a significantly greater rate for this group of children and young people for permanent and fixed-period exclusion, than for those with the next highest rates. Whilst this may not be surprising, it does suggest that this is an area of need for which we need to explore how senior leaders, teachers and practitioners can develop practice to support this group of children and young people with accessing the social and academic aspects of school.

Conclusion

There are some striking patterns recorded within these figures. It is alarming that the greatest proportion of children and young people being given the sanction of exclusion is made up of our most vulnerable children and young people. One example of this is the stark difference between the children and young people with education, health and care plans (or statements of SEN where those have not yet been converted) and those with no SEN need. Another example is that of the sharp difference in the number of children and young people with social, emotional and mental health needs who were excluded as compared to other areas or types of SEN need.

This suggests that children and young people who start from a disadvantaged position in relation to other peers in their cohort at school are at risk of interruptions to their education, which sets up further challenges to their progress in relation to social and academic learning. This potentially may also impede relationships with adults and peers within their school and adds to the risk factors affecting self-belief, self-esteem, resilience and mental health.

The DfE (2018) report and tables provide further detail and offer opportunities to dig deeper into statistics which relate to the characteristics of your school population, which you may find helpful to explore.

Reflection

How does your school data in relation to excluded pupils or those at risk of exclusion compare with the national data?

How do you think the wider policy context influences the broader environment in which your own school or setting operates?

How do you think the wider policy context influences inclusion and exclusion in your own school or setting?

References

Adams, P. (2014) *Policy and Education: Foundations of Educational Studies*. London: Routledge.

Alisauskas, A., Alisauskiene, S., Kairiene, D. and Jones, S. (2011) '"Meeting of pupils" special needs in the context of inclusive education: UK experience'. *Special Education*, 1(24), pp. 91–104.

Ball, S.J. (2006) *Education Policy and Social Class: The Selected Works of Stephen J. Ball*. Abingdon: Routledge.

Ball, S.J. (2013) *The Education Debate*. Second Edition. Bristol: The Policy Press.

Bloxham, S. and Boyd, P. (2007) *Developing Effective Assessment in Higher Education: A Practical Guide*. Maidenhead: Open University Press.

Brodie, I. (2001) *Children's Homes and School Exclusion*. London: Jessica Kingsley Publishers.

Centre for Social Justice. (2016) *Selective Education and Social Mobility*. Available at: www.centreforsocialjustice.org.uk/core/wp-content/uploads/2016/12/161201-Grammar-School-Report.pdf. (accessed 18 August 2018).

Centre for Studies on Inclusive Education. (2018). Available at: www.csie.org.uk.

Chitty, C. (2014) *Education Policy in Britain*. Third Edition. Basingstoke: Palgrave Macmillan.

Cooper, P., Drummond, M.J., Hart, S., Lovey, J. and McLaughlin, C. (2000) *Positive Alternatives to Exclusion*. London: RoutledgeFarmer.

Cowne, E. (2003) *Developing Inclusive Practice: The SENCo's Role in Managing Change*. London: Fulton.

Denziloe, J. and Dickens, M. (2004) *All Together: How to Create Inclusive Services for Disabled Children and Their Families*. Second Edition. London: National Children's Bureau.

Department for Education (DfE). (1992) *Exclusions: A Discussion Paper*. London: HMSO.

Department for Education (DfE). (1995) *National Survey of LEAs' Policies and Procedures for the Identification of and Provision for, Children Who Are Out of School by Reason of Exclusion or Otherwise*. London: Pupils and Parents Branch, DfE.

Department for Employment and Education (DfEE). (1997) *Excellence in Schools*. London: The Stationery Office, Cm 2681.

Department for Education and Skills. (2004) *Every Child Matters: Change for Children in Schools*. DfES/1089/2004/. Available at: https://dera.ioe.ac.uk/7670/7/DFES-1089-200MIG748_Redacted.pdf (accessed 18 August 2018).

Department for Education and Families (DfES). (2006) *Education and Inspections Act*. Available at: www.educationengland.org.uk/documents/acts/2006-education-and-inspections-act.pdf. (accessed 17 August 2018).

Department for Education (DfE). (2012) *The School Discipline (Pupil Exclusions and Reviews) (England) Regulations*. Available at: https://www.legislation.gov.uk/uksi/2012/1033/made (accessed 18 August 2018).

Department for Education (DfE). (2014) *National Award for Special Educational Needs Co-ordinator: Learning Outcomes*. Available at: www.gov.uk/government/publications/national-award-for-sen-co-ordination-learning-outcomes (accessed 24 February 2015).

Department for Education (DfE). (2015) *Special Educational Needs and Disability Code of Practice: 0 to 25 Years. Statutory Guidance for Organisations Which Work With and Support Children and Young People Who Have Special Educational Needs or Disabilities.DFE-00205–2013*. London: DfES. Available at: www.gov.uk/government/publications/send-code-of-practice-0-to-25 (accessed 24 February 2015).

Department for Education (DfE). (2017) *Exclusion From Maintained Schools, Academies and Pupil Referral Units in England: Statutory Guidance for Those With Legal Responsibilities in Relation to Exclusion*. Available at: www.gov.uk/government/publications/school-exclusion (accessed 16 June 2018).

Department for Education (DfE). (2018) *Permanent and Fixed Period Exclusions in England: 2016 to 2017*. Available at: www.gov.uk/government/statistics/permanent-and-fixed-period-exclusions-in-england-2016-to-2017 (accessed 8 March 2019).

Department of Health. (2015) *New Mental Health Act Code of Practice*. Available at: www.gov.uk/government/news/new-mental-health-act-code-of-practice (accessed 20 July 2018).

Dyson, A. and Gallannaugh, F. (2007) 'National policy and the development of inclusive school practices: A case study'. *Cambridge Journal of Education*, 37(4), pp. 473–488. https://doi.org/1080/0305764070105690.

Dyson, A., Gallannaugh, F. and Millward, A. (2003) 'Making space in the standards agenda: Developing inclusive practices in schools'. *European Educational Research Journal*, 2(2), pp. 228–244. https://doi.org/10.2304/eerj.2003.2.2.3.

Elton, L. (1989) *Discipline in Schools*. Report of the Committee of Enquiry chaired by Lord Elton. London: H.M.S.O.

Forrester, G. and Garratt, D. (2016) *Education Policy Unravelled*. Second Edition. London: Bloomsbury.

Glazzard, J. (2011) 'Perceptions of the barriers to effective inclusion in primary school: Voices of teachers and teaching assistants'. *International Journal of Research in Special Educational Needs*, 26(2), pp. 56–63.

Glazzard, J. (2013) 'A critical interrogation of the contemporary discourses associated with inclusive education'. *International Journal of Research in Special Educational Needs*, 13(3), pp. 182–188.

Glazzard, J., Stokoe, J., Hughes, A., Netherwood, A. and Neve, L. (2015) *Teaching and Supporting Children With Special Educational Needs and Disabilities in Primary Schools*. Second Edition. London: SAGE.

Hall, K., Collins, J., Benjamin, S., Nind, M. and Sheehy, K. (2004) 'SATurated models of pupildom: Assessment and inclusion/exclusion'. *British Educational Research Journal*, 30(6), pp. 801–817. https://doi.org/10.1080/014119204000279512.

Hayden, C. (1997) *Children Excluded From Primary School: Debates, Evidence, Responses*. Buckingham: Open University Press.

Hodkinson, A. (2012) '"All present and correct?" Exclusionary inclusion within the English education system'. *Disability and Society*, 27(5), pp. 675–688. https://doi.org/10.1080/09687599.2012.673078.

Hodkinson, A. (2016) *Key Issues in Special Educational Needs and Inclusion*. Second Edition. London: SAGE.

Imich, A.J. (1994) 'Exclusions from school: current trends and issues'. *Journal of Educational Research*, 36(1), pp. 3–11. https://doi.org/10.1080/0013188940360101

Kane, J. (2005) 'Exclusions from school. Different voices', In J. Rix, K. Simmons, M. Nind and K. Sheehy (eds.), *Policy and Power in Inclusive Education: Values Into Practice*. London: RoutledgeFarmer, pp.107–117.

Kane, J. (2011) *Social Class, Gender and Exclusion From School*. London: Routledge.

Lamb Enquiry (2009) *SEN and Parental Confidence*. Nottingham: DCSF.

McCluskey, G., Riddell, S., Weedon, E. and Fordyce, M. (2016) 'Exclusion from school and recognition of difference'. *Discourse: Studies in the Cultural Politics of Education*, 37(4), pp. 529–539.

Munn, P., Lloyd, G. and Cullen, M.A. (2000) *Alternatives to Exclusion From School*. London: Paul Chapman Publishing.

O'Brien, J. (2016) *Don't Send Him in Tomorrow: Shining a Light on the Marginalised, Disenfranchised and Forgotten Children of Today's Schools*. Carmarthen: Independent Thinking Press.

Office for Standards in Education [Ofsted]. (1993) *Exclusions: A Response to the DfE Discussion Paper*. London: OFSTED.

Office for Standards in Education [Ofsted]. (1996) *Exclusions from Secondary School*. London: HMSO.

Office for Standards in Education [Ofsted]. (1999) *The Annual Report of Her Majesty's Chief Inspector of Schools Standards and Quality in Education 1997/98*. London: OFSTED.

Office for Standards in Education [Ofsted]. (2004) *Special Educational Needs and Disability: Towards Inclusive Schools*. London: Ofsted.

Office for Standards in Education [Ofsted]. (2010) *The Special Educational Needs and Disability Review*. Reference 090221. London: Ofsted.

Ostler, A. (1997) *Exclusion from School and Racial Equality*. London: Commission for Racial Equality.

Parkes, B. (2012) 'Exclusion of pupils from school in the UK'. *The Equal Rights Review*, 8, pp. 113–129. Available at: www.equalrightstrust.org/ertdocumentbank/ERR8_Brenda_Parkes.pdf (accessed 17 July 2018).

Pomeroy, E. (2000) *Experiencing Exclusion*. Stoke-on-Trent: Trentham Books.

Rix, J. and Simmons, K. (2005) 'Introduction: A world of change'. In J. Rix, K. Simmons, M. Nind and K. Sheehy (eds.), *Policy and Power in Inclusive Education: Values Into Practice*. London: RoutledgeFarmer, pp. 1–9.

Scrivens, K. and Smith, C. (2013) *Four Interpretations of Social Capital: An Agenda for Measurement*. OECD Statistics Working Papers. Available at: www.oecd-ilibrary.org/economics/four-interpretations-of-social-capital_5jzbcx010wmt-en.

Slee, R. (2011) *The Irregular School: Exclusion, Schooling and Inclusive Education*. Abingdon: Routledge.

Slee, R. and Allan, J. (2005) 'Excluding the included: A reconsideration of inclusive education'. In J. Rix, K. Simmons, M. Nind and K. Sheehy (eds.), *Policy and Power in Inclusive Education: Values Into Practice*. London: RoutledgeFarmer, pp. 13–24.

Smith, R.A.L., Florian, L., Rouse, M. and Anderson, J. (2014) 'Special education today in the United Kingdom'. In A.F. Rotatori, J.P. Bakken, F.E. Obiakor and S. Burkhardt (eds.), *Advances in Special Education*. Volume 28. Bingley: Emerald Publishing, Bingley, Yorkshire, pp. 109–145. https://doi.org/10.1108/S0270-401320140000028011 (accessed 18 August 2018).

Standards & Testing Agency (STA). (2018) *Assessment and Reporting Arrangements (ARA) October 2018*. Available at: www.gov.uk/government/publications/2019-key-stage-2-assessment-and-reporting-arrangements-ara (accessed 28 March 2019).

Tomlinson, S. (2005) *Education in a Post-Welfare Society*. Second Edition. Maidenhead: Open University Press.

Trussler, S. and Robinson, D. (2015) *Inclusive Practice in the Primary School: A Guide for Teachers*. London: SAGE.

Tutt, R. (2016) *Rona Tutt's Guide to SEND and Inclusion*. London: SAGE.

Tutt, R. and Williams, P. (2015) *The SEND Code of Practice 0–25 Years: Policy, Provision and Practice*. London: SAGE.

UNESCO. (1994) *The Salamanca Statement and Framework for Action on Special Needs Education*. Paris: UNESCO. Available at: http://unesdoc.unesco.org/images/0009/000984/098427eo.pdf (accessed 18 August 2018).

Waugh, D. (2015) 'England: Primary schooling'. In C. Brock (ed.), *Education in the United Kingdom*. London: Bloomsbury, pp. 9–34.

Webster, R., Russell, A. and Blatchford, P. (2016) *Maximising the Impact of Teaching Assistants: Guidance for School Leaders and Teachers*. London: Routledge.

Wright, C., Weekes, D. and McGlaughlin, A. (2000) *'Race' Class and Gender in Exclusion From School*. London: Falmer Press.

Chapter two
INFORMAL AND INTERNAL EXCLUSION

Introduction

The previous chapter outlined the authors' definition of exclusion and exemplified English policy and guidance linked to exclusion. The majority of the literature addressing school exclusion focuses on formal exclusion where learners are sent away from school. This chapter will focus on manifestations of exclusion for which growing concern in reports, research and the media is evident. These types of exclusion are informal, in as much as the learner is not officially sent away from the school and school records do not show that the learner has been excluded. In addition to informal exclusion, where the learner is asked or directed to stay at home, but not recorded as having been excluded, this chapter will also consider internal exclusion. Internal exclusion is where a learner is moved away from the learning environment of their peers and remains in the school grounds. This approach is commonly resourced through 'seclusion units', also referred to as 'isolation units', where strict codes of behaviour and supervision are enforced.

What is informal exclusion?

Informal exclusion, simply described, is where a pupil is asked to leave the school or not to come in to school for a period of time without formal exclusion procedures being followed. This approach is clearly identified in statutory guidance as an unlawful exclusion:

> 'Informal' or 'unofficial' exclusions, such as sending a pupil home 'to cool off', are unlawful, regardless of whether they occur with the agreement of parents or carers. Any exclusion of a pupil, even for short periods of time, must be formally recorded.
>
> (DfE, 2017a).

An example of informal exclusion was given by the *Daily Telegraph* (Barrett, 2015) where a secondary school in Wiltshire allegedly told children and young people to stay home for the duration of an Ofsted inspection. The Annual Ofsted Report 2016/17 (December 2017) identified pupils with SEN as a particular group who experience informal exclusion.

It is difficult to identify the scale of the practice of informal exclusion, which is being experienced by too many children and young people with SEN (IPSEA, 2018). There are no official figures for informal exclusion to support Adoption UK's claim that, 'The percentage of children who had ever been "informally" excluded from school was virtually the same as that of children who had ever received a fixed period exclusion' (Adoption UK, 2017, p. 24). However, the Children's Commissioner (2017) used the NFER Teacher Voice survey of over 1000 teachers in identifying that this practice is, 'affecting thousands of children in several hundred schools across the country' (Children's Commissioner, 2017, p. 7) with 6.7 per cent of schools having sent pupils home without following formal exclusion procedures. This report also identified the specific impact on pupils with Statutory identification of SEN: '2.7 per cent of schools have sent children with statements of SEN home when their carer or teaching assistant is unavailable; if these were evenly spread across the country, it would represent 650 schools, or an average of more than four in every local authority' (Children's Commissioner, 2017, p. 25).

This is a parent's report of a school's informal exclusion of their child:

Told to stay home during Ofsted visit. Not even considered eligible for year 6 residential. Cannot guarantee safety of others.

(CBS, 2019, p. 17)

This notion of 'staying at home' is not the same as home education, which is a choice made by parents and carers and children and young people, rather than being imposed by a school. However there have been cases recently reported in the press, which blur the distinction, where schools have been accused of encouraging parents and carers to home educate as a way to avoid exclusion (Staufenberg, 2017; IPSEA, 2018) or are recorded as being educated off-site, whilst the parents and carers understand that their child is excluded.

There is a further aspect to informal exclusion which is emerging through media reports and The Annual Ofsted Report 2016/17 (December 2017), where schools 'off-roll' young people in Year 10 or Year 11, prior to GCSEs. It is suggested that schools take this action in order to improve the prospect of positive exam results. Concerns have been raised that in 2016/17, of the 22,281 pupils who left state education before the end of Year 11, 6,200–7,700 pupils appear to have remained in England whilst receiving no education (Nye and Thomson, 2018).

What is internal exclusion?

There are many accounts of practice in previous decades where learners with identified SEN or disabilities have been enrolled in settings which, on the surface, have appeared to include the learners with mainstream peers, whilst in reality the learners were segregated or excluded. An example of this approach is recounted by Mavis Parris (2018) who describes a segregated setting in the 1950s where the 'bottom of the school was the "physically handicapped" and the upper school was ordinary children and they had their own entrance and we had our own entrance'.

It can be argued that legislation and policy has moved on from the 1950s and that following key documents, from the Warnock Report (Warnock, 1978) to the Equality Act (Legislation. co.uk, 2010), the Children and Families Act (DfE, 2014) and the SEND Code of Practice (DfE, 2015), such direct exclusion of learners is no longer common practice. However, there is the argument that whilst there have been improvements in the experience of exclusion for many learners, more subtle and insidious forms of exclusion continue to be experienced. For some learners with SEN in mainstream settings, the experience can be that of frequently leaving the class for a small group or one-to-one work away from the majority of their class and the class teacher (Webster and Blatchford, 2013). This practice, although usually approached with positive educational aims at the fore, can be considered as a form of internal exclusion.

Recent discussions in policy fora and the education media highlight the experiences of learners with SEN being informally excluded and internally excluded within school settings. A particular focus of this discussion is the experience of learners who present behaviour challenges as a result of social, emotional and mental health difficulties.

The Department for Education (2017) has published clear statutory guidance which outlines procedures and functions of those with responsibilities in schools for exclusion processes. What is missing from this statutory guidance is any reference to internal exclusion.

The coalition government, via the Department for Children, Schools and Families, provided schools with 'Internal Exclusion Guidance', defining internal exclusion as:

> an internal process within the school and is used when the objective is to remove the pupil from class, not from the school site, for disciplinary reasons. It may be a formal process within the school but it is not a legal exclusion so exclusions legislation and the department's guidance on exclusion from school does not apply.
>
> (DCFS, 2009, p. 1)

Hodkinson identifies internal exclusion in more broad terms as, 'forced absence of children from their classrooms' (2012, p. 678). We acknowledge the point of children and young people being removed from their usual environment without choice being made by Hodkinson, but feel that as a definition this does not allow for consideration of contextual factors and practical implications which may be experienced by schools. For example, children and young people may not be permitted into their classroom during a break time as there is no supervision available.

In this book, we define internal exclusion as a short- to medium-term strategy, used in response to learner challenges to schools' behaviour or discipline policies. It is an approach which moves the child or young person away from learning alongside their peers to a situation where they are constrained to a specific room or area for extended periods as a consequence of their actions.

Internal exclusion is different from planned interventions where students may have sessions outside their mainstream class, for example as part of a Pupil Premium or SEN provision, to support their learning. Such learning situations, where a child or young person may be in an environment away from their peers, at a different location or with a different member of staff will have been planned with educational outcomes at the fore and will be identified within provision mapping.

A short-term time-out from a learning environment is not the same as internal exclusion. Short-term time-out, rather than being implemented as a result of contraventions of school policies, is a strategy used to proactively manage behaviour. It will usually be a planned-for approach where, as identified behaviours are being seen to escalate, the opportunity for the learner to leave the situation is provided in order to break the pattern of escalation. This strategy is non-punitive and return to the learning environment is expected within a short period of time.

Seclusion units

Barker *et al.* (2010) identify and explore seclusion units as the most common organisation of internal exclusion in secondary schools in England. In the DfE guidance on 'Behaviour and Discipline in Schools' (2016), seclusion or isolation rooms are identified as a strategy within a behaviour management approach. The DCSF includes 'remove rooms' (2008) within this category of internal exclusion approaches.

Barker *et al.* state that 'seclusion units' as a provision have developed in response to 'political pressure to raise educational standards and attainment, to reduce levels of exclusion from school and to remove the threat of the presence of "undesirable" young people in public space during school hours' (2010, 379). These pressures can be linked to changes in government rhetoric around exclusion. In 1998 the government set targets for the reduction of schools exclusions by one-third (Social Exclusion Unit, 2002, p. 2), however in response to an annual increase of 11 per cent in 2001, Secretary of State for Education and Skills Estelle Morris reported as being, 'not too upset' about this, qualifying the approach: 'There has got to be a clear message to young people that behaviour is important. If boundaries are crossed, consequences take place' (2002). As with the broader issue of internal exclusion, there is little statutory guidance on the appropriate use of seclusion units, with most recent documentation identifying that it is up to individual schools to decide upon reasonable use of this strategy (DfE, 2016).

The broad use of seclusion units can be evidenced by the range of job adverts which can be found online, seeking staff for internal seclusion units or internal exclusion rooms across the country. Within a number of these, it is expressly stated that the approach is an alternative to fixed term formal external exclusions (North East Jobs, 2017).

The Centre for Social Justice identify that secondary schools are more likely to have internal exclusion units, whilst in primary settings this is more likely to occur in somewhere such as the head-teacher's office (Centre for Social Justice, 2011).

Internal exclusion through the use of seclusion units will, in the short term, provide schools with an additional procedure or stage in behaviour management approaches, which can be seen to delay a formal exclusion. This delay can be recognised as a strategy which can support schools in maintaining a more positive return on exclusion numbers as part of the School Census, which is returned to the DfE three times a year (DfE, 2017b). The reduction of exclusion numbers through the use of isolation is evidenced by Galton and MacBeath (2008), however they also identify that those pupils with SEN are significantly over-represented in seclusion units.

The use of seclusion units is also identified as a form of punishment. In the DfE information for parents on 'School Discipline and Exclusions' (2018), this internal exclusion approach is specifically identified as a punishment. Alongside Woollard (2010) who questions the effectiveness of punishment in the context of behaviourism, the authors question the evidence-base for the use of punishment, in the form of exclusion, as a way of securing a long-term change in behaviour or as a way of leading a child or young person to learn the social and emotional skills needed to regulate their own behaviours.

Figure 2.1 Example of isolation booths available to schools, taken from a furniture supplier's catalogue

Source: www.cofltd.co.uk/project/isolation-booths/

The use of seclusion units is challenged by a number of authors within the perspective of human rights; the Centre for the Advancement of Positive Behaviour Support (CAPBS, 2015) questions the use of seclusion on the grounds that it is likely to contravene Article 5 of the Human Rights Act which enshrines the right to liberty and security (Gov, 1998) by restricting the child or young person and depriving them of liberty.

The impact on children and young people who are placed into seclusion units has been identified as having a negative long-term impact on them. In the Mental Health Act Code of Practice the use of seclusion is identified as being potentially traumatic and having, 'adverse implications for the emotional development of a child or young person' (Department of Health, 2015, pp. 26, 57). This guidance goes on to outline that such 'restrictive interventions' should only be used as part of a positive behaviour support plan where there has been input from the child or young person and their family (Department of Health, 2015, pp. 26, 53). In a short survey of school behaviour/exclusion policies available online conducted by the authors, 35 per cent of policy documents stated that in the case of an internal exclusion parents are involved, whilst 40 per cent do not mention contacting parents and 25 per cent state that parent contact is not a routine procedure.

Internal exclusion – what is it like?

The experience of internal exclusion on the part of the child and young person is a key aspect for practitioners to consider. Barker *et al.*'s research presents the testimony of a Seclusion Unit supervisor, who said, 'Well a lot of them do say they feel that they're in prison. I explain to them it isn't a prison and the door isn't locked, as it would be in prison. But a lot of them say they feel as though this is what prison would feel like' (2010, p. 381). This identifies the extreme and challenging nature of the learner's experience.

A key aspect of the practice of internal exclusion is the isolation of the individual away from other learners. In some settings, this extends to learners being kept after the end of the school day for extended periods of time to prevent them from mixing with peers as they leave the school. Many settings also enforce the exclusion during lunch and break times.

The 2011 Centre for Social Justice report identifies a 'considerable variation in its quality. For example, pupils can be supervised by staff who have no or little experience in relation to their complex behavioural difficulties' (p. 139).

Barker *et al.* (2010, p. 381) provide this graphic testimony from a learner in a Seclusion Unit: 'You're not allowed to interact with other students . . . you just work on your own, you're not allowed to speak until break, there are boards in-between (desks) so you're not allowed to talk to other people while you're doing your work and stuff.'

> This is a testimony from a young person placed in 'isolation' in their school:
>
> *The windows, the bare walls. It was that every day. Every single day. They put me in a room on my own, I was in isolation. . . . It made me feel there was no point to learning. . . . I locked myself into my room every day after I came home and shut the blinds. . . . It felt like being isolated was normal. I wouldn't expect them to treat a dog like that. It was just vile.*
>
> (Titheradge, 2018)

A recent parliamentary question by GP Dr Paul Williams (HC deb 6 June 2018) identified the potential negative effect of internal exclusion, in the form of isolation, on children and young people's mental health. The authors concur with this view and have cited evidence to support this. Internal exclusion is presented in policy and legislative documentation as being something of less concern than formal school exclusion. The reporting and procedural expectations are significantly smaller than with formal school exclusion. However, we suggest that the impact of internal exclusion, in the use of isolation rooms or other approaches, can be as significant as with formal school exclusion. This will be explored further in the next chapter.

References

Adoption UK. (2017) *Adoption UK'S Schools & Exclusions Report*, November 2017. Available at: www.adoptionuk.org/FAQs/adoption-uks-schools-exclusions-report (accessed 5 June 2018).

Barker, J., Alldred, P., Watts, M. and Dodman, H. (2010) 'Pupils or prisoners? Institutional geographies and internal exclusion in UK secondary schools'. *Area*, 42(3), pp. 378–386.

Barrett, D. (2015) 'Disruptive pupils "hidden" by school during ofsted visit'. *Daily Telegraph*, 13th February 2015.

CAPBS. (2015) *The Use of Seclusion, Isolation and Time Out*. Available at: www.bild.org.uk/capbs/pbsinformation/ (accessed 16 July 2018).

Centre for Social Justice. (2011) *No Excuses: A Review of Educational Exclusion*. Available at: www.centreforsocialjustice.org.uk/library/no-excuses-review-educational-exclusion (accessed 16 July 2018).

Challenging Behaviour Foundation (CBS). (2019) *Reducing Restrictive Intervention of Children and Young People: Case Study and Survey Results January 2019*. Available at: www.challengingbehaviour.org.uk/cbf-articles/latest-news/restraintseclusionnews.html?fbclid=IwAR0xJGzmi8IUHJLTwJXI12wFxtm3O_ZdlXVxmvkV6kLJ6BC8anOv8U6bDik (accessed 28 March 2019).

Children's Commissioner. (2017) *"Always Someone Else's Problem" Office of the Children's Commissioner's Report on Illegal Exclusions*. Available at: www.childrenscommissioner.gov.uk/wp-content/uploads/2017/07/Always_Someone_Elses_Problem.pdf (accessed 16 July 2018).

DCFS. (2009) *Internal Exclusion Guidance*. Available at: http://dera.ioe.ac.uk/712/1/DCSF-00055-2010. pdf (accessed 17 June 2018).

Department of Health. (2015) *Mental Health Act 1983: Code of Practice*. Available at: www.gov.uk/ government/publications/code-of-practice-mental-health-act-1983 (accessed 16 July 2018).

DfE. (2014) *Children and Families Act*. Available at: https://www.legislation.gov.uk/ukpga/2014/6/ contents (accessed 16 July 2018).

DfE. (2015) *Special Educational Needs and Disability Code of Practice: 0 to 25 Years. Statutory Guidance for Organisations Which Work With and Support Children and Young People Who Have Special Educational Needs or Disabilities*. DFE-00205-2013. London: DfES. Available at https://www.gov.uk/government/ publications/send-code-of-practice-0-to-25 (accessed 24 February 2015).

DfE. (2016) *Behaviour and Discipline in Schools*. Available at: https://assets.publishing.service.gov.uk/ government/uploads/system/uploads/attachment_data/file/488034/Behaviour_and_Discipline_in_ Schools_-_A_guide_for_headteachers_and_School_Staff.pdf (accessed 16 July 2018).

DfE. (2017a) *Exclusion From Maintained Schools, Academies and Pupil Referral Units in England: Statutory Guidance for Those With Legal Responsibilities in Relation to Exclusion*. Available at: www.gov.uk/ government/publications/school-exclusion (accessed 16 July 2018).

DfE. (2017b) *A Guide to Exclusion Statistics*. Available at: https://assets.publishing.service.gov. uk/government/uploads/system/uploads/attachment_data/file/642577/Guide-to-exclusion-statistics-05092017.pdf (accessed 16 July 2018).

DfE. (2018) *School Discipline and Exclusions*. Available at: www.gov.uk/school-discipline-exclusions (accessed 16 July 2018).

Galton, M.J. and MacBeath, J.E.C. (2008) *Teachers Under Pressure*. London: Paul Chapman.

Gov. (1998) *Human Rights Act*. Available at: www.legislation.gov.uk/ukpga/1998/42/contents (accessed 16 July 2018).

HC Deb. (6 June 2018) *Written Question 150770*. Available at: www.parliament.uk/business/publications/ written-questions-answers-statements/written-question/Commons/2018-06-06/150770/ (accessed 2 August 2018).

Hodkinson, A. (2012) '"All present and correct?" Exclusionary inclusion within the English education system'. *Disability and Society*, 27(5), pp. 675–688.

IPSEA. (2018) *Response to Home Education – IPSEA's Response to the Call for Evidence and Revised DfE Guidance*. Available at: www.ipsea.org.uk/news/home-education-not-always-what-it-seems (accessed 17 July 2018).

Legislation.gov.uk. (2010). *Equality Act 2010*. Available at: http://www.legislation.gov.uk/ukpga/2010/15/ contents (Accessed 11 Jan. 2018)

McCluskey, G., Riddell, S., Weedon, E. and Fordyce, M. (2016) 'Exclusion from School and recognition of difference'. *Discourse: Studies in the Cultural Politics of Education*, 37(4), pp. 529–539.

Morris, E. (2002) 'Today Programme'. *BBC Radio 4*, 23rd May 2002.

North East Jobs. (2017) *Internal Exclusion Manager 163888*. Available at: www.northeastjobs.org.uk/job/ Internal_Exclusion_Manager/163888 (accessed 16 July 2018).

Nye, P. and Thomson, D. (2018) *Who's Left 2018, Part One: The Main Findings*. Available at: https://ffteducationdatalab.org.uk/2018/06/whos-left-2018-part-one-the-main-findings/ (accessed 16 July 2018).

Ofsted. (2017) *The Annual Report of Her Majesty's Chief Inspector of Education, Children's Services and Skills 2016/17*. Available at: https://assets.publishing.service.gov.uk/government/uploads/system/uploads/attachment_data/file/666871/Ofsted_Annual_Report_2016-17_Accessible.pdf (accessed 16 July 2018).

Parris, M. (2018) *How Was School: Never the Twain Shall Meet*. Available at: http://howwasschool.org.uk/audio/never-the-twain-shall-meet/ (accessed 16 July 2018).

Social Exclusion Unit. (2002) *Truancy and School Exclusion*. Available at: http://dera.ioe.ac.uk/5074/2/D5074New.pdf (accessed 16 July 2018).

Staufenberg, J. (2017) 'Oasis Academy Trust Denies Encouraging Parents to "Home Educate" Disruptive Pupils'. *Schools Week*, 5th June 2017.

Titheradge, N. (2018) 'Hundreds of pupils spend week in school isolation booths'. *BBC News, Family & Education*, 12th November 2018. Available at: www.bbc.co.uk/news/education-46044394 (accessed 28 March 2019).

Warnock, M. (1978) *Special Educational Needs: Report of the Committee of Enquiry Into the Education of Handicapped Children and Young People*. London: H.M.S.O

Webster, R. and Blatchford, P. (2013) 'The educational experiences of pupils with a statement for special educational needs in mainstream primary schools: Results from a systematic observation study'. *European Journal of Special Needs Education*, 28(4), pp. 463–479.

Woollard, J. (2010) *Psychology in the Classroom: Behaviourism*. Abingdon, Oxon: Routledge.

Chapter three
IMPACT OF EXCLUSION

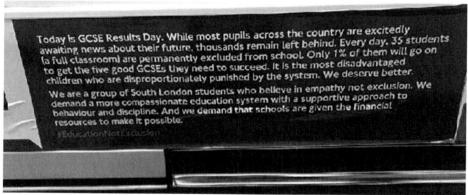

Figure 3.1 Posters spotted on Northern Line, 23 August 2018

Source: Photos taken by Tristan Middleton

Pomeroy (2000, p. 3) argues that 'Exclusion has a serious detrimental effect on young people, their families and society'. This was echoed some 16 years later by McCluskey et al. (2016, p. 530) who identified that, 'Children and young people excluded from school are already more likely to be disadvantaged, and . . . the experience of exclusion often further reduces their life chances'. In this final chapter of Part I, we explore the impact of exclusion upon the excluded pupil, their families and upon wider society in order to investigate the effects. Our analysis of literature identified six key dimensions which may potentially be affected by exclusion shown in Figure 3.2.

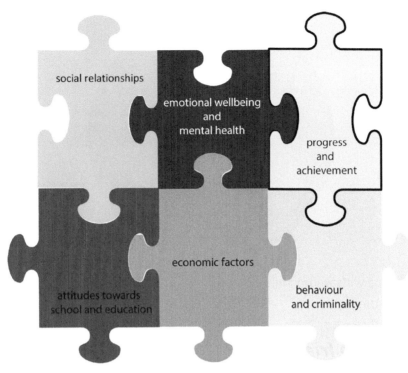

Figure 3.2 Dimensions which may be affected by school exclusion

Many of the research studies investigating experiences of exclusion for learners, parents and school staff have been small-scale studies owing to the resource implications of undertaking in-depth interviews. This does mean that the findings of each small-scale study may not be generalised across the whole population of children and young people excluded from school. Nevertheless, the mosaic built from the studies contribute to building a picture of the impacts of exclusion upon children and young people and their families (Munn, Lloyd and Cullen, 2000). These studies are also valuable in that the researchers offered opportunities for children and young people to share their perceptions of their experiences. This is because children and young people are able to provide an authoritative account of their own perceptions of their experiences, and researchers who examine children and young people's views within their investigation provide a valuable addition to building an ethical and genuine understanding of children's lived-experiences (Sargeant and Harcourt, 2012).

Each dimension identified within Figure 3.2 will be discussed within the remainder of this chapter. There are real-life testimonies included to illustrate the key points identified from the research and literature.

Social relationships

Figure 3.3 presents key people with whom children and young people interact and relate with in relation to the school context. The arrows are included to acknowledge that these people will also hold perceptions of and have some interactions with one another.

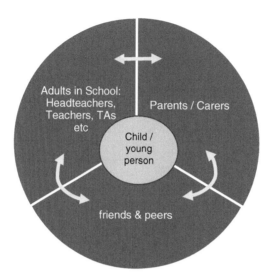

Figure 3.3 Key people with whom children and young people have a social relationship in relation to the school setting

Relationships with friends and peers

Internal and external exclusion mean that young people are separated from their friends and peers and shared experiences within school. This leads to the young person feeling isolated, lonely and bored (Brodie, 2001). Students interviewed for Pomeroy's research (2000) reported that they felt exclusion from school impacted negatively upon their social relationships. The separation from peers engendered a feeling of difference to their peers. Osler and Osler (2005) also note that the excluded learner may experience feelings of isolation and rejection. This feeling of isolation may continue when the learner returns to school as children and young people may be rejected by some of their peers when they return to school (Munn, Lloyd and Cullen, 2000). Exclusion sanctions which require longer periods of internal or external exclusion for learners during the social aspects of the school day, reduce opportunities for these young people to interact with their peers. O'Brien (2016) argues that children and young people's social development is hampered owing to the separation from peers during social activities.

It is important to acknowledge that young people who experience difficulties with social interaction and friendships may engage in actions to self-exclude themselves from school. Osler and Vincent (2003) in their research upon girls and exclusion identified that some girls self-excluded themselves from school owing to difficulties with social relationships.

Relationships within the family

Exclusion may cause strain on relationships within the family. Kane (2011) identified that there may be blame for the child's challenging behaviour attributed by the parents or carers towards one another. She also noted reports from some children and young people of being punished physically by parents or carers or isolated from the rest of their family in their room as a consequence of exclusion. Indeed in situations in which a child or young person presents with challenging behaviours in both home and school settings, some parents or carers may feel the strain of having to manage their child's difficult behaviour for longer periods as they do not have the respite which the school day normally offers (Munn, Lloyd and Cullen, 2000).

Relationships with adults in school

The exclusion of a child or young person from school or the individual classroom impacts upon their relationship with the key adults involved. The exclusion may be considered to offer a breathing space for the pupil, their peers and the school staff (Kane, 2005; Cooper, 2002). This breathing space may act positively for all concerned and their relationships if it is used to gain help and plan for the student's return (Cooper, 2002). However, the gap in time during which the pupil is not within the school environment interacting with their peers and adults, may negatively impact upon their relationships. One example of how this may negatively affect relationships is that of missing out on shared experiences; shared experiences which support building and strengthening connections between people.

It is important to acknowledge that sometimes there is a need to exclude in order to protect adults and children and young people; for example, in the case in which a pupil has assaulted members of staff or pupil(s). For the remaining pupils and staff therefore, there is a positive outcome in that a potential safety risk has been removed. This may be accompanied by contrasting emotions such as relief regarding safety and sadness about not being able to meet all of the child's needs so that they could stay in the school's community (O'Brien, 2016).

McCluskey *et al.* (2016) contend that employment of the exclusion sanction denotes failures within the relationships within school which are then at risk of not being resolved. This is because time away from school may hinder chances for building positive relationships with teachers and peers (Osler and Vincent, 2003). Schools play a vital role in socialising young people (Brodie, 2001), which includes adults modelling pro-social behaviours to pupils. McCluskey *et al.* (2016, p. 535) offer this explanation of how exclusion provides a negative model for pupils: '[exclusion] models little that we would want children and young people to learn about effective and pro-social ways of relating to and communicating with others. It rarely offers authentic opportunity for acknowledgement of harm done, conflict to be resolved or discussion of ways to repair relationships, all of which have been found to be helpful to schools and children themselves.'

Emotional wellbeing and mental health
The pupil

The pupil who is excluded may experience a range of emotions across the time of the implementation of the exclusion, the period away from school and upon the reintegration back into school (Munn, Lloyd and Cullen, 2000). Within the array of initial emotions experienced in relation to the initial implementation of the exclusion sanction identified by excluded pupils (interviewed for research studies) are included intense feelings of anger, distress, devastation and anxiety about parental and carer reactions to the news of exclusion (Osler and Osler, 2005; Cooper, 2002; Munn, Lloyd and Cullen, 2000; Hayden, 1997). Munn, Lloyd and Cullen (2000) reviewed a number of studies and noted that excluded pupils reported feeling rejected, annoyed, that they have been treated unfairly, feared and branded as menaces. They note that the unfairness was owing to the perception that there was a lack of consistency between teachers' application of the sanctions for rule breaking.

Over time, other emotions experienced included feelings of isolation, loneliness and rejection together with a negative impact upon self-esteem (Osler and Osler, 2005). Some children and young people were reported to have had feelings of isolation exacerbated owing to the punishments issued at home in response to exclusion, such as being confined to their rooms with little interaction with other family members (Munn, Lloyd and Cullen, 2000). Some children and young people reported feeling bored owing to the lack of work set from school, meaning there was little for them to do (Munn, Lloyd and Cullen, 2000). Additionally, children and young people reported that they continued to experience some of these emotions upon reintegration into school, for example in response to negative comments or actions from peers or adults within school. In her research, Kane (2011) reported that pupils expressed concern about how exclusion may impact their lives in the future.

Munn, Lloyd and Cullen (2000, p. 9) present their findings regarding the phased affects upon children and young people's emotions across the episodes within a period of exclusion. This ranges from initial intensity to later worries about the longer-term implications arising from having an exclusion recorded on their schooling record. Figure 3.4 sets out a spectrum of emotions across phases of exclusion.

This consideration of affective aspects of exclusion raises questions about whether exclusion may impact upon the excluded pupil's mental health. Parker and Ford (2013) state that there is limited evidence which points to exclusion impacting negatively on mental health, however there is a clear gap in literature. This view is echoed by the Children's Commissioner Report (Apland *et al.*, 2017).

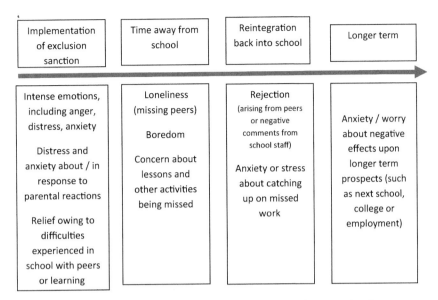

Figure 3.4 Spectrum of potential emotions across phases of an exclusion

Source: Adapted from Munn, Lloyd and Cullen (2000, p. 9)

Parents and carers

As an initial reaction to the news of the sanction of exclusion being instigated, parents or carers may experience feelings of anger, shock or devastation (Hayden, 1997). Cooper (2002) reported that some teachers had observed that parents felt the emotions of anger and shame in response to their child being excluded. Parental anger may have also been accompanied with some resignation, particularly in the circumstances of the exclusion being justified by reasons of health and safety issues (McCluskey *et al.*, 2016).

Some parents and carers may also feel helpless or powerless in response to the exclusion (Kane, 2011, 2005; Hayden, 1997). This may be compounded by Hayden's (1997) observation that some parents identified that they lacked confidence with regard to communicating with school.

Frustrations may arise from parental perceptions that the schools are not meeting their child's needs and/or that the schools hold a negative perception of their child (Cooper, 2002; Munn, Lloyd and Cullen, 2000). Cooper (2002) noted that parents felt that school staff did not listen to their concerns. He also identified that parents reported frustrations owing to the denials being given from schools in response to parents asking schools for help or requests for actions to gain support from outside agencies. This often led to further stress and anxiety for parents and feelings of isolation owing to the lack of support following the exclusion of their child. In a similar vein, Munn, Lloyd and Cullen (2000) reported parental feelings of frustration owing to the perception that schools were not being supportive of parents' difficulties with meeting their child's needs and from their observations that exclusion did not support positive changes in children and young people's behaviours. They noted that frustrations also arose from the way in which exclusion processes were applied.

Parents and carers may also experience feelings of anxiety or vexation about their child's education owing to the time away from formal education and from their worries about what would happen regarding their child's education and their future prospects (Cooper, 2002; Munn, Lloyd and Cullen, 2000).

School staff

The focus within the literature explored was upon excluded children and young people and their parents' emotional responses and actions in response to exclusion. Hayden (1997) noted distress together with a sense of frustration identified within teacher's accounts of exclusion; the frustrations arose from difficulties in engaging support from the child's parents or external agencies. She reported that some frustrations were elicited from the difficulties experienced with managing challenging behaviour and supporting mental health needs which were underlying these behaviours.

Emotional development for children and young people

There are some pupils who experience difficulties with regulating their emotions and need explicit teaching to develop their emotional awareness and competences with emotional regulation (O'Brien, 2016). In addition to implementing specific teaching to develop emotional understanding and skills, schools provide opportunities for children and young people to practise these skills with peers in structured and unstructured activities. An inference may potentially be drawn that children and young people who need this teaching and practice will miss out on these opportunities if they have been excluded.

This account was provided by a senior leader in an alternative provision school:

Steven first came to my APS after his permanent exclusion. I had to abandon his first induction meeting as he was very escalated running around the room, climbing on the furniture and kicking the door to get out. He told me clearly that he did not want to be in my school and that it was shit and he was never coming again. His Mother told me at the meeting that Steven had been excluded for hitting out at staff. The exclusion paperwork did not mention this. It detailed persistent disruption of learning, absconding, refusal to follow instructions, threatening staff, climbing and damaging equipment. The school had helpfully included pictures of damage done and of Steven messing up a room. This must have been highly distressing for him to have his picture taken in an escalated state.

Progress and achievement

Exclusion from school represents the most direct way in which schools can exercise their power to prevent children from participating in education.

(Brodie, 2001, p. 19)

Students interviewed for Pomeroy's research (2000) reported that they felt exclusion from school impacted negatively upon their educational opportunities and achievements. Examples cited by the students included the much reduced number and breadth of lessons they had access to within the provision provided during their exclusion and subjects they were able to take formal qualifications in. This view is supported by Osler and Vincent (2003, p. 14) who contend that 'students who are barred from school or who absent themselves for significant periods of time are unlikely to realise their full academic potential'. Similarly, Osler and Osler (2005) contend that the period of exclusion may impact negatively upon progress and attainment. Within their research, they cite an example of a pupil excluded twice during their GCSE year without any work of guidance for studies provided, in addition to missing out on the opportunity to sit for mock exams providing practice for the real exams.

Further negative influences upon progress may be drawn from Kane (2011) who identifies within her research that the requirement for work to be set by school for the excluded child or young person may be regarded negatively by both school staff and pupils. She noted that some excluded pupils were reported to have refused to complete the work set, and that some teachers regarded this as a tokenistic task and did not reflect upon what may be needed to ensure continuity for the child or young person's learning.

Excluded children and young people may experience difficulties with settling back into school following an exclusion. Their self-esteem may also be negatively impacted. Osler and Vincent (2003) contend that this has the potential to directly and indirectly influence attainment. Mackenbach *et al.* (2015) provide a sobering reflection upon the longer-term outcomes in their assertion that those with poorer education on average live six years less than their better educated peers.

This reflection was provided by a specialist advisory teacher working in a behaviour support team for a local authority:

one thing we see quite a lot of is pupils being permanently excluded on the back of a reintegration following a fixed term exclusion. They . . . often put the pupils into isolation/consequence room on their return as well.

Attitudes towards school and education

The previous section has noted that some researchers have identified that excluded children and young people experience a lowering of motivation and self-esteem. Cooper (2002) reported that one of the consequences of exclusion included lowering of self-esteem in children and young people is a loss of trust in school. Time not attending school may lead to children and young people experiencing difficulties with settling back into a routine for learning and attendance (Osler and Vincent, 2003). Indeed, excluded children and young people interviewed for Cooper's research (2002, p. 32) reported that they experienced difficulties with settling into 'a structured education programme'. Many of these children and young people had not had any work set for them and thus were out of the routines of working. This also left gaps of continuity in topics within each of subjects being studied which may have a negative impact upon learning. Teachers interviewed for Cooper's research felt that exclusion would impact negatively upon their child's feeling of belonging to the school community.

Parents and carers of children and young people who are permanently excluded from their schools need to find a new school placement for their child. Cooper (2002) maintains that the influence of market forces within education often means that children and young people who have been excluded cannot secure a place at a popular school. Indeed, data analysis by Gill, Quilter-Pinner and Swift (2017) shows once a child or young person is excluded, they are twice as likely to be taught by an unqualified teacher and twice as likely to have a supply teacher. In addition, some children and young people who may not return to formal schooling are at risk of disappearing from education and care systems (Kane, 2011; Daniels and Cole, 2010; Pomeroy, 2000).

Economic factors

Exclusion may have a negative financial impact upon the family in the circumstances in which a parent or carer has to take time off work in order to be at home to supervise their excluded child (Brodie, 2001). Brodie (2001) argues that this can further exacerbate social exclusion for disadvantaged families. The child's exclusion impacted negatively upon the parent's ability to do their job, or to seek better paid employment, owing to needing to be at home to supervise their child or to collect and return to school for lunchtime detentions (Cooper, 2002). Thus, the implementation of regular demands to remove children and young people from school sites, for example during lunchtimes may impact upon parental work and finances (O'Brien, 2016). For some families the need to provide the child or young person with a midday meal, owing to exclusion, places a strain upon family finances (Pomeroy, 2000). In 2007, New Philanthropy Capital estimated the total lifetime cost of a permanent exclusion from school to be £14,187 to the individual arising from future lost earnings (NPC, 2007, p. 12).

In Chapter 1, we explained that the political discourse from all major parties has embodied the notion that a key purpose of schooling is to educate children and young people for their future employment. Exclusion may place obstacles in the path for children and young people to gain paid employment. Kane (2011 p. 137) identified that 'Repeated experience of school exclusion was seen to undermine and sometimes destroy pupils' participation in schooling and to deny them the benefits accruing from education and formal credentials'. This is supported by Daniels and Cole (2010) who report that one person interviewed for the research identified that they experienced difficulties with securing paid employment owing to having an exclusion recorded on their school records. Daniels and Cole also noted that social isolation for the excluded pupils meant that they did not have relationships which might have helped them with finding and securing employment.

There may be financial burdens for wider society linked to school exclusions. Pomeroy (2000) contends that there are costs arising from exclusion of children and young people from school which impact upon a range of services, including education, police and justice system and social care. This is supported by Gill, Quilter-Pinner and Swift (2017) who identify that every cohort of permanently excluded pupils will go on to cost the state an extra £2.1 billion in education, health, benefits and criminal justice costs.

Behaviour and criminality

There is some difficulty with proving a causal link between exclusion and criminality. Some researchers have suggested that exclusion from school facilitates time for young people to become engaged in behaviours which leads them into illegal actions. This is owing to the lack of structure, which triggers feelings of boredom and heightens risks for involvement in criminal activity (Cooper, 2002; Pomeroy, 2000).

Osler and Vincent (2003, p. 20) identified that 'there appears to be a strong link between school exclusion and juvenile crime; a study conducted for the Home Office found that 98 per cent of boys and 61 per cent of girls who were excluded from school admitted to offending'. Osler and Vincent (2003) cite research from the Audit Commission in 1996 which identified 42 per cent of offenders who were of school age had been excluded from school, and from the Metropolitan Police which identified that 35 per cent of juvenile crime had been perpetrated during school hours. The Centre for Social Justice (2011) identified that, in a survey conducted in 2010 by HM Inspectorate of Prisons and the Youth Justice Board of 15–18 year-olds held in custody, '90 per cent of the young men and 75 per cent of the young women had been excluded from school'. This is supported by Daniels and Cole (2010, p. 20) who identified that 'many of the young people retained limited horizons, lacked self-belief and their marginalisation tended to increase, sometimes associated with increasing offending'.

Conclusion

It is interesting to note that parents and carers, children and young people and teachers identify similar emotions experienced in response to exclusion, such as frustration, distress, anxiety. Within the literature reviewed, some parents perceived that the school viewed their child negatively, and did not implement strategies and interventions to meet their child's needs. Contrary to this, some teachers expressed frustration regarding the lack of resources and professional knowledge, which impeded their abilities to understand and meet needs appropriately. They also cited difficulties with engaging support from external agencies and sometimes from parents.

Brodie (2001) argues that schools play a vital role in socialising young people and thus exclusion from the school environment may heighten risks of breaching societal expectations and rules regarding participation in society. Indeed, exclusion from school has been linked to social exclusion and poor long-term outcomes, such as employment (McCluskey *et al.*, 2016; Se1lman *et al.*, 2002).

We end this chapter with a quotation from McCluskey *et al.* (2016, p. 535) for you to reflect upon:

> In view of the large body of international evidence on the relationship between disciplinary exclusion and under-achievement, long-term unemployment, poverty and involvement with the criminal justice system, it seems evident that disciplinary exclusion has no place in the education system.

This account of an experience of exclusion is provided by a member of the police force responsible for training recruits, looking back at his experiences as a young person:

I still recall some parts vividly. . . . I was in a play fight with a year 7 student and I was in year 10. It escalated and I hurt him. I remember being shocked at what I did. . . . I was made to sit outside the headmasters office. The headmaster, who had spend the last four years of calling me Jim, suddenly was able to use my actual name. He was very cross and shouted that he was sick of my behaviour. This was also a surprise as the behaviour I had, I felt, was no better or worse than many of my peers. His was red faced and shouted at me . . . Initially I was sent to the desk outside of his office. . . . It was also next to the school office and after about an hour I heard one of the admin ladies talking on the phone. Afterwards, her voice became loud whilst she talked to the deputy. She said she had spoken to the mother of the boy and the mother was furious at me. The deputy appeared and apologised that I had over heard what had been said. I'll never know to this day, but I suspect that it was deliberate that I over heard what I later thought was a staged event. . . . I felt guilty and wanted to apologise to the boy. However I wasn't allowed to and had to write a letter instead. A letter that I feared would be poked fun at by the boy's friends. I was told that I was being internally excluded for the day, and so I carried out some work at the desk. It was probably the most focussed I'd ever been. When I turned up for school the next day, I sat in registration then went to my first lesson. My German teacher was surprised to see me. She said that my exclusion was meant to be for a second day. She also said how surprised she had been when the head told all of the teachers in the morning about what happened, and the teacher thought he'd made a mistake. . . . I went to the head who told me I was excluded for another day. I was upset that this had not been told to me. I had thought, as I had not been told, the punishment was over.

References

Apland, K., Lawrence, H., Mesie, J. and Yarrow, E. (2017) *Children's Voices: A Review of Evidence on the Subjective Wellbeing of Children Excluded From School and in Alternative Provision in England*. Available at: www.childrenscommissioner.gov.uk/wp-content/uploads/2017/11/CCO-Childrens-Voices-Excluded-from-schools-and-alt-provision.pdf (accessed 8 March 2019).

Brodie, I. (2001) *Children's Homes and School Exclusion*. London: Jessica Kingsley Publishers.

Centre for Social Justice. (2011) *No Excuses: A Review of Educational Exclusion*. Available at: www.centreforsocialjustice.org.uk/core/wp-content/uploads/2016/08/CSJ_Educational_Exclusion.pdf (accessed 10 January 2019).

Cooper, C. (2002) *Understanding School Exclusion: Challenging Processes of Docility*. Nottingham: Education Now Publishing.

Daniels, H. and Cole, T. (2010) 'Exclusion from school: Short term set back or a long term of difficulties?'. *European Journal of Special Needs Education*, 25(2), pp. 115–130.

Gill, K., Quilter-Pinner, H. and Swift, D. (2017) *Making the Difference Breaking the Link Between School Exclusion and Social Exclusion*. Institute for Public Policy Research. Available at: www.ippr.org/publications/making-the-difference (accessed 9 March 2019).

Hayden, C. (1997) *Children Excluded From Primary School: Debates, Evidence, Responses*. Buckingham: Open University Press.

Kane, J. (2005) 'Exclusions from school: Different voices'. In J. Rix, K. Simmons, M. Nind and K. Sheehy (eds.), *Policy and Power in Inclusive Education: Values Into Practice*. London: RoutledgeFarmer, pp. 98–106.

Kane, J. (2011) *Social Class, Gender and Exclusion From School*. London: Routledge.

Mackenbach, J. P., Menvielle, G., Jasilionis, D. and De Gelder, R. (2015) *Measuring Educational Inequalities in Mortality Statistics*. OECD Statistics Working Papers. https://doi.org/10.1787/5jrqppx182zs-en.

McCluskey, G., Riddell, S., Weedon, E. and Fordyce, M. (2016) 'Exclusion from school and recognition of difference'. *Discourse Studies in the Cultural Politics of Education*, 37(4), pp. 529–539.

Munn, P., Lloyd, G. and Cullen, M.A. (2000) *Alternatives to Exclusion From School*. London: Paul Chapman Publishing.

New Philanthropy Capital. (2007) *Misspent Youth: The Costs of Truancy and Exclusion*. London: New Philanthropy Capital.

O'Brien, J. (2016) *Don't Send Him in Tomorrow: Shining a Light on the Marginalised Disenfranchised and Forgotten Children of Today's Schools*. Carmarthen: Independent Thinking Press.

Osler, A. and Osler, C. (2005) 'Inclusion, exclusion and children's rights'. In J. Rix, K. Simmons, M. Nind and K. Sheehy (eds.), *Policy and Power in Inclusive Education: Values Into Practice*. London: RoutledgeFarmer, pp. 107–117.

Osler, A. and Vincent, K. (2003) *Girls and Exclusion: Rethinking the Agenda*. London: RoutledgeFalmer.

Parker, C. and Ford, T. (2013) 'Editorial perspective: School exclusion is a mental health issue'. *Journal of Child Psychology and Psychiatry*, 54(12), pp. 1366–1368.

Pomeroy, E. (2000) *Experiencing Exclusion*. Stoke-on-Trent: Trentham Books.

Sargeant, J. and Harcourt, D. (2012) *Doing Ethical Research with Children*. Maidenhead: Open University Press.

Sellman, E., Bedward, J., Cole, T. and Daniels, H. (2002) 'Thematic review a sociocultural approach to exclusion'. *British Educational Research Journal*, 28(6), pp. 889–900.

PART II

Part II explores different views of inclusion and presents the authors' theoretical framework of the six dimensions of inclusion. This section of the book also explores the challenges for leading inclusive practice and proposes approaches for leading inclusive practice through the dimensions of our proposed framework.

Chapter one
DEFINITIONS OF INCLUSION

This section of the book will explore different views of inclusion making reference to academic literature. It will clarify key vocabulary related to inclusion, including reflecting upon notions of equality, equal opportunity, equity, diversity and social justice (Lumby and Coleman, 2016) and will also explore the need for a shared understanding between professionals of the language and concepts involved within inclusion and exclusion.

What is inclusion?

> Inclusion is not about figures, politics or . . . dogma, it is, about beliefs, faith, caring and the creation of community. . . . It is about human rights and human beings.
>
> (Allan, 2003, p. 178)

The Salamanca Agreement, which was signed by 92 governments in 1994, enshrined a human-rights perspective on education and outlined that countries should, 'concentrate their efforts on the development of inclusive schools' (UNESCO, 1994). This document had a significant impact upon the debate surrounding access to education in the context of learners with Special Educational Needs and Disability, as well as for other inclusion groups. It led towards the call by many for the closing of all special schools. Some writers have identified that as a result of this inclusion became the fashionable (Armstrong, Armstrong and Spandagou, 2010) new orthodoxy of education (Allan, 1999). A quarter of a century on from this significant event in the development of the understanding of inclusive education, this chapter will explore the evolving concept of inclusive education and identify a working understanding for practitioners.

Grenier (2010) suggested that inclusion should be considered as a philosophical concept rather than something concerned with school structures and organisation and Lumby and Coleman (2016) assert the importance of language in the exploration and understanding of concepts. They extensively examine key concepts related to inclusion which were identified by Blackmore (2009, p. 3) as equity, equality, equal opportunity, affirmative action, social justice and diversity. Lumby and Coleman's (2016) conclusions around four of the key concepts are summarised here.

Equality

This concept relates to 'sameness' and treating people in the same way. Equal treatment is likely to reinforce existing inequalities, which has the consequence of offering unequal opportunities and resulting in unequal outcomes.

Equal opportunity

By providing equal opportunity, individuals' differences may be recognised and compensated for, through treating people differently. This approach has the aim of enabling the outcomes for individuals being the same or similar. The perspective of equal opportunity is reflected in the OECD's definition of inclusion in education, where they identify the aim of all learners reaching a similar minimum level of skills (2012, p. 9).

Equity

This concept is founded upon the understanding of difference and relates to individuals choosing the activities they value and their achievements, reflecting their interests and passions. As such, individuals will be treated differently and outcomes for individuals will be different.

Social justice

The notion of social justice links closely to the view of education as a basic human right (Ekins, 2017, p. 2). Key values within an understanding of social justice are 'distributive justice', 'cultural justice' and 'associational justice'. Distributive justice, which is more simply summarised as sharing, relates within schools to resources and learning opportunities being spread fairly amongst all learners. Cultural justice relates to different groups and ensuring that a particular group does not dominate or lead curricula or access. Discrimination related to race, gender, sexuality and other inclusion groups is a key issue within this area. Associational justice concerns the engagement of all people in decision-making for factors which affect their lives.

The concepts of equity and social justice are those which the authors present as being an important part of the foundation for an understanding of inclusive education.

The notion of equity stands in opposition to the approach of integration, which was a prevalent framework for educational practitioners and policy makers towards the millennium and beyond. The approach of integration is based upon the assumption that there is a norm within a group or organisation, towards which all members need to move. If a learner arrives at a school setting and the approach taken is to aim to integrate them within the setting, this makes the assumption that the learner needs to change in some way, in order to fit the 'norm'. This places the learner's differences within the context of being problematic and needing to be altered and has the consequence of problematising their differences. It places the difference as a deficit within the learner, which needs to be altered or a situation where adaptations need to be made in order to overcome the barriers presented by the difference.

Integration – an example

If someone arrives in the UK unable to speak English or without an understanding of the culture, to integrate they need to learn the language and understand the culture in order to become part of society.

The contrast between inclusion and integration is reflected in two well-established and different views of disability: the medical model and the social model.

The medical model of disability

Disability is a problem which lies within the individual and the individual needs to be changed. Medical professionals are in a position to cure the person's impairment
(ALFIE, 2018a).

This model has a strong focus on interventions and treatments which aim to impact on the perceived deficit or impairment.

The social model of disability

Disability is not something within an individual, but an oppressive social relationship 'imposed on top of our impairments'
(Union of the Physically Impaired Against Segregation, 1976, p. 14).

A further model of disability which is useful to consider, which is closely linked to the 'associational' aspect of social justice, is the affirmative model. This model, whilst underpinned by the social model seeks to challenge negative attitudes about disabled people (Tregaskis, 2004). It moves forward to identify impairment as a common and ordinary part of human life (Cameron, 2014, p. 6) rather than a deviation from the norm. This model emphasises difference as a positive part of society, including impairment and disability, and recognises that difference leads to a range of needs, desires and values. As such, it is not for those who are part of the dominant culture to make decisions for others. Rather, alongside other inclusion groups, disabled people have a right to have their voice heard and to have control over decisions which are made when they relate to them (Swain and French, 2000).

> An affirmative model of disability has emerged that seeks to encourage us to support disabled people's individual and collective aspirations, asserted value and validity to impairment; celebrate difference; and recognise disabled people's right to have control of what is done to their bodies.
>
> (Davis, 2014, p. 158)

> The difference between 'integration' and 'inclusion' is that integration was concerned with assimilating those with special needs into the school existing system without changing that system in any significant way, while inclusion is concerned with fundamentally transforming the way the educative process is organised and conducted in schools.
>
> (Barton, 2003)

The authors present a fundamental attitude inherent in an inclusive approach, which is one of valuing difference and viewing difference as normal and a positive attribute which contributes to the group or organisation. Underpinning human existence is the notion of difference. Part of our identity as a human is our individuality or difference and the notion of choice or agency. Different people, cultures, traditions and beliefs can be considered to make our world a richer and more rewarding place in which to exist and to enrich and strengthen our communities (ALFIE, 2018b). By applying this to our educational contexts, we will be placing our institutions within an inclusive process of searching, 'to find better ways of responding to diversity. It is about learning how to live with difference and learning how to learn from difference (Ainscow, 2005, p. 119).

Where the medical model is used, it is likely that difference will be viewed within a binary context of able/disabled or can-do/can't-do (Tomlinson, 2017, p. 165). Using the social model, difference is viewed as something to be expected and ability will be understood within the context of the expectations placed on others. The affirmative model will lead to those who may be seen as being different having a voice in framing ideas of ability. This links closely to the notion of empowerment, which is implied within the concept of social justice and will be discussed further.

Ekins (2017) suggests that in order to develop an understanding of inclusion we need to relate the concept to the notion of the purpose of education. Some argue that school structures in England have developed as a means to create uniformly prepared automatons to service our industrial manufacturing requirements and that our education system is struggling to move on from this legacy. Claxton (2006) suggests that a generational change has been happening, with the focus of education moving away from the transmission of knowledge, through the development of skills to support learners to assimilate the knowledge more successfully. He suggests that the focus has reached a point where education has become concerned with developing lifelong learning skills and attributes, where teachers become facilitators. The authors recognise this trajectory whilst also acknowledging that policy, guidance, accountability measures and practices within education presenting contrasting approaches, with underpinning philosophies or values which are frequently in conflict. Current practitioners will be familiar with professional development materials which communicate expectations that learning opportunities will be individualised and provide choices for learners, whilst also experiencing demands for standardised evaluations of learning and progress against narrow subject descriptors. Nevertheless, there is an identifiable move towards approaches which are underpinned by pedagogies of choice, empowerment and outcomes related to learning attributes rather than accumulated knowledge. This is, in no small part, as a result of the increasing pace of change and development in our societies, where, for example there are estimates that between 10 per cent and 50 per cent of jobs will be highly susceptible to being replaced by technology in 2030 (Sellar, 2018).

No one would think of lighting a fire today by rubbing two sticks together. Yet much of what passes for education is based on equally outdated concepts.

(Dryden and Vos, 1994)

In times of change, learners will inherit the earth, while the learned will find themselves beautifully equipped to deal with a world that no longer exists.

Attributed to Eric Hoffer

All of these factors lead towards a direction of travel in education practices away from a didactic dissemination of established packets of knowledge which are tested and subsequently conclusions of individual ability are drawn. Instead pedagogy is moving towards enabling learners to develop skills and understanding which will support them to be a lifelong learner within their own contexts of needs and interests. This direction challenges approaches of conformity based upon norms and the aims of mass production in education (Armstrong, Armstrong and Spandagou, 2010, p. vii). This links back to the concepts of equity and cultural and associational justice and a philosophical understanding of inclusion (Grenier, 2010).

In order to explain the concept of inclusion, the authors have focused on concepts and values, as, when we expand diversity in our educational systems, it becomes increasingly difficult to identify specific practices, techniques and approaches which may be inclusive. Instead, an inclusive approach to education can be defined as 'a never-ending process which involves the progressive discovery and removal of limits to participation and learning' (Booth and Ainscow, 2011, p. 40). Inclusive education is a dynamic concept which is about developing organisations and practice, with a diverse community, within the principles of empowerment, emancipation and equity (Argyropoulos and Nikolaraizi, 2009) based upon the concepts of equity and social justice.

References

Ainscow, M. (2005) 'Developing inclusive education systems: What are the levers for change?'. *Journal of Educational Change*, 6(2), pp. 109–124.

ALFIE. (2018a) *Models of Disability*. Available at: www.allfie.org.uk/definitions/models-of-disability/ (accessed 2 August 2018).

ALFIE. (2018b) *Our Principles*. Available at: www.allfie.org.uk/about-us/our-principles/ (accessed 17 July 2018).

Allan, J. (1999) *Actively Seeking Inclusion: Pupils With Special Needs in Mainstream Schools*. London: Falmer

Allan, J. (2003) 'Productive pedagogies and the challenge of inclusion'. *British Journal of Special Education*, 30(4), pp. 175–179.

Argyropoulos, V. and Nikolaraizi, M. (2009) 'Developing inclusive practices through collaborative action research'. *European Journal of Special Needs Education*, 24(2), pp. 139–153.

Armstrong, A.C., Armstrong, D. and Spandagou, I. (2010) *Inclusive Education: International Policy & Practice*. London: SAGE.

Barton, L. (2003) *Inclusive Education and Teacher Education: A Basis of Hope or a Discourse of Delusion?* Inaugural Professorial Lecture delivered at the Institute of Education, University of London, 3rd July 2003.

Blackmore, J. (2009) 'Inclusive education: What does it mean for students, teachers, leaders and schools?'. *Professional Voice*, 7(1), pp. 11–15.

Booth, T. and Ainscow, M. (2011) *Index for Inclusion: Developing Learning and Participation in Schools.* Third Edition. Bristol: CSIE.

Cameron, C. (ed.). (2014) *Disability Studies: A Student's Guide.* London: SAGE.

Claxton, G. (2006) *Learning to Learn – The Fourth Generation: Making Sense of Personalised Learning.* Bristol: TLO Ltd.

Davis, J.M. (2014) 'Disability and childhood: A journey towards inclusion'. In J. Swain (ed.), *Disabling Barriers – Enabling Environments.* Third Edition. London: SAGE, pp. 157–164.

DfES. (2004) *Removing Barriers to Achievement: The Government's Strategy for SEN.* Nottingham: DfES.

Dryden, G. and Vos, J. (1994) *The Learning Revolution: A Lifelong Learning Program for the World's Finest Computer: Your Amazing Brain.* Rolling Hills Estate, CA: Jalmar Press.

Ekins, A. (2017) *Reconsidering Inclusion: Sustaining and Building Inclusion Practices in Schools.* London: Routledge.

Grenier, M. (2010) 'Moving to inclusion: A socio-cultural analysis of practice'. *International Journal of Inclusive Education*, 14(4), pp. 387–400.

Lumby, J. and Coleman, M. (2016) *Leading for Equality: Making Schools Fairer.* London: SAGE.

OECD. (2012) *Equity and Quality in Education: Supporting Disadvantaged Students and Schools.* Available at: www.oecd.org/education/school/50293148.pdf (accessed 17 July 2018).

Sellar, S. (2018) *Rewiring Education Studies: The Methodological Challenges of Researching Datafication in Schooling.* Keynote Speech, British Education Studies Annual Conference, University of Bolton, 29th June 2018.

Swain, J. and French, S. (2000) 'Towards an affirmation model of disability'. *Disability & Society*, 15(4), pp. 569–582.

Tomlinson, S. (2017) *A Sociology of Special and Inclusive Education: Exploring the Manufacture of Inability.* Abingdon, Oxon: Routledge.

Tregaskis, C. (2004) *Constructions of Disability: Researching the Interface Between Disabled and Non-disabled People.* London: Routledge.

UNESCO. (1994) *Final Report: World Conference on Special Needs Education: Access and Quality.* Paris: UNESCO.

Union of the Physically Impaired Against Segregation. (1976) *Fundamental Principles of Disability.* London: UPIAS.

Chapter two

THEORETICAL FRAMEWORK FOR AN INCLUSIVE APPROACH

In the previous chapter the authors explored concepts of inclusive education. They concluded that valuing difference and the concepts of social justice and equity were fundamental to an understanding of inclusive education.

In this chapter the authors present a theoretical framework for an inclusive approach to education, which practitioners can use as they make pedagogical decisions.

Some argue that there is a 'need to stop trying to define and recreate a polished version of inclusion' (Ekins, 2017, p. 135), and the authors recognise the dynamic nature of the concept of inclusion. However, in order for practitioners to develop their practice in an inclusive way, a framework within which to consider practice is needed. The authors will, therefore, provide a working definition of inclusive education and discuss the implications of the definition for practice in schools and in particular supporting children and young people with SEN.

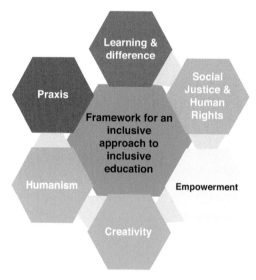

Theoretical framework for an inclusive approach, presented within six dimensions

The authors' theoretical framework for an inclusive approach to education is presented within six dimensions:

- Learning and difference

- Social justice and human rights

- Empowerment

- Creativity

- Humanism

- Praxis

These six dimensions are explained and explored in the following sections.

Learning and difference

As pedagogues, our key concern is learning. Whilst it may be problematic and raise conflicts when measures of successful learning and the arenas in which learning occurs are discussed, it is not controversial to state that learning is about change. Learning moves us as humans from one position to another, to a different place. Learning is about exploring and understanding different approaches, positions and outcomes from different perspectives. These perspectives can be more diverse when the diversity of learners and teachers are widened and, as such, pedagogues need to value difference in order to enhance learning opportunities. When curricula welcome and value difference, learning can be enhanced. Whether we believe learning is socially constructed (Vygotsky, 1986) and situated (Lave and Wenger, 1991), experiential (Dewey, 1958; Kolb, 1984) and discovery-based (Bruner, 1966) or even based within direct instruction (Clark, Kirchner and Sweller, 2012), bringing diverse learners and teachers will offer enhanced learning opportunities. This welcoming and valuing of difference will also have the impact of emancipating those who have been disabled by society, by removing stigma and discrimination (Mazurek and Winzer, 2015).

> Learning is about change and difference. As professionals concerned with learning, valuing difference is at the core of our practice.

Social justice and human rights

Notions of inclusive practice have a theoretical basis within the belief in fundamental human rights. The notion of 'equity' is founded upon the belief, as expressed in Article 1 of the

Universal Declaration of Human Rights that, 'All human beings are born free and equal in dignity and rights' (United Nations, 1948). This right is linked to education in Article 26.

A social justice approach is based upon the belief that there are fundamental human rights. One of these is the right to education.

'Everyone has the right to education' (United Nations, 1948). Article 22 (United Nations, 1948) presents the statement that everyone is a member of society and that the elements of society should promote human rights, dignity and 'free development of his personality'. This article links human rights to social justice, indicating that society should be actively promoting human rights and, therefore, justice. Schools, as significant institutions in societies, therefore have a key role in securing human rights and delivering social justice. Article 26 further states that education, 'shall promote understanding, tolerance and friendship among all nations, racial or religious groups, and shall further the activities of the United Nations for the maintenance of peace'(United Nations, 1948).

Empowerment

In order to provide all members of society with education which is appropriate to their diverse needs and interests, all of their voices need to be heard and their views need to be represented in decisions. School structures and mechanisms continue to reflect both dominant ideologies (Illich, 1973) and specific attitudes towards learning. A parallel with attitudes to disability in society can be drawn. 'Disabled people, like children, are meant to be seen and not heard: they are meant to be grateful, not angry, they are meant to be humble, not proud' (Shakespeare, 2006, p. 67). In school settings, this attitude to disability, or diversity, can be seen as being compounded because the learners are also children or young people. By listening and involving diverse children and young people in making decisions about their education, they will be empowered directly. This empowerment will also have implications beyond school settings, as this validation of their views and importance is likely to strengthen and affirm their identity in society.

Diverse members of communities need to be enabled and empowered to have their voices heard and views represented. By engaging all people in planning and decision-making about their education, curricula will move towards inclusivity.

This approach of empowerment links closely to the theory, critical pedagogy. Critical pedagogy has the aim to 'build more egalitarian power relations, to strengthen the voices of learners, and to inspire critical consciousness, in order to promote social change' (Cho, 2013, p. 1). This theory can be contextualised when viewed in the context of wider critical theory approaches, which focus on the power which exists within societal structures as a result of historical events. The critical theory view is well summarised in an educational context by Smith (2012, p. 131): 'We should ask if we want educational systems to perpetuate social and economic inequalities. It is possible for schools to engender understanding and tolerance, include all children and enable them to learn together. Today education segregates and divides.'

By empowering those who have been disenfranchised as a result of societal structures and attitudes, we can open new avenues and potentials for learning, as expressed by the phrase from critical pedagogy: the 'language of possibility' (Giroux, 1997).

Creativity

When we accept that learning is about change and difference, creativity becomes a key aspect to inclusive education. The drive of creativity is well defined as the desire to 'add variation and diversity to society and culture, rather than mimic other's successes or otherwise support the status quo' (Moran, Cropley and Kaufman, 2014, p. 281). If we understand that creativity in education is not, necessarily, about 'creative' subjects, such as art or drama, but about 'originality, novelty or newness' (Gajda, Karwowski and Beghetto, 2017, p. 272), then valuing diversity can be regarded as part of the creative process or creative flow encompassing the expansive tendency of creativity (Csikszentmihalyi, 1996, p. 11). The importance of creativity within the context of inclusive education is that the focus is towards a wide range of outcomes for learning activities. This contrasts with curricula and assessments where narrow, tick-list outcomes define success. When visiting early years and primary settings during the December term, the author was often surprised to be shown 'creative' outcomes drying on a line and see 30, almost identical, festive cards. In this case, when an inclusive and creative approach was taken, one would expect to see 30 very different cards waiting to go home. Where we recognise and value the diverse experiences and backgrounds of learners it is necessary to provide space for different outcomes.

Where we recognise and value the diverse experiences and backgrounds of learners it is necessary to provide space for different outcomes.

Humanism

Humanism is a philosophical concept which puts humans at the centre of existence. It believes that there are core, positive traits which humans live by and also links closely to the belief that there are human rights. It contrasts philosophical arguments which espouse ideas about universal truths and instead maintains a focus on views which are concerned with the ethics of human existence.

> Making ethical and reasoned decisions based on evidence and with concern for other human beings.

The roots of humanism are suggested to have arisen as part of the Renaissance in sixteenth-century Italy as a reaction to restrictive totalitarian and dogmatic religious power (Russell, 1989) and later developing in response to the rise of fascism (Davies, 2008).

Whilst there continue to be debates about the definition of humanism, the key elements of this concept are that the core to being human is bound within moral values where humanity stands in opposition to barbarity and inhumanity and makes ethical decisions based on scientific reasoning. The psychologist Carl Rogers, used the base of humanism to focus on the importance of relationships in human development. This notion of positive psychological relationships underpinning successful learning and resulting in motivated, independent learners (Rogers, 1967) is a key element to a humanist dimension.

Praxis

Praxis (Freire, 1996) is a term which encompasses the use of theory to improve practice with a values-based goal in mind. Praxis in inclusive educational approaches means using research evidence to improve learning in practice within a specific ideological framework, or values-based evidence informed practice.

> Using evidence informed practice to improve learning for all.

Where education practitioners engage with research evidence, both reading and conducting their own, practice can be significantly improved. In order to ensure that the evidence supports inclusive educational approaches, it needs to be approached in a critical way. Critical realism (Cruickshank, 2003) can offer practitioners a useful lens through which to consider the evidence and help practitioners make informed choices. Rather than viewing evidence as providing a complete truth which when followed results in specific outcomes, this lens supports the consideration of evidence as presenting descriptions of causal relationships. These causal relationships can be considered by practitioners and their relevance and applicability to their own settings and contexts can be considered. Critical realism is also a values-based theoretical approach, recognising that science, or research, embodies particular values (Bhaskar, 1989). As such this approach fits well with the other dimensions presented here.

Implications

The implications upon practice of adopting an inclusive approach, based on the six dimensions, will be explored in later sections of this book. It may, however, be useful to consider here the implications for practitioners. In adopting a change in practice towards an inclusive approach, it is likely that there will be implications and change which are widespread for the practitioner, reaching beyond the boundaries of their professional interactions with learners.

[T]he world of the individual person; the neighborhood he lives in; the school or college he attends; the factory, farm or office where he works. Such are the places where every man, woman, and child seeks equal justice, equal opportunity, equal dignity without discrimination. Unless these rights have meaning there, they have little meaning anywhere. Without concerted citizen action to uphold them close to home, we shall look in vain for progress in the larger world.

Eleanor Roosevelt, Chair of the United Nations Commission that wrote the Universal Declaration of Human Rights in 1948

Changes in the language which practitioners use can often be a significant factor. The use of specific language will be discussed in later chapters, however it is important to recognise how the language we use carries implications for social and cultural values (Holmes and Wilson, 2017) and how frequently the language we use can have a negative impact on different learners. A consequence of this for practitioners is that they can feel that they become very self-conscious about all the language they use and that they need to develop new habits in their word choice.

Adopting an inclusive approach is closely linked to challenging the status quo and is a political decision, as part of 'liberation politics' (Shakespeare, 2006, p. 53). Practitioners will find themselves challenging systems, structures and practice where exclusionary practices continue (Ruairc, 2013) and this will lead towards political discussions. The tensions for educators between their role and expressing political views has long been recognised. In a recent revision to government advice, a warning about expressing political views was issued (DfE, 2018, p. 25). This tension is something which practitioners may find challenging and will need to reflect upon.

A further likely impact of adopting an inclusive approach is that the practitioner may experience a challenge to their professional power. The empowerment of those previously marginalised (Shakespeare, 2006, p. 64) is likely to introduce a new balance in professional relationships which can challenge the practitioner's established relationships.

> The oldest and strongest emotion of mankind is fear, and the oldest and strongest kind of fear is fear of the unknown.
>
> (Lovecraft, 1927)

It is important to acknowledge that the challenges which moving towards an inclusive approach can present are likely to be scary for the practitioner. They will be moving into a new and unknown professional and personal arena. This can be an emotionally challenging journey and these factors could easily prevent the practitioner from making changes to their practice.

It is by remembering the ethical, or moral, imperative to provide access to education for all and by considering their own support networks and not making these changes alone that a practitioner can successfully take forward the principles of an inclusive approach to education, using the framework suggested, and make a positive change for the learners they encounter.

> Inclusive education entails reaching out to all learners and addressing all forms of exclusion and inequalities in access, school participation, and learning outcomes. Effective models for inclusion can help children with disabilities flourish and ultimately play an important and active role in society. Inclusive education is also beneficial for all learners with its focus on diversity and quality and its responsiveness to the different needs of children.
>
> (Unesco/IIEP, 2018)

References

Bhaskar, R. (1989) *Reclaiming Reality: A Critical Introduction to Contemporary Philosophy*. London: Verso.

Bruner, J.S. (1966) *Towards a Theory of Instruction*. London: Oxford University Press.

Cho, S. (2013) *Critical Pedagogy and Social Change: Critical Analysis on the Language of Possibility*. New York: Routledge.

Clark, R.E., Kirchner, P.A. and Sweller, J. (2012) 'Putting students on the path to learning: The case for fully guided instruction'. *American Educator*, Spring 2012, pp. 6–11.

Cruickshank, J. (2003) 'Critical realism: A brief definition'. In J. Cruickshank (ed.), *Critical Realism: The Difference It Makes*. London: Routledge (Routledge studies in critical realism, 6), pp. 1–14.

Csikszentmihalyi, M. (1996) *Creativity: Flow and the Psychology of Discovery and Invention*. First Edition. New York: HarperCollins.

Davies, T. (2008) *Humanism*. London: Routledge.

Dewey, J. (1958) *Democracy and Education: An Introduction to the Philosophy of Education*. New York: The Macmillan Company.

DfE. (2018) *Staffing and Employment Advice for Schools: Departmental Advice for School Leaders, Governing Bodies, Academy Trusts and Local Authorities*, September 2018. Available at: https://assets. publishing.service.gov.uk/government/uploads/system/uploads/attachment_data/file/738024/ Staffing_and_employment_advice_for-schools-18.pdf (accessed 20 September 2018).

Ekins, A. (2017) *Reconsidering Inclusion: Sustaining and Building Inclusive Practices in Schools*. New York: Routledge.

Freire, P. (1996) *Pedagogy of the Oppressed*. New Revised Edition. London: Penguin.

Gajda, A., Karwowski, M. and Beghetto, R. (2017) 'Creativity and academic achievement: A meta-analysis'. *Journal of Educational Psychology*, 109(2), pp. 269–299.

Giroux, H.A. (1997) *Pedagogy and the Politics of Hope: Theory, Culture, and Schooling: A Critical Reader*. Boulder: Westview Press (The Edge, Critical Studies in Educational Theory).

Holmes, J. and Wilson, N. (2017) *An Introduction to Sociolinguistics*. Fifth Edition. Abingdon, Oxon: Taylor and Francis (Learning About Language).

Illich, I. (1973/2002) *Deschooling Society*. London: Marion Boyars.

Kolb, D.A. (1984) *Experiential Learning: Experience as the Source of Learning and Development*. Englewood Cliffs, NJ: Prentice Hall.

Lave, J. and Wenger, E. (1991) *Situated Learning: Legitimate Peripheral Participation*. Cambridge: Cambridge University Press.

Lovecraft, H.P. (1927/1973) *Supernatural Horror in Literature*. London: Dover Publications.

Mazurek, K. and Winzer, M. (2015) 'Emancipation through education: Views on the convention on the rights of persons with disabilities'. *Interdyscyplinarne Konteksty Pedagogiki Specjalnej*, 10, pp. 201–213.

Moran, S., Cropley, D. and Kaufman, J. (2014) *The Ethics of Creativity*. Basingstoke: Palgrave Macmillan.

Rogers, C.R. (1967) *On Becoming a Person: A Therapist's View of Psychotherapy*. London: Constable & Company.

Ruairc, G.M. (2013) 'Including who? Deconstructing the discourse'. In G.M. Ruairc, E. Ottesen and R. Precey (eds.), *Leadership for Inclusive Education: Studies in Inclusive Education*. Volume 18. Rotterdam: SensePublishers Rotterdam, pp. 9–18.

Russell, B. (1989) *A History of Western Philosophy*. London: Unwin Hyman Ltd.

Shakespeare, T. (2006) 'Disabled people's self-organisation: A new social movement?'. In L. Barton (ed.), *Overcoming Disabling Barriers: 18 Years of Disability and Society*. London: Routledge (Education Heritage Series), pp. 53–69.

Smith, E.D. (2012) *Key Issues in Education and Social Justice*. London: SAGE.

UNESCO/IIEP. (2018) *Technical Round Table: Inclusive Education for Children With Disabilities*, 18th June 2018. Available at: www.iiep.unesco.org/en/technical-round-table-inclusive-education-children-disabilities-4523 (accessed 13 September 2018).

United Nations. (1948) *Universal Declaration of Human Rights*. Available at: www.un.org/en/universal-declaration-human-rights/ (accessed 23 August 2018).

Vygotsky, L. (1986) *Thought and Language*. Transl. and ed. A. Kozulin. Cambridge, MA: The MIT Press.

Chapter three
CHALLENGES

Current context of support services

The wider context in which schools operate has experienced, and continues to experience, a period of exceptional changes (Ekins, 2015). These changes arise from the impact of global economic recession, different government and wide-ranging reforms to education, and changes within the wider services from which schools may seek support to analyse and meet the needs of children and young people with SEN. Ekins (2015) argues that the drivers for the changes made with and alongside the Children and Families Act (DfE, 2014) arose from:

- The influencing factors of political policy drivers

- Economic challenges

- The acknowledgement that the existing system (at that time) of assessment and provision for SEN needed to be changed

These wider influences were discussed in greater detail within Chapter 1 in Part I of this book.

Anecdotal evidence from postgraduate students, who are practitioners in schools at a variety of levels of seniority within schools, suggests that schools are experiencing difficulties with securing support from outside agencies. Two factors appear to influence this:

- Difficulties with securing funding within the constraints of the school budget to pay for external expertise

- Difficulties finding expertise owing to local services being much reduced (or long waiting lists for such services)

Diverse strategic management structures across schools

The education landscape has changed. The responsibility for schools within a specific area has changed from local government, through the education authority within the area, to a combination of public and private bodies. This has led to a diverse approach to leadership and management within schools. Positions of responsibility may be held by people who work in the school all of the time may or these positions may be organised so that they are shared across a cluster of schools. An example of this is the role of the SENCO, which may be held by a member of staff of the school or by a teacher who holds responsibility across two or more schools within a federation or Multi-Academy Trust (MAT). Where this happens it is likely to present challenges related to factors including:

- Communication – restrictions or constraints in frequency of communication or responses to requests for information

- Resource – time for building relationships and working with colleagues, parents and carers and pupils as it may be absorbed by the administrative duties within the role

- Access – challenges for colleagues to be able to consult with the SENCO or share information owing to the need for the SENCO to move between sites

In situations in which senior and middle leadership roles are shared across schools, there may be challenges with developing a shared ethos and vision which fits each unique institution within the partnership. Indeed, the ethos of a school may lead to tensions between the values held by different practitioners within the setting, arising from whether this orientated towards having greater focus upon developing knowledge and measuring performance or developing potential and accommodating diversity (Norwich, 2013). The vision of schools may seek to encompass many elements within this range of foci; Norwich (2013) notes that the weighting accorded to each of these elements may be varied for individual settings.

Challenges

The challenges to inclusive approaches within schools will be discussed within three components:

- Perspectives of those within inclusion groups

- The perspective of individual need

- Challenges within schools for those working to develop an inclusive approach

Perspectives of those within inclusion groups

Ekins (2015) contends that practice for children and young people with SEN should be reflected upon not as a separate entity but within the broader demands and challenges which impact upon education. She notes that there is dissonance between the objectives of policy and actual experience of vulnerable learners. This will influence whether these learners feel a sense of belonging within the school community (Tutt, 2016).

Crow (2010) discusses the positive impact the social model of disability has had upon the lives of those with disabilities arising from the change in focus away from the individual towards work to change barriers within the physical environment and moving away from negative standpoints within societal views. She proposes that the notion of impairment is still important to reflect upon owing to the impact upon life experiences (such as pain, mental health and so on) caused from the nature of the impairment the individual has. She suggests that the negative perception of the medical model has problematised the use of the word impairment within dialogue about learners' profiles. This provides a rationale for the notion that through dialogue, it is possible to plan meaningful ways in which the nature of the difficulties and the social and physical context can all be included (Crow, 2010). Thus, impairment needs to be separated from the notion of disaster and sadness as this engenders anxiety which hinders purposeful reflections and discussion. Impairment needs to be considered within a functional explanation of the difficulties being experienced by the individual rather than another's perception of those difficulties. In making this argument, Crow is not advocating support for the medical model of disability, rather that an individual's experience of any impairment should be incorporated with the application of the social model of disability. Our contention is that within education, we need to consider the strengths and difficulties the learner has or experiences together with the physical and social environment to support planning for them. This holistic approach does need to include the learner and parent or carer in order to develop a greater depth of understanding. Their previous life experiences and insights are vital to support problem-solving.

Connors and Stalker's (2010, p. 144) findings from their small-scale study exploring children and young people's experiences of disability suggest that children and young people perceived their disability through four lenses: 'impairment, difference, other people's reactions and material barriers'. The children and young people within this study were reported to discuss their impairment pragmatically in terms of its impact upon everyday life. They also highlighted similarities between themselves and their peers rather than differences. The researchers suggest that this may have been owing to the children and young people having a limited lexicon to draw upon for this topic. Interestingly, Connors and Stalker report that some of the schools attended by the children and young people in their study were keen that attention should not be drawn to difference and that all should be regarded and handled in the same manner. They cite an example given to them by the parents of a child with a physical disability who had ended up alone inside the school building during a fire drill to support their argument that this approach does have inherent risks. This study also found that occasions where difference had not been appropriately handled, such as the rationale for specific actions not being fully discussed with the child or young person, or inappropriate labels used which elicited upsetting feelings and feelings of exclusion for the children and young people concerned. The study reported that insensitive behaviour from others (such as inappropriate actions or comments) impacted negatively upon these learners' emotions and self-belief. Additionally, the participants in this study discussed the impact of material barriers in terms of the limitations this placed on the children and young people's opportunities to join in with activities. These material barriers included factors such as:

- Barriers within the physical environment of clubs and activities

- The limited local offer of leisure activities

- Challenges with transportation

- The availability of support for communication

(Connors and Stalker, 2010, p. 148)

This is important for schools to reflect upon in light of any extra-curricular activities and clubs they offer.

Reflection

Does your school consider the diversity within the school population in the planning of their offerings of extra-curricular activities?

Are there activities within the local community that learners can access outside of school?

Jarvis, Iantaffi and Sinka (2010) reviewed a study of deaf and hearing children and young people's experiences of school and noted the importance of there being more than one deaf child or young person in a school to support positive self-image and a positive ethos within the school. The children and young people highlighted the negative impact that poor teacher knowledge of effective teaching strategies and approaches to support within whole class teaching has upon accessing the curriculum. The support of TAs was analysed in a similar vein. Support from friends was reported to be essential to positively augment their school experience. This highlights the positive influence of a holistic approach to inclusion and the importance of professional development for all school personnel.

Challenges within perspectives regarding individual needs

Norwich (2013) reminds us that SEN is a relatively recent addition to educational terminology across the historical landscape of education. The phrase SEN was introduced during the 1970s. Norwich notes that Professor Ron Guilford is credited with this phrase which was espoused by the Warnock Committee and implemented within legislation in the UK to replace the existing categories (such as handicap) to redirect focus from classifications emphasising the deficit models to more positive stances. However, the lack of clarity surrounding the definition of SEN hinders the development of both identification of SEN and provision to meet needs, which leads to varying quality across schools and settings (Tutt, 2016; Norwich, 2013). Furthermore, this encourages a perception that the focus should be upon having specialist teaching and interventions, rather than acknowledging the importance of high quality teaching for all (Norwich, 2013, 2014). The categorisation of learners as having SEN has been argued to encourage negative perceptions of these learners. This may be observed within low expectations for the achievements or progress for learners with SEN held by some practitioners. This ambiguity highlights the need for critical conversations involving the practitioners from all levels of seniority to explore these terms and the differing stances which are held in regard to the definitions and related practices and work to develop a shared collective understanding.

These conversations will also need to reflect upon views held in the wider community and indeed involve parents and carers. These views may take stances which practitioners may not have previously been made aware of. An example of such a circumstance is provided by Jarvis, Iantaffi and Sinka (2010) who note that an argument presented against this inclusion is that deaf children and young people miss the opportunity to be part of deaf community culture. This means that they may not become secure with British Sign Language (BSL) and miss out on access to role models from within the deaf community. This may lead to deaf children and young people being excluded from the deaf community owing to not fully understanding it. A counter argument to this stance highlights the fact that where deaf children and young people live with family members who can hear, they need to be part of the hearing community and culture. Jarvis, Iantaffi and Sinka (2010) note that the practicalities around access are an important factor here. They identify issues such as the teaching of the curriculum being interpreted from the teacher's explanations by a TA, thus the deaf child or young person is not being taught directly by the teacher unless the teacher can use BSL. Another consideration they raise is that there may also not be another peer who uses BSL to interact with. The child's communication may thus be mediated between teachers and peers through the TA which may be isolating for the child. Indeed, both social and learning conversations can be fast moving and thus deaf children and young people may experience difficulties following and joining in with these dialogues.

Current practitioners studying for an education postgraduate qualification report that they are observing increasing challenges and complexities for schools within the needs of their school population. Tutt (2016) concurs with this and reports that increasing medical knowledge and skills has resulted in greater numbers of children surviving premature birth, traumatic incidents or illnesses and increased awareness and diagnosis of rare syndromes and other neurodevelopment conditions (such as foetal alcohol spectrum disorder [FASD], pathological demand avoidance (PDA)). This requires high quality professional development and research to facilitate planning to meet diverse needs and making adaptations to different populations than may have previously been experienced by practitioners (Tutt, 2016).

Increasing numbers of young children are starting school with difficulties or constraining factors with their language and communication skills (nasen, 2017; Tutt, 2016). This may present as observed behaviour which includes difficulties with expressing themselves in sentences or holding conversations and a reduced lexicon of vocabulary (Bercow, 2018). This impacts upon all aspects of school, including both academic and social-emotional development (Tutt, 2016). In relation to the focus of this book, one example of how this may negatively influence behaviour is that having a limited lexicon of emotion words affects skills with articulating feelings and experiences. Thus the child or young person may use behaviour to communicate frustrations or perceived unmet needs; some of these behaviours may include aggressive verbal or physical outbursts.

Chapter 1 of this book explained that the requirements of the SEND CoP (2015) are that the views of the learner should be take into account within planning and setting of targets or goals for them. There may be challenges to gaining pupil voice owing to issues of:

- Language or maturational development
- Pupil trust of teachers or other adults
- Constraints of time
- Lack of knowledge or confidence in using differing approaches to gain pupil views (e.g. visual methods)

Norwich (2013, p. 119) cites research undertaken by Norwich and Kelly (2004) which identified 'promising practice but inconsistencies between policy and practice'.

He also notes that pupils may be frustrated by the length of time it takes for any changes they request to be implemented by school staff. This reminds us of an experience from one of the author's professional practice. A colleague (specialist teacher) was supporting a secondary school pupil with a physical disability. The pupil was to transition to a new school after the summer holiday. The colleague had planned to visit the school with the pupil for a tour so that they could work with the staff to identify areas of the building which may be tricky for the pupil to negotiate. This colleague had found that the pupil was a good problem-solver and was often able to identify practical and workable solutions to such difficulties that adults were finding difficult to resolve. This was the rationale for the tour with the pupil, however, whilst they were very willing to work with the specialist teacher, the new school refused to include the pupil within the tour and planning.

Challenges for those within schools working to develop an inclusive approach

In seeking solutions to issues within practice, tensions arise at times when values sit in opposition to one another (Norwich, 2013). At such times there are difficult questions to answer and choices to be made. Norwich (2013) observes that those final choices may not sit comfortably owing to the degree of concession of those values which may have to be made by those involved. This can trigger or contribute to tensions between practitioners. Opinions regarding the use of labels or categories, values related to curricular matters including what should be prioritised as foci to programme design and pedagogical approaches are all embroiled within these debates, concerns and tensions.

Schools exist within complex contextual influences and demands placed upon them by national and local policies. This presents some challenges to meeting a range of diverse strengths and needs. An example of one such challenge may be drawn from Tutt (2016) who cites views from a senior leader who argued that the government's focus on metrics and targets related to a narrow range of subjects which did not include arts, and sports appeared of less importance. This leader felt that this set up a challenge to schools catering to the needs of children and young people whose strengths and interests do not lie within the narrow range of subjects. Interestingly, the January 2019 guidance published for consultation from Ofsted (2019) appears to support this view as it is promoting the broad and balanced curriculum for all learners. Further challenges may arise from issues of resources. This may not only be in the form of concerns regarding funding but also of time in which to provide activities, such as sensory breaks, owing to concerns about being able to cover the curriculum sufficiently. Allied to this concern may be concerns about space in which such activities may be provided.

The resource of time may also be limited in terms of finding spaces within the planning of professional development for:

- Discussions to work to identify a collective agreement regarding terminology related inclusion

- Work to develop a shared approach to, and responsibility for, inclusive pedagogy

- CPD for professional learning related to meeting diverse needs of learners, including approaches to measuring and monitoring the progress of learners with SEN

Summary

This chapter has outlined some of the challenges which schools face in developing inclusive practice. These include tensions which are elicited from external contextual influences, such as the policy context and the economic environment, and from internal influences, such as the multiple perspectives of inclusion and pedagogy within the school community, the increasing complexity of needs with the school population, issues of resource and of developing knowledge, skills and understanding of inclusive pedagogical approaches. Reframing these challenges as opportunities for developing inclusive practice may support ways of moving forward.

References

Connors, C. and Stalker, K. (2010) 'Children's experiences of disability. Pointers to a social model of childhood disability'. In J. Rix, M. Nind, S. Kieron, K. Simmonds and C. Walsh (eds.), *Equality, Participation 1: Diverse Perspectives*. Second Edition. London: Routledge and The Open University, pp. 141–152.

Crow, L. (2010) 'Including all of our lives. Renewing the social model of disability'. In J. Rix, M. Nind, S. Kieron, K. Simmonds and C. Walsh (eds.), *Equality, Participation 1: Diverse Perspectives*. Second Edition. London: Routledge and The Open University, pp. 124–140.

DfE. (2014) *Children and Families Act*. Available at: https://www.legislation.gov.uk/ukpga/2014/6/contents (accessed 16 July 2018).

Ekins, A. (2015) *The Changing Face of Special Educational Needs: Impact and Implications for SENCOs, Teachers and Their Schools*. Abingdon: Routledge.

Jarvis, J., Iantaffi, A. and Sinka, I. (2010) 'Inclusion in mainstream classrooms. Experiences of deaf pupils'. In J. Rix, M. Nind, S. Kieron, K. Simmonds and C. Walsh (eds.), *Equality, Participation 1: Diverse Perspectives*. Second Edition. London: Routledge and The Open University, pp. 225–239.

Nasen. (2017) '83.6% increase in the number of pupils with SLCN as the primary area of need'. *News Report*, 27th June 2017. Available at: www.nasen.org.uk/newsviews/newsviews.83-6-increase-in-the-number-of-pupils-with-slcn-as-the-primary-area-of-need.html (accessed 17 August 2018).

Norwich, B. and Kelly, N. (2004) 'Pupils' views on inclusion: Moderate learning difficulties and bullying in mainstream and special schools.' *British Educational Research Journal*, 30(1), pp. 43–65.

Norwich, B. (2013) *Addressing Tensions and Dilemmas in Inclusive Education: Living With Uncertainty*. London: Routledge.

Norwich, B. (2014) 'Changing policy and legislation and its effects on inclusive and special education: A perspective from England'. *British Journal of Special Educational Needs*, 41(4), pp. 403–425. https://doi.org/10.1111/1467-8578.12079.

Office for standards in Education [Ofsted]. (2019) *The Education Inspection Framework Draft for Consultation*. Available at: https://assets.publishing.service.gov.uk/government/uploads/system/uploads/attachment_data/file/770924/Proposed_education_inspection_framework_draft_for_consultation_140119.pdf.pdf (accessed 28 March 2019).

Tutt, R. (2016) *Rona Tutt's Guide to SEND & Inclusion*. London: SAGE.

Chapter four

APPROACHES FOR LEADING INCLUSIVE PRACTICE

We open this chapter with a quotation to reflect upon. This is from Ekins (2015), who acknowledges the complexities within planning for inclusive approaches. She highlights the need to ask ourselves (and all of our colleagues) those tricky critical questions regarding existing practices, and reminds us that at the heart of our practice are all of the learners in our school population.

Please take some time to read this quotation and reflect upon how this resonates with current practices and perceptions of inclusion in your own context.

> [I]nclusion is not just about something that is 'done' to pupils with SEN and/or disabilities. Rather, it involves complex consideration and challenging questions about the appropriateness of educational experiences for ALL pupils. This is a principled approach to education that, in this time of changing policies and practices, really does need to be clearly and consistently articulated.
>
> Ekins (2015, p. 5)

In Chapter 2 we presented our theoretical framework for an inclusive approach to education which is set out within six dimensions.

The operationalisation of inclusion engages schools in extending their capacity to respond to and meet a range of diverse needs (Norwich, 2013). This capacity building is one of the core purposes of strategic leadership. The enactment of this strategic approach engages leaders in an analysis of how current systems and practices constrain inclusive approaches and working to enhance these. It is important to acknowledge that the definition of leadership in school settings is not restricted to headteachers and the Senior Leadership Team. There are a range of educational professionals in schools who have leadership roles. These roles may

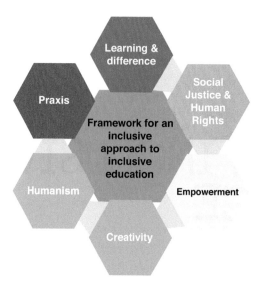

Theoretical framework for an inclusive approach, presented within six dimensions

be formally acknowledged, as in the case of formally recognised middle leaders (Bennett and NCSL, 2003). However the focus on the leadership aspect of the SENCO role varies widely from setting to setting (Tissot, 2013). Leadership in schools may also be informal, through, for example, mentoring, or individual practitioner experiences and interests. As such, the authors' discussion of leadership in this chapter needs to be viewed within the context of diverse models of leadership. We will now discuss approaches to leading inclusive approaches through the dimensions of our theoretical framework.

Learning and difference

For those leaders focusing upon the dimension of learning and difference through which to develop inclusive approaches, an analysis of how all people (children and young people and adults) are received within the school community will be essential. Thus, in order to develop an inclusive approach through the dimension of learning and difference, consideration of the values, beliefs and professional confidences which feed into the enactment of school vision statement and ethos is needed. The ethos of a school or setting acts as a conduit for inclusive approaches either positively, as an enabler, or negatively, drawing up barriers. The influence of the way in which diversity is not only perceived but also embraced or rebuffed, has been noted by Trussler and Robinson (2015) in their analysis of Jordan, Schwartz and McGhie-Richmond's (2009) longitudinal research from Canada. This research identified a relationship between teacher's values and beliefs and their approach to inclusive practice. These factors relating to learning and difference were identified by Trussler and Robinson:

• Views as whether ability and learning was fixed or was responsive to teaching and could change

- Acceptance that responsibility for all learners was their own (SEN does not 'belong' to someone else)

- Engages with children and young people with SEN rather than handing them over to other adults.

This suggests the importance of leaders engaging their staff in critically reflecting upon, and analysing, the principles and values which act as the foundation for current practices in their context (Ekins, 2015). Although justifying the creation of space for these critical dialogues within the busy schedule of a school development plan may seem daunting, this serves a constructive function of positively embracing diversity and styles of learning within the school culture and a shared vision owned by all. This also serves the important purpose of keeping the school ethos active and alive.

Social justice and human rights

Ekins (2015) reminds us that processes within education should not just reflect changes within the policy context but also draw upon values of inclusion and social justice. This cannot be reduced to a checklist of basic needs, rather a holistic approach is warranted which Watson *et al.* (2012, p. 205) frame as an 'ethics of care'.

In order to develop an inclusive approach through the dimension of social justice and human rights, a consideration of these elements is needed by leaders:

- Social-emotional relationships

- School environment

- Physical and emotional wellbeing

- Opportunities to succeed and for self-reflection

- Encouragement of aspirations and of widening horizons

Underpinning the development of actions to support each of these elements is the importance of dialogic relationships between adults and between adults and learners (Watson *et al.*, 2012). Another vital ingredient is constructing an ethos in which all members of the community value one another, thus engendering sense of belonging to the school for every individual.

Empowerment

In Chapter 2 in Part II, we explained that by listening to children and young people and involving them in making decisions about their education, they will be empowered and this offers opportunities for opening new possibilities for learning. The longitudinal research discussed by Trussler and Robinson (2015), referred to earlier, also identified that deep listening to pupils was integral within an inclusive approach.

In order to develop an inclusive approach through the dimension of empowerment, consideration of what is involved in deep or active listening, and how this may be enacted with children and young people with diverse learning characteristics, is needed.

Listening and talking with children and young people through a reflexive approach supports sense making of their experiences; children and young people feel that their perspectives have been considered with plans that are made. This also enables teachers to develop a deeper understanding of their learners and of supportive factors for social and academic learning. Thus, in this way dialogue with children and young people is used to facilitate formulating solutions collaboratively (Watson *et al.*, 2012).

Creativity

The notion of creativity being a vital component within inclusive education, acknowledges not only the desire and need to meet the needs of diverse characteristics within our learners and offer opportunities for differing outcomes, but also that pedagogical approaches are situational, responsive to the individual within the context.

In order to develop inclusive approaches through the dimension of creativity, consideration of these components is needed:

- Developing a variety of ways in which success and evidence of summative achievements are framed and celebrated

- Proactive encouragement of practitioners to build confidence and their engagement in utilising creative approaches to assessment and the way in which learning is demonstrated by learners

- 'Thinking-outside-of-the-box' approaches to developing flexible modes of responding to factors which may act as constrainers upon a learner's engagement with learning opportunities with regard to the:
  - Physical environment
  - Sensory environment
  - Social-emotional environment
- Creative and proactive planning for organising
  - Transition times
  - The organisation across the school day (Lever (2011) suggests reflecting upon Maslow's hierarchy of need and factors such as concentration span, importance of providing opportunities for hydration and movement to inform this.

As discussed within the learning and difference section earlier, enacting creative approaches to meeting diversity will require leaders to be proactive, engaging in critical reflection upon current practices to inform planning for each of the areas identified.

Humanism

The humanism dimension of an inclusive framework focuses upon the importance of positive relationships within developing social, emotional and academic knowledge, skills and understanding. In order to develop an inclusive approach through the dimension of humanism, leaders need to consider how to create a nurturing community for the school population. Tutt (2016) advocates that putting holistic or caring goals at the centre of school vision and core purpose can support a positive ethos and eradicate bullying, as well as developing motivation within practitioners and learners (Gagné and Deci, 2005). The modelling (Bandura, 1986) of a humanist approach may also be considered by leaders as a way of developing inclusive practice.

Praxis

Praxis engages teachers in developing inclusive educational approaches informed from evidence which has been critically considered. It is important to acknowledge that there is no one-size-fits-all mode of inclusion which will guarantee success. Ekins (2015, p. 6) offers this advice: 'For me, the development of inclusive practice will always be individualised, and will involve critical consideration of the underlying values and principles impacting upon the particular context.' She notes that this means that there are challenges in providing clear directions or instructions for practice, rather it requires schools to critically analyse and reflect upon the influences which underpin their current practices.

In order to develop an inclusive approach through the dimension of praxis, leaders need to consider the strategy to be used to develop inclusive pedagogical approaches. Conceptualising exploring and enhancing practice within the notion of school development rather than school improvement encapsulates both an acknowledgement of the complexity of schools' social and cultural contexts, and that development is a process (rather than a short or singular activity). To enact this, leaders need to create an ethos in which there are spaces in which questions and ideas or initiatives can be debated collaboratively. This will be supported by the employment of analysis and practitioner-inquiry to critically explore practice (Ekins, 2015). To facilitate beneficial and constructive change, this process needs to include the school staff, parents and carers, learners and wider agencies.

Pedagogy for SEN may be conceptualised in two ways:

being part of high quality teaching for all learners, which offers flexible approaches and reasonable adjustments	Or	A specialist pedagogy

The conceptualisation, held by teachers, of the pedagogical approaches for SEN influences their confidence with, and enactment of, learning activities. Trussler and Robinson (2015) draw upon the research within the fields of dyslexia and ASD to illustrate their argument that while labels and diagnoses provide an overview of the characteristics and likely strengths and difficulties for the learner, each learner is unique. This notion requires teachers to reflect upon:

- The learner

- The learning context

- Knowledge of the diagnosed difficulty or disability and of appropriate pedagogical approaches

Trussler and Robinson (2015) support Norwich's proposition which frames inclusive pedagogy within the model of knowledge of the learner, of learning and teaching and specific approaches which support inclusive practice, rather than a specialist pedagogy stance.

We have heard the phrase 'it's not rocket science' used many times in relation to designing pedagogical approaches. Indeed we believe that it is about using knowledge and understanding to support research-informed practices, whether that is about the nature of the strategy used or the intensity of application.

Implications for leading an inclusive approach

Norwich (2013) notes that vocabulary such as 'inclusion' or 'inclusive' is used widely across societal organisations to discuss issues relating to welcoming others and feelings of belonging or acceptance. He identifies that these words in modern-day usage encompass a 'mix of the values of equal opportunity, social respect and solidarity' (Norwich, 2013, p. 154) and suggests that this amalgam of these values is a factor in the confusion surrounding a shared comprehension of inclusion. These ambiguities elicit tensions between practitioners who may have differing interpretations of inclusion and its enactment.

Ekins (2015, p. 3) proposes that 'it is essential that practitioners working in schools take time to critically consider the "unique" opportunities that they have to change and develop existing practices to ensure a meaningful impact for the pupils they serve'. She advocates that all professionals across phases of education and in wider services should reflect critically and review existing practices for learners with SEN, and the underlying assumptions which inform those practices.

In school, this means creating opportunities to engage in these critical conversations and reflect upon whether the current practice, systems and processes within the school or cluster of schools (e.g. federated schools or MATs) are working effectively to meet pupil needs. These critical dialogues need to encompass working together to develop a shared definition of inclusion and of approaches to inclusive practice. This highlights the challenges and importance of developing a school's ethos in relation to inclusive practices and welcoming of diversity which is embraced, owned and enacted by all staff.

This notion of collaborative reflective work of sense-making in relation to inclusion is supported by Alila, Maatta and Uusiautti (2016) who contend that:

> If you think that . . . your school is an inclusive school, you cannot just plan it by yourself, but you have to collaborate with others.
>
> (k822,80)

and point out that there are other parties to draw into this collaboration:

> And then also the collaboration relationships . . . other teachers and the work community, and parents.
>
> (k225,21)

They also offer advice for leaders in their contention that supervision supports the change of the whole school culture towards inclusion. Supervision helps develop new practices by adjusting them to the prevailing school culture. In addition, supervision can serve as a tool to lead the change in a controlled manner (Alila, Maatta and Uusiautti, 2016).

A useful tool to support the reflections, creative and critical questioning may be provided by using Booth and Ainscow's (2002) broad principles for inclusion to support analysis of practice:

- Reduce barriers to learning

- Increase participation and access to learning

- Support diversity

All of this work will be supported through dialogical relationships (Watson *et al.*, 2012) in which deep listening and honest respectful exchanges are both an expectation and honoured by all within the community.

References

Alila, S., Maatta, K. and Uusiautti, S. (2016) 'How does supervision support inclusive teacherhood?'. *International Electronic Journal of Elementary Education*, 8(3), pp. 351–362.

Bandura, A. (1986) *Social Foundations of Thought and Action: A Social Cognitive Theory*. Englewood Cliffs: Prentice-Hall (Prentice-Hall Series in Social Learning Theory).

Bennett, N. and National College for School Leadership (NCSL). (2003) *The Role and Purpose of Middle Leaders in Schools: Summary Report*. Nottingham: National College for School Leadership.

Booth, T., Ainscow, M. and Centre for Studies on Inclusive Education. (2002) *Index for Inclusion: Developing Learning and Participation in Schools*. Bristol: CSIE.

Ekins, A. (2015) *The Changing Face of Special Educational Needs: Impact and Implications for SENCOs, Teachers and Their Schools*. Abingdon: Routledge.

Gagné, M. and Deci, E.L. (2005) 'Self-determination theory and work motivation'. *Journal of Organizational Behavior*, 26, pp. 331–362.

Jordan, A., Schwartz, E. and McGhie-Richmond, B. (2009) 'Preparing teachers for inclusive classrooms'. *Teaching and Teacher Education,* 24(4), pp. 535–542.

Lever, C. (2011) *Understanding Challenging Behaviour in Inclusive Classrooms*. Harlow: Pearson.

Norwich, B. (2013) *Addressing Tensions and Dilemmas in Inclusive Education: Living With Uncertainty*. London: Routledge.

Tissot, C. (2013) 'The role of SENCos as leaders'. *British Journal of Special Education*, 40(1), pp. 33–40.

Trussler, S. and Robinson, D. (2015) *Inclusive Practice in the Primary School*. London: SAGE.

Tutt, R. (2016) *Rona Tutt's Guide to SEND & Inclusion*. London: SAGE.

Watson, D., Emery, C. and Bayliss, P. with Boushel, M. and McInnes, K. (2012) *Children's Social and Emotional Wellbeing in Schools*. Bristol: The Policy Press.

PART III

Part III explores targeted and individual strategies and programmes.

INTRODUCTION

Thus far, this book has explored the wider contextual influences upon decision-making about pedagogical approaches and the impact of exclusion upon children and young people, their families and schools and wider society. We have proposed a theoretical framework through which senior leaders, SENCOs, teachers, TAs and practitioners can engage in critical reflection to inform decisions about inclusive approaches and significantly reduce or eradicate exclusion.

Part III moves the process from a focus upon the inclusive ethos of the school and universal approaches, to explore targeted and individual strategies and programmes. It provides suggestions for practical strategies and approaches to promote inclusion and reduce exclusion within each of the sections. This seeks to support teachers to meet their responsibilities as teachers of every child in their class (DfE, 2015). The focus is upon understanding the factors underlying the behaviour and using this information to work to reduce the incidence of those behaviours and thus the risk of exclusion.

Each chapter follows a framework of questions to lead the reader through understanding the focused approach or intervention, the theoretical underpinnings, the positive impact the approach can have, implementing the approach in addition to signposting sources of support for further exploration. The framework of questions is set out in the following figure.

1) What is the approach for working in partnership?

2) Why might it reduce exclusion?

3) How does it fit within our definition of inclusive pedagogy?

4) What is the practice for working in partnership?

5) What is the background / theoretical underpinning?

6) What would you need in order to use this approach?

7) Further reading / resources / websites

Framework to support exploration of pedagogical approaches and interventions

Part III starts with exploring strategies for working in partnership with learners, their parents and carers and external agencies, followed by approaches to support different dimensions of need within the context of inclusive practice. The information provided in answer to the questions posed in the framework will support teachers, teaching assistants and SENCOs in their dialogue with parents and carers and senior leadership, explaining and persuading them of the reasons why the strategy is worth using.

Reference

DfE. (2015) *Special Educational Needs and Disability Code of Practice: 0 to 25 Years. Statutory Guidance for Organisations Which Work With and Support Children and Young People Who Have Special Educational Needs or Disabilities.DFE-00205–2013*. London: DfES. Available at: www.gov.uk/government/publications/send-code-of-practice-0-to-25 (accessed 24 February 2015).

Chapter one
EFFECTIVE INCLUSIVE PARTNERSHIPS

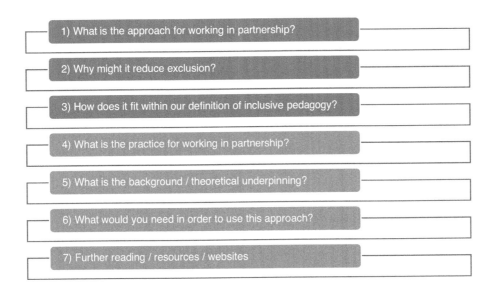

1) What is the approach for working in partnership?

2) Why might it reduce exclusion?

3) How does it fit within our definition of inclusive pedagogy?

4) What is the practice for working in partnership?

5) What is the background / theoretical underpinning?

6) What would you need in order to use this approach?

7) Further reading / resources / websites

What is the approach for working in partnership?

Working in partnership refers to collaborative work, which is undertaken by key actors to work together to seek resolutions to issues and to meet the needs of children and young people. Hodkinson (2016, p. 132) identifies some components which characterise working in partnership:

- Mutually agreed aims.
- There are inputs and activity from all partners: a shared responsibility in working to fulfil aims.
- Expertise and accountability is acknowledged to be jointly owned.
- A belief that working collaboratively is a positive strategy to meet needs underlies partnership working.

Implied within these components is the notion that everyone's contributions will be valued and accepted, and that trust and respect form foundations for working in partnership with others (Ekins, 2015). We would add active listening and keeping an open mind to these elements.

Working in partnership with others is an approach which is often employed for developing provision to meet needs of children and young people with SEN, especially when there are complex needs or the child or young person is at risk of being excluded.

There are different dimensions of working in partnership:

- Partnership with children and young people

- Partnership with parents and carers

- Partnership with a wider group (including parent and carer, and child or young person) – the purpose of these partnerships is to draw upon expertise outside of the school

The wider group may include:

- Professionals who hold specific specialist roles (e.g. educational psychologist, speech and language therapist, school nurse, paediatrician, specialist advisory teacher, social worker)

- Charities who have developed particular expertise or who are able to offer practical support (e.g. Families First, Home Start)

- Members of the local authority SEN Casework team (e.g. SEN caseworker) – especially when an application for statutory assessment is planned

- Practitioners from other schools who have expertise which is pertinent to the focus of concern

- Wider family members or practitioners who have a role in parent support (e.g. family support workers, parent advisers, parent partnership)

- Other practitioners from the local authority (e.g. education welfare officers)

Why might working in partnership reduce exclusion?

The work to develop positive working relationships between school staff, learner and parents and carers may sometimes involve a problematic journey to attain that goal, and does require an investment of time. Positive working relationships support building trust between the partners. This is important because it supports engendering a sense of belonging to the school community and the individual's personal sense of being valued (Roffey, 2011). Working to develop effective relationships with parents was a key element of the Achievement for All pilot. Gross (2013) notes that this research identified that the number of schools that reported excellent relationships with parents increased significantly, and that those reporting poor relationships decreased by a large amount.

Positive relationships support encouraging parental confidence in the school and their positive engagement. Parents and carers are thus more likely to be willing to share key information, essential to support understanding of issues, and to work cooperatively and collaboratively with school staff to support meeting the needs of children and young people. This shared communication helps identify issues and factors which can be addressed. The final report of the Lamb Enquiry (2009) identified that systems are more effective when parents and carers, schools and local authorities work together positively (Tutt, 2011).

Roffey (2011) argues that working in partnership with children and young people to empower them increases the likelihood of their sense of responsibility for their actions, and their abilities to analyse positive and negative aspects of a situation to inform their decision-making. Positive relationships usually engender interactions which are more likely to be respectful rather than challenging or discourteous (Lever, 2011). In addition, this work may reduce incidents of attention-seeking behaviour and increase learners' willingness to collaborate with others (Roffey, 2011), and their motivation for learning (Tutt, 2011).

Multi-agency working offers the opportunity to reframe the concern regarding a child or young person's behaviour as a shared concern, rather than being an issue heaped upon the responsibility of one or a few. This may support reducing the heightened tensions and anxiety which have been triggered from the challenging behaviour and the difficulties being experienced by the practitioners, parents and carers and child or young person. Additionally, other organisations can offer impartial advice or advocate for the child or young person (Ekins, 2015). 'Team around the Child' is one term used to refer to multi-agency working. The Team around the Child approach facilitates a holistic approach to the child or young person's education and wellbeing. This is because the Team around the Child will be able to draw on a variety of expertise in relation to the multiple needs experienced by a child or young person with SEN (Hodkinson, 2016). This holistic approach can support identification of wider needs underlying the behaviours of concern and identifying approaches and resources which can meet those needs. If we recollect that behaviour is a form of communication, which communicates unmet needs in addition to other factors such as anxiety, then the holistic approach will support reducing or eradicating those behaviours. In this way the risk of exclusion is similarly reduced or eradicated.

The positive outcomes of good working relationships may support reducing the risk of exclusion through a shared understanding, willingness to communicate respectfully, honestly and work collaboratively to support needs and reduce incidents of negative behaviours. Indeed, Osler and Vincent (2003) reported that the girls participating in their research perceived that when parents and carers and schools worked in partnership together, there appeared to be a greater desire to avoid the sanction of exclusion.

How does it fit within our definition of inclusive pedagogy?

Working to develop positive working relationships with children and young people, parents and carers and wider (external) groups fits within our theoretical framework for inclusion in that:

- It acknowledges learning differences through genuine engagement to work jointly to identify factors underlying needs or challenging behaviours and the collective planning of how these factors might best be supported to facilitate success.

- It acknowledges the rights of the individual to be heard, respected and to have access to education.

- Learners are given agency through their increased sense of belonging to, and value within, the school community and are thus empowered to achieve.

- Active listening and involving learners and parents and carers in seeking solutions informs part of responding creatively to learners' differing needs and valuing the diversity within our learning community.

- It responds to a humanistic approach of acting ethically and with concern for others.

- Employing evidence-based approaches to develop positive relationships embodies developing practice (Praxis).

In order to support reflections upon, and planning for, working collaboratively with parents and carers, learners and others, it can be helpful to consider with the team the elements which feed into positive relationships. There are some questions in the reflective activity to support your own reflection and to support analysis and reflection with your team.

Reflective activity

What factors do you think contribute to effective partnership working?
What factors do you think hinder/provide barriers to effective partnership working?

Think about an example of working in partnership with parents and/or outside agencies from your own experience:

What elements or activities do you think supported the successes?
What elements or activities do you think hindered working effectively?

There are two elements within working in partnership:

- Working in partnership to identify strengths, needs and aspirations of the child or young person

- Working in partnership to plan and implement strategies and approaches to address needs

The second element will also engage the partnership in identifying and agreeing a priority order of addressing needs and concerns, and the objectives which will drive the work to meet needs.

The next part of this chapter explores working in partnership with others within three sections: pupil voice, partnership with parents and carers and partnership with external agencies.

Pupil voice

What is the approach?

The requirement upon schools to listen to pupil views and involve them in making decisions about their learning and school life come from a variety of standpoints:

- Legal requirements (e.g. Children Acts 1989, 2004) which require that we should have regard to the ascertainable wishes and feelings of the child.

- Accord with Human Rights: UNCRC Article 12, explained in Part I, Chapter 1.

- The SEND CoP (2015 1 · 9, p. 21) requires that schools and local authorities have information, advice and support to facilitate their involvement in discussions and decisions made about their support.

- Moral reasons – The moral purpose for listening to pupils' views and opinions has been provided through policies such as Every Child Matters (HMS Treasury, 2003), in order to ensure better outcomes for children and young people.

This is captured by Tutt (2011, p. 10) in her contention that 'Learning in school is no longer viewed as an experience where teachers are the active participants and pupils the passive recipients'. This aligns with the perspective offered by Gross (2013) who believes that there has been cultural change in schools to be more proactive and creative in the ways in which pupil voice is collected. Norwich (2013) notes that the UNCRC has acted as a catalyst for the child's voice, but advises that there is potential for tensions to arise between what is the child's best interest and their views, not least because their standing in societal hierarchy means that an adult is required to act for the child.

What is the practice for hearing the voice of the learner?

Three factors have been identified within positive relationships: acceptance, congruence and empathy (Rogers, 1962 cited by Lever, 2011). Essential actions to support these factors include:

- Displaying a non-judgemental acceptance of the child or young person's emotions
- Sincerity
- Correct perception of emotions
- Listening actively

The modes of communication employed by adults play a key role within this. Ekins (2015) cites research from Bradbury *et al.* (2010) who identify that communication systems need to be meaningful and appropriate for the learner; they also note the importance of being aware that our assumptions may influence our interpretation of what children and young people say. Indeed some issues will need time and sensitivity to support exploring these. This means that we will need to explore and be prepared to use a variety of modes of communication to support learners' understanding of information given, and questions asked, and for expressing their views and questions.

What is the background/theoretical underpinning?

Seeking children and young people's views for differing aspects of school life supports empowering them, enhancing their sense of belonging and their motivation for learning (Tyrrell and Woods, 2018; Tutt, 2011). Tutt (2011) contends that this has particular significance for children and young people with SEN as they can often feel marginalised. This approach also recognises that children and young people with SEN often have deep acumen into their strengths and needs. Pupils are able to provide valuable insight into factors which are influencing their learning and are able to offer solutions to issues affecting their access to learning (Ekins, 2015). This belief is supportive of the notion that pupils should be involved in identifying and setting, at least some of, their own targets.

Further rationale for this perspective may be drawn from Roffey (2011, p. 120) who identifies positive links between learner voice and behaviour:

- Encourages sense of belonging to the school community and their personal sense of being valued
- Involvement with their community enriches emotional wellbeing and resilience
- May reduce attention-seeking behaviour

- Working to develop children and young people's agency increases likelihood of their sense of responsibility for their actions and their abilities to analyse positive and negative aspects of a situation to inform their decision-making

- Supports developing positive relationships

- May influence change of perceptions of the pupil by adults

- Encourages motivation, thinking skills, creativity, positive self-belief and willingness to collaborate with others

What would you need in order to use this approach?

It is important that strategies used to gather pupils' views do need to be meaningful and match developmental stages of pupils (Ekins, 2015). Here are some ideas of strategies that may be used:

- Engaging pupils in an activity (e.g. art activity, playing a game) and introducing discussions about their school experiences alongside the activity. This may help diffuse any anxiety or shyness which the pupil may feel.

- Using symbol supported communication – questions are presented in text supported by symbols (e.g. Widgit) with symbols/pictures to support pupils with expressing their views.

- Using a range of pictures (e.g. photographs, picture postcards) and asking pupils to select the one that matches their experience or feeling about a particular aspect of school life.

- Asking children and young people to draw pictures representing their experiences or take photographs of aspects of school life.

- Using approaches such as comic strip conversations (Gray, 1994). This approach was developed by Carol Gray and is predicated on the belief that visual approaches can support people who experience difficulties with social communication skills to make sense of social situations. Simple drawings are drawn to show the content of a conversation between two or more people who are discussing a present or past event or planning for future events. Comic strip conversations are often used to work through situations that have been challenging and support understanding of the child's perceptions and actions and to help the child understand others' perceptions and actions. It also helps with developing strategies or solutions for future similar events.

- Modifying the phrasing of questions to match the developmental level of children and young people.

Sometimes, we pose questions to children and young people and a response is not forthcoming. Norwich (2013) cites Lewis (2010, p. 20) who argues that silence 'is not neutral or empty' and thus should be heard within the process of listening to learners. Thus, practitioners do need to develop the skills of reading non-verbal cues and the nuances within the sound of silence to formulate hypothesis about the pupil's views which may then be explored through other means.

In preparation for seeking children and young people's views, there are elements which are useful for practitioners to consider to inform their planning:

- An appraisal of children and young people's capacity to evaluate the available options.

- Is there any likelihood of children and young people complying with an assertive opinion from key adults, such as parents and carers?

- Is there any likelihood of children and young people giving answers to questions which are aimed to please, rather than provide their actual views and thoughts?

- The validity and durability of the opinions expressed by children and young people and how this may judged.

- The delicate balancing act between encouraging children and young people to have aspirations and also to be able to amend their dreams to enable them to be attainable.

- Plan strategies for managing conflicts between opinions of children and young people and others (e.g. parents and carers).

- The communications skills of children and young people and planning the strategies and approaches which will enable children and young people to be able to express views and be involved with planning and decisions in a meaningful way.

- Plan strategies to manage situations in which there is a need to explain to children and young people that having listened to their views we are or are not undertaking a particular action.

(Lewis and Porter, 2007; Bradbury, Feeney and Gager, 2011)

Further reading/resources/websites

Comic Strip Conversations: www.erinoakkids.ca/ErinoakKids/media/EOK_Documents/Autism_Resources/Comic-Strip-Conversations.pdf
www.autism.org.uk/about/strategies/social-stories-comic-strips.aspx
Widgit Symbols: www.widgit.com/

Working in partnership with parents and carers
What is the approach?

Working in partnership with parents and carers has been recommended and required over time through a number of official reports and legislation. Working to construct authentic partnerships may be problematic in some circumstances, particularly for those pupils who are at high risk of exclusion (Hayden, 1997). Hayden (1997) notes that this may be especially difficult for children and young people who are in care, particularly if they are not in a settled foster placement.

A vignette from one of the authors

A child who often presented with challenging behaviours both in and out of school was moved to different foster placements several times. This proved challenging for communication and working co-operatively together with foster carers, particularly when the child was being brought to and from school by taxi. Often the foster carers felt they did not have the capacity to attend meetings or engage in discussions to plan strategies. They explained that they could not cope with the behaviour the child exhibited outside of school, which together with the responsibilities for their other foster children and the distance they had to travel, restricted their capacity to engage. Now perhaps we could try more creative approaches such as using Skype – but this and other solutions offered via information technology were not available to us at that time.

The perception practitioners (or schools) hold of parenting and how this should be enacted influences the way in which parents and carers' views are listened to, regarded and acted upon (Norwich, 2013). These perceptions or judgements can act as enablers or barriers to working collaboratively with parents and carers. Postgraduate students studying for MA Education courses have observed in discussions, that while there is a requirement for schools to engage with parents and carers, there is no such requirement for parents and carers. This presents an interesting dichotomy that schools working to reach out to those families which are considered to be 'hard to reach' are all too aware of. The reasons underlying barriers to parental engagement relate to a range of factors, including parental experiences of school, social capital, physical and emotional health, language barriers, time owing to work or caring roles and to circumstances related to children and young people being in care. Norwich (2013) suggests that parental perspectives of their child's disability and of the influence that a diagnosis has upon access to resources, together with school and societal attitudes may elicit tensions for parents and carers. School ethos, and the approaches used to communicate with and involve parents and carers, also contribute to this complex mix.

What is the practice for working in partnership with parents and carers?

A range of formal systems exist in schools to communicate with parents and carers, such as parent evenings, review meetings, annual reviews of ECH Plans, Team Around the Child (TAC) meetings, parent groups and letters sent home. Ekins (2015) highlights the importance of critically reflecting upon the effectiveness of the approaches being used in school, to facilitate improving parental and pupil voice within decision-making and reviews. Support for this notion may be drawn from Ofsted (2010) which identified parents feeling that schools often took a combative approach to discussions about SEN needs.

Gross (2013) reports that research suggests that working with parents remains challenging for schools. She cites research from Pinkus (2005) who identified that parents of children and young people with SEN reported that they struggled with the jargon used, felt that they were not offered opportunities to express their views or be involved in decision-making for their child. She also draws from the work of Lindsay *et al.* (2010) to support her advice that greater success in partnerships with parents and carers is facilitated through actions such as teachers and leaders being willing to:

- Meet with parents and carers and listen sensitively to their views

- Use flexible approaches with children and young people to support access the curriculum and demonstrate learning

- Recognise strengths as well as difficulties

- Acknowledge and tackle the social-emotional impact of social-emotional difficulties

A vignette from a secondary school SENCO

The parents of one of the pupils with SEN needs always appeared apprehensive when I met with them. It was difficult to encourage them to say much about how they felt about the reports they had of their child's academic progress and behaviour and to share information and ideas with me (or other staff). In addition to being the SENCO, I also taught PE. On one occasion, I had a meeting arranged and owing to circumstances did not have the time I had thought I would have to change into my usual smart clothes for the meeting. Thus, I met the parents in my PE kit. The parents were much more relaxed during this meeting and opened up to share their thoughts, feelings and some valuable information to help me understand their child much more deeply. Reflecting upon the change and the success of this meeting led me to plan the venue of meetings (e.g. formal meeting room or more relaxed area with soft chairs/sofas) and how I presented myself (e.g. PE kit or suit) in preparing for all my meetings with parents. Parents have a variety of life experiences and expectations and it helps to reflect on this ahead of any meeting. As a result, I hope that parents are made to feel more at ease and that this supports the success of our partnership.

Parents and carers may be generally involved in many ways in the life of a school (e.g. voluntary help in classrooms and on school trips, parent/carer representatives on the trustees board or school governing body or fund-raising organisations). A newer development is the introduction of parent/carer councils which may provide useful consultation on specific issues for the school leadership and/or governors (Tutt, 2011)

A vignette from a secondary school SENCO

Starting my post at a new school which had previously had an inspection which left lots of action points to work on for SEN provision at the school felt both exciting and daunting. The parents of the pupils with SEN gave very negative reports of their previous experiences with the school in my early meetings with them. I felt strongly that if I was going to be able to positively turn the SEN provision around, I needed to ensure that parents were involved and that I worked to develop a good working partnership with parents. In order to facilitate this, I started a parents' group for the parents of children with SEN. Providing tea and biscuits or cake seemed to encourage parents to come along to meetings and helped to create a welcoming relaxed atmosphere. I used this forum to seek parents' views on how we could best communicate with them, the SEN provision in the school and other aspects of school life, such as access to extra-curricular activities for pupils with SEN. I also consulted with them on other issues, such as the action plan I had for developing our provision. Initially this was a small group, but these parents became advocates for the forum and encouraged other parents to attend.

What is the background/theoretical underpinning?

The Lamb Enquiry (2009) was set up to research parental confidence in the assessment and statement process and how this might be enhanced. In the final report, Lamb argued that systems are more effective when parents and carers, schools and local authorities collaborate together positively. This perspective is supported by other studies, such as Osler and Vincent (2003) who identified that parents and carers and children and young people in their research study cited parental involvement and good home–school communication as being vital to engagement and motivation in learners.

O'Brien (2016) reports that involving parents and carers in meetings about their child helps reassure them that the professionals understand the child's needs. In practical terms, parents and carers can contribute information to their child's learning passport/individual profile document.

What would you need in order to use this approach?

Roffey (2011) contends that dialogue with parents that frequently includes a long list of negative reports about their child is not conducive to building positive relations. Thus it can be helpful to think back over conversations with parents and carers and analyse the content of what was said, how and where the conversation took place and the responses of all involved.

These strategies are helpful to support reflection with colleagues on the elements which help to build positive relationships with parents and carers:

- Communicate positive reports to parents and carers regularly and work to keep good communication

- It may be helpful to have informal dialogues with parents and carers to support building relationships

- Acknowledge parents' and carers' expertise on their child

- Frame communications positively – start with positive reports as this will show parents and carers that a balanced approach with the best interests of the learner is being adopted

- Maintain focus on the learner's needs

- Work to identify shared understanding and shared decision-making

- Use knowledge of family circumstances to inform planning of meetings, for example time, notice and offer of opportunity to bring someone to support them

- Ensure parents and carers have opportunities to articulate their views

(Roffey, 2011)

The notion of creating spaces, presented in the introduction of this book, also extends to working with parents and carers. Parents and carers may be feeling exhausted or overwhelmed by their child's SEN needs and they may need space to talk about their concerns and experiences (O'Brien, 2016). Professionals need to engage in active listening within these spaces to enable them to understand the lived-experiences of parents (O'Brien, 2016). This is particularly pertinent for the times when professionals need to take on the role of advocate for parents and carers.

It is helpful to have a range of communication channels, from formal meetings to emails and telephone calls. The use of IT, perhaps through allowing access to the school's virtual learning environment, can be helpful to keep parents informed about activities in school. However, this does require an investment of time for teachers to be able to engage with this, which may require creative approaches to generate this time in order to facilitate collaboration with parents and carers (Gross, 2013).

Some parents benefit from practical ideas of activities they can do at home to support their child's learning. Gross (2013) suggests it may be helpful to consult with parents on what kind of help they want to support their child's learning. She advocates offering non-threatening activities (e.g. crafts with children and young people, tea and cake, etc.) and then using these activities to develop skills. There are some programmes which offer activities which can be used to support parents, for example the DfE's Social Emotional Additional Learning (SEAL) curriculum had a programme of parental activities which schools could use.

Practical workshops with parents

One of the authors supported a primary school to set up workshops for parents to learn about and try out activities to support literacy skills at home. The school's SENCO had learned from conversations with parents, that when they were asked by their child's teacher to support their child's reading or spelling or writing at home, parents felt willing but were uncertain of what to do.

The workshops focused upon practical activities which could be done with resources easily available to parents. Parents were able to try out the activities, ask questions and share comments in small groups in addition to a short session of information –question and answer session at the beginning and end. The school reported positive feedback from parents.

The Achievement for All pilot required the schools involved to employ an approach for working with parents called structured conversations. Gross (2013) notes that within the pilot schools, the number of schools reporting excellent relationships with parents increased significantly and those reporting poor relationships decreased by a large amount. Parents were reported to feel valued and listened to. One of the authors worked at a school involved in the pilot and recollects that schools involved in the pilot willingly shared good practice with one another to support engaging parents who had previously been hard to reach. Structured conversations have a framework for schools to follow, structured into four stages (explore, focus, plan and review) (Gross, 2013) and offer a longer time period for the meeting than would traditionally be offered in parent evening type discussions. Following the framework carefully and accurately is highly important to its successful implementation and does require training. The benefits of this approach include:

- Raising aspirations of parents and children and young people (Gross, 2013)

- The focus on constructing a holistic view of children and young people has supported building 'genuine relationships' between parents and school staff (Humphreys and Squires, 2011, p. 8)

- Better understanding by school staff on child's profile and other important contextual information (Gross, 2013)

- Parents feeling greater empowerment and inclusion in their child's education (Humphreys and Squires, 2011)

- Creative approaches utilised by schools to support working in partnership with parents who have been hard to reach, such as meeting in places other than the school site, having support of wider family or other parents and flexibility in scheduling the meetings (Humphreys and Squires, 2011)

One SENCO reported an experience of working with teachers to support them with structured conversations. The teachers had frequently complained that two of their learners never did homework and questioned why their parents did not ensure their children completed their homework. The SENCO worked with teachers to develop active listening skills. This was aimed to support the implementation of the structured conversation approach for meeting with parents and carers. The SENCO reported that after the meetings, the teachers had reframed their thinking about homework. Hearing about the parent's experiences of trying to do homework with their child had changed their thinking from 'why don't they' to 'how can we change what we do to better support these parents and the learners with practising skills taught in class'. The SENCO also reported that the views of the learners and their parents and carers, articulated in structured conversations, led to a more creative and holistic approach being taken to planning extra-curricular activities. The outcome was greater opportunities for learners with SEN.

Some practical strategies to encourage parental involvement in structured conversations identified by Gross (2013) include:

- Reassurance offered to parents and carers ahead of the meeting, which may be through means such as telephone conversation

- Providing parents and carers with some questions to think about before the meeting to help them to feel prepared for the meeting

- Reminders of the meeting which could be in the form of a text message

- Offering flexibility in terms of venue for the meeting and time of the meeting

- Inviting the parent or carer to bring along someone for support if needed (e.g. wider family member or friend)

Vignette from a SENCO

Parents and carers may be apprehensive about attending meetings in schools because of their own experiences. We offer to meet them at home or in a neutral place, such as a local café, to help with building a trustful relationship.

Further reading/resources/websites

Achievement for All (EEF report): https://educationendowmentfoundation.org.uk/projects-and-evaluation/projects/achievement-for-all/

nasen booklet Working in partnership with parents and carers: www.google.co.uk/url?sa=t&rct=j&q=&esrc=s&source=web&cd=5&ved=2ahUKEwiE2JPgkejeAhVpIcAKHaOzDlgQFjAEegQIARAC&url=http%3A%2F%2Fwww.nasen.org.uk%2Futilities%2Fdownload.4186A2D0-EABF-49C7-9206A7C7B6A8C314.html&usg=AOvVaw07Lby9BGaooaJon-zz6apK

Autism Tool Box Working with parents: www.autismtoolbox.co.uk/partnership-with-families/

Working in partnership with external agencies

What is the approach?

Multi-agency working has been a headline within policy over quite some time, but this approach may still be problematic owing to difficulties in communication and understanding. Ekins (2015) contends that it is not possible for one person alone to fully meet the needs of learners with SEN or learners at risk of exclusion and thus developing effective approaches to working with others is important. Potential external sources of support to meet the needs of learners have been listed at the beginning of this chapter. Working with external agencies or other schools may facilitate access to specialist expertise, or provide opportunities to work together to develop practice (Tutt, 2011).

What is the practice for working in partnership with external agencies?

Tutt (2011) cites research from Cameron *et al.* (2009) which identified four forms of inter-agency working:

1 Parallel working – agencies are co-located but there are few instances of collaborative work

2 Multi-agency casework – agencies working together on specific cases; does not necessarily involve any structural change or co-location

3 Project teams – short time period during which professionals have some of their time allocated to working with others on particular projects.

4 Work groups – professionals work together as a multi-professional team to take a holistic approach to children and young people's education and wellbeing

In schools, these meetings may be referred to as Team around the Child (TAC) meetings or multi-agency meetings. These may take the form of multi-agency casework or work groups within the provided list.

What is the background/theoretical underpinning?

Edwards *et al.*'s (2010) research study examined inter-professional work. In their case studies of five secondary schools, they conceptualised this collaborative work as the creation of 'spaces' to build relationships; interestingly the drivers were often centred upon learner achievement. They noted that roles and role boundaries for people were regularly negotiated and renegotiated with schools. This notion of concerns regarding standards and achievement being used to stimulate ways to develop inclusive practice has been identified by Ainscow, Booth and Dyson (2006).

Research studies investigating multi-agency working have identified positive outcomes for children and young people. Characteristics and factors which have been identified in effective multi-agency working are:

• Shared understanding of the purpose of the group with clearly identified aim and goals

• Shared understanding of terminology

- Clear communication

- Sufficient resource of time for regular meetings

- Mutual respect for the skills of individuals

- Willingness of individuals to critically reflect on their practice and relax professional boundaries

- The appointment of a key worker or coordinator to act as a single point of contact

(Soan, 2012; Walker, 2008; Bertram *et al.*, 2002)

What would you need in order to use this approach?

It will be useful for the SENCO and senior leadership to work to build their knowledge of the work of charities; what resources, activities and support they are able to offer as this can help with planning for learners and meeting needs holistically (Tutt, 2011). Ekins (2015) notes that other organisations (e.g. charities) can play a valuable part in relation to offering impartial advice and advocating for the child or young person within their involvement in multi-agency work.

Proactive planning to develop working in partnership with external agencies and with parents and carers is supported by reflection upon components which influence success or hinder this work. Leaders need to create time to engage in this reflection and dialogue with the school team to support and inform the development of practice. This may be helped by considering principles which help, and potential barriers to, collaborative work.

Key components influencing barriers are (Tutt, 2011):

- Challenges of funding and resources

- Lack of shared language

- Managing other priorities

- Complications arising from different management streams and balancing differing interest.

Ekins (2015) proposes these principles to support successful collaborative work:

- Clear focus of the needs of the learner

- Commitment from all involved to meeting those needs

- Trust

- Shared respect

- Team approach

- Shared understanding of everyone's perspectives

- Valuing and accepting one another's expertise

- Clear protocols for sharing information

- Development of a clear action plan, agreed by all, which sets out responsibilities, actions and date for review

- Time

Further reading/resources/websites

National College for Teaching and Leadership (Effective multi-agency teams): www.nationalcollege.org.uk/transfer/open/adsbm-phase-5-module-6-managing-programmes/adsbm-p5m6-s3/adsbm-p5m6-s3t7.html

There are implications for parents in working collaboratively with a multi-professional team. Earlier in this chapter, two elements of working in partnership were identified: identifying need and planning and implementing strategies and approaches to support the child or young person. The second element may lead to parents being asked to take on specific actions within the action plan. This may be to employ strategies agreed in the planning for their child at home, in order to work with school for consistency of approach or work with another agency on an issue outside of school.

One approach which may help to facilitate both elements of multi-agency working is person-centred planning. The next section of this chapter explores person-centred approaches and how this may be implemented in practice.

Person-centred approaches

What is the approach?

Person-centred planning is a way to include parents and carers and children and young people's aspirations and wishes within planning for the child or young person (Gross, 2013). The process involves examining things that are working well as well as those which need to be amended.

What is the background/theoretical underpinning?

Ekins (2015, p. 144) contends that 'person-centred planning has at its heart, a clear focus on a more holistic understanding of the child, utilising the various experiences and understandings of the child as a whole person, rather than a narrow focus on a particular diagnosis or label'.

This approach to working with parents and children and young people is underpinned by empathy, trust and respect for one another's perspectives and experiences (Ekins, 2015).

What would you need in order to use this approach?

Person-centred planning may involve wider family members, not just parents (e.g. grandparents, siblings) and the wider circle of others involved with the child or young person (e.g. social worker, SaLT, other professionals, club leaders). The child or young person is involved. The meeting(s) will be facilitated (or chaired) by a nominated person (e.g. SENCO, EP).

Gross (2013) notes that the focus starts with everyone's aspirations and then works to identify and agree priorities, and the practical steps which will support reaching those goals. These discussions will also involve an analysis of anxieties, barriers and things which will be supportive. It is important that strengths and key interests will be incorporated within these discussions.

Many of the approaches utilised to facilitate person-centred planning involve some element of visual strategies to record the ideas discussed and the actions which are agreed upon (Sakellariadis, 2010). An example of this is where one person within the meeting draws out the key points discussed and agreed upon on a large sheet of paper using symbols, words and pictures. People attending the meeting may be asked to sign the sheet to show their support and agreement of the plan.

During the meeting, the child or young person is asked at regular intervals their views or responses to the points being made by others (Bradbury *et al.*, 2010). In order for this to happen, careful planning on the modes of communication will best facilitate the child or young person to be able to understand what has been said, ask questions and communicate their views. As discussed in the section about pupil voice, this will need to be personalised to the learner. Additionally, it may be felt that a specific person who will act as advocate for the child or young person should be nominated (this was discussed in the section on pupil voice) and present at the meeting.

One of the issues which need to be considered is how the facilitator of the meeting will handle times when sensitivity is needed in order to manage opposing perspectives and desires, to arrive at shared understanding and goals especially in relation to issues which are tricky or difficult (Bradbury *et al.*, 2010).

There are some specific strategies which set out a process for a person-centred planning meeting, for example Planning Alternative Tomorrows with Hope (PATH) and Making Action Plans (MAP). Links for information to these are provided in the following section.

Further reading/resources/websites

Inclusive Solutions have information and video clips about person-centred planning: https://inclusive-solutions.com/person-centred-planning/

Kirklees Council have information and examples: www.kirklees.gov.uk/beta/special-education/pdf/path.pdf

Foundation for people with learning disabilities: www.mentalhealth.org.uk/learning-disabilities/a-to-z/p/person-centred-planning-pcp

West Sussex Local Offer has video clips about 'What is a MAP?' and other resources: https://westsussex.local-offer.org/information_pages/388-person-centred-planning-pcp-map-tools

Conclusion

Ekins (2015) notes that there is not a discrete chapter in the SEND CoP about working with parents; she suggests this may be interpreted as showing that the expectation is that working in effective partnerships with parents is integral to developing provision for children and young people.

It is helpful to keep in mind that relationships are revealed through both words and actions, and from what is communicated through both these modes about values and expectations (Roffey, 2011). These factors can support developing genuine partnerships which empower parents and pupils (Ekins, 2015):

- Mode and nature of communication utilised

- Honesty and trust

- Active listening

- Nature of language used within communication (e.g. jargon)

- Flexibility in the form of support provided

- Respecting the parents' and child or young person's expertise

Participation, also framed as working collaboratively with others, underlies principles of inclusion and may act as one measure for an analysis of inclusion (Norwich, 2013). Norwich (2013) reminds us that participation refers to listening, and responding, to the views of parents and children and young people. This means that their views are better understood and included with decision-making for children and young people.

References

Ainscow, M., Booth, T. and Dyson, A. (2006) 'Inclusion and the standards agenda: Negotiating policy pressures in England'. *International Journal of Inclusive Education*, 10(4), pp. 295–308.

Bertram, T., Pascal, C., Bokhari, C., Gasper, M. and Holtermann, S. (2002) *Early Excellence Centre Pilot Programme Second Evaluation Report 2000–2001*. DfES Research Report No 361. London: HMSO.

Bradbury, B., Feeney, A. and Gager, A. (2010) 'Hearing the voice of the child: Ensuring authenticity'. In F. Hallet and G. Hallett (eds.), *Transforming the Role of the SENCO: Achieving the National Award for SEN Coordination*. Maidenhead: Open University Press, pp. 207–215.

Cameron, C., Moss, P., Owen, C., Petrie, P., Potts, P., Simmon, A. and Wigfall, V. (2009) *Working Together in Extended Schools and Children's Centres: A Study of Inter-professional Activity in England and Sweden*. Available at: dcsf.gov.uk/everychildmatters/research.

Edwards, A., Lunt, I. and Stamou, E. (2010) 'Inter-professional work and expertise: New roles at the boundaries of schools'. *British Educational Research Journal*, 36(1), pp. 27–45.

Ekins, A. (2015) *The Changing Face of Special Educational Needs: Impact and Implications for SENCOs, Teachers and Their Schools*. Abingdon: Routledge.

Gray, C. (1994) *Comic Strip Conversations*. Arlington, TX: Future Horizons.

Gross, J. (2013) *Beating Bureaucracy in Special Educational Needs*. Second Edition. Abingdon: Routledge.

Hayden, C. (1997) *Children Excluded From Primary School: Debates, Evidence, Responses*. Buckingham: Open University Press.

HMS Treasury. (2003) *Every Child Matters*. Available at: www.gov.uk/government/publications/every-child-matters (accessed 28 March 2019).

Hodkinson, A. (2016) *Key Issues in Special Educational Needs and Inclusion*. Second Edition. London: SAGE.

Humphreys and Squires. (2011) *Achievement for All National Evaluation*. Research Report DFE-RR123. ISBN978-1-84775-926-9.

Lamb Enquiry. (2009) *SEN and Parental Confidence*. Nottingham: DCSF.

Lever, C. (2011) *Understanding Challenging Behaviour in Inclusive Classrooms*. Harlow: Pearson.

Lewis, A. 2010. 'Silence in the context of "choice" voice'. *Children and Society*, 24, pp. 14–23.

Lewis, A. and Porter, J. (2007) 'Research and pupil voice'. In L. Florian (ed.), *The SAGE Handbook of Special Educational Needs*. London: SAGE, pp. 222–232.

Lindsay, G., Cullen, M., Cullen, S., Dockerell, J., Strand, S., Arweck, E., Hegart, S. and Goodlad, S. (2010) *Evaluation of Impact of DfE Investment in Initiatives Designed to Improve Teacher Workforce Skills in Relation to SEN and Disabilities*. London: DfE.

Norwich, B. (2013) *Addressing Tensions and Dilemmas in Inclusive Education: Living With Uncertainty*. London: Routledge.

O'Brien, J. (2016) *Don't Send Him in Tomorrow: Shining a Light on the Marginalised Disenfranchised and Forgotten Children of Today's Schools*. Carmarthen: Independent Thinking Press.

Ofsted. (2010) *The Special Educational Needs and Disability Review*. Reference 090221. London: Ofsted.

Osler, A. and Vincent, K. (2003) *Girls and Exclusion: Rethinking the Agenda*. London: RoutledgeFalmer.

Pinkus, S. (2005) 'Bridging the gap between policy and practice: Adopting a strategic vision for partnership working in special education'. *British Journal of Special Education*, 32(4), pp. 184–187.

Roffey, S. (2011) *Changing Behaviour in Schools: Promoting Positive Relationships and Wellbeing*. London: SAGE.

Sakellariadis, A. (2010) 'The challenge of supporting the supporters in the inclusive school'. In F. Hallett and G. Hallett (eds.), *Transforming the Role of the SENCO: Achieving the National Award for SEN Coordination*. Croydon: Open University Press, pp. 24–36.

Rogers, C. R. (1967) *On Becoming a Person: A Therapist's View of Psychotherapy*. London: Constable & Company.

Soan, S. (2012) 'Multi-professional working: The way forward?'. In J. Cornwall and L. Graham-Matheson (eds.), *Leading on Inclusion: Dilemmas, Debates and New Perspectives*. London: Routledge, pp. 87–97.

Tutt, R. (2011) *Partnership Working to Support Special Educational Needs and Disabilities*. London: SAGE.

Tyrrell, B. and Woods, K. (2018) 'Gathering the views of children and young people with ASD: A systematic literature review'. *British Journal for Special Educational Needs*, 45(3), pp. 302–328.

Walker, G. (2008) *Working Together for Children: A Critical Introduction to Multi-Agency Working*. London: Continuum.

Chapter two
SPEECH, LANGUAGE AND COMMUNICATION SKILLS

| 1) What is the approach? |
| 2) Why might it reduce exclusion? |
| 3) How does it fit within our definition of inclusive pedagogy? |
| 4) What is the practice? |
| 5) What is the background / theoretical underpinning? |
| 6) What would you need in order to use this approach? |
| 7) Further reading / resources / websites |

What is the approach?

Speech language and communication skills are made up of different components which interact together:

- Attention and listening

- Receptive language (comprehension)

- Expressive language

- Pragmatic language (social use of language)

It may be helpful to think of the components which are part of the complex processes involved in language and communication as being like a well-oiled machine. If a difficulty is experienced in one or more components, then this affects the working of the machine.

Speech, language and communication needs (SLCN) is an umbrella term used to denote that a learner is experiencing difficulties in one or more areas of language and communication skills. Difficulties with speech, language and communication may be a primary need or may be part of more complex needs such as autism, ADHD, dyspraxia (Hayden and Jordan, 2015). SLCN may be hidden because whilst some areas of difficulties may be easy for practitioners to be aware of (e.g. speech difficulties), others may be much more difficult to identify.

Speech, language and communication skills are important for:

- Facilitating the communication of our needs, opinions and ideas to other people

- Supporting the development of cognitive skills

- Facilitating social interaction

- Providing opportunities for self-regulation of behaviour and responses

(Westwood, 2015, p. 17)

Additionally, language is the principle means through which learning activities in school are conducted (Westwood, 2015). These points are also recognised within research studies and reports, for example Cambridge Primary Review (2010) and Bercow Report (2008). Bercow Ten Years On (2018) highlighted the vital role played by communication towards the opportunities children and young people gain access to and that understanding among decision-makers is insufficient. SLCN may negatively influence the development of academic skills and social-emotional skills (Hayden and Jordan, 2015).

The rationale for including a section on speech, language and communication needs within this book is that research has identified links between SLCN and behaviour difficulties; that SLCN is a risk factor for problematic behaviours (Clegg et al., 2015; Yew and O'Kearney, 2013).

[P]eer problems, emotional difficulties and impaired prosocial behaviour are the most significant types of difficulty experienced by children and young people with SLCN.

(Lindsay and Dockrell, 2012, p. 22)

Behaviour serves a function for the individual and is a means of communication (Long, 2014; Porter, 2007). Many of the behaviours we consider to be negative or challenging may be indicators of the learner's attempts to have needs met and surmount problems (Long, 2007). Long (2007) reminds us that while behaviour is serving a function, it becomes problematic when the behaviour does not match our expectations for that particular social situation. Our observation is that age expectations also play a role here, for example tantrums from a two–three-year-old may be understood but not from older children and young people.

The key point we are making here is that behaviour considered problematic may have SLCN as an underlying factor or one of the factors within a complex profile of needs. Children and young people who do not have the language skills to effectively communicate their feelings or needs may thus use behaviour as a mode of communicating. SLCN is an area of need which is invisible in its nature, thus may be difficult to detect; the presenting challenging behaviour can obscure adults to the existence of SLCN as a potential underlying need. Thus, the observed behaviours rather than any underlying needs become the focus of everyone's attention and planning for the pupil (Allenby *et al.*, 2015).

> To change your child's behaviour you will need to be able to make sense of that behavior.
>
> (Hanbury, 2007, p. 5)

Why might it reduce exclusion?

As mentioned in the previous section, research has identified links between SLCN and problematic behaviour. This is explored in greater depth in the section looking at theoretical underpinning. Look back at the four components of speech, language and communication that we listed at the beginning of this chapter. Difficulties in any of those areas of language may present differing difficulties for children and young people in their interactions with their surroundings, which highlights the need for careful assessment to inform planning tailored support for these learners (Anderson, Hawes and Snow, 2016). Should a learner be identified as having SLCN, strategies, approaches and intervention programmes can be implemented to support meeting their language and communication needs. These interventions and strategies may also be part of a package of support aimed at different areas of need experienced by the learner, with the overall goal of reducing behaviours considered problematic. The work targeting specific difficulties with aspects of speech, language and communication skills may help to reduce the problematic behaviour which was underpinned by those specific difficulties (Law and Plunket, 2009). This may reduce the risk of exclusion.

How does it fit within our definition of inclusive pedagogy?

A willingness to consider and explore potential factors which may underlie the behaviours we observe in children and young people, reflects a holistic perspective of learners and planning for their learning and wellbeing. Speech, language and communication is one of the factors which should be considered. In exploring a learner's speech, language and communication profile, we are acknowledging difference and diversity and seeking to empower learners through identifying needs and working to meet those needs. The problem-solving nature of this work is a creative endeavour to respond positively to learners' needs. This relates to working to fulfil a social justice and human rights agenda to enable all learners to access education and have the potential for positive long-term outcomes. This aligns with the six dimensions of our theoretical framework of inclusion.

What is the practice?

The implications of this for practice are:

- Assess the language skills of children and young people for whom behaviour is of concern

- Use assessment (from formal assessments, informal assessment and observations) to inform planning of specific tailored interventions and pedagogical approaches to use with the learner

What is the background/theoretical underpinning?

Research studies have noted connections between SLCN and emotional-behaviour needs (Clegg *et al.*, 2015). Clegg *et al.* (2015) note that the degree of strength between those connections has varied between studies and suggest that this discrepancy might be owing to factors including sample size, the age of the learners and the variety of definitions used in relation to SLCN and socio-emotional-behavioural needs. Potential difficulties may be considered within the areas of social relationships, pro-social behaviours, externalising and internalising behaviours and self-esteem and self-belief.

Within the scope of this section, we are not able to bring an in-depth presentation of the research studies but present a succinct overview for each of these four areas.

Social relationships

A number of research studies have identified that children and young people with SLCN are at greater risk of experiencing difficulties with social relationships and social interaction (for example, Bakopoulou and Dockrell (2016), Dockrell *et al.* (2014), Lindsay and Dockrell (2012), St. Clair *et al.* (2011)). They are also at greater risk of being involved in incidents of bullying, as victims or perpetrators, than typically developing peers (Yew and O'Kearney, 2015). It should be noted that the language of risk is being used here; these statements are not an inescapable outcome for the child or young person (Dockrell *et al.*, 2014).

Difficulties with speech, language and communication may hinder or reduce opportunities to have conversations and interact with others, which may contribute to barriers to social relationships (Lindsay, Dockrell and Strand, 2007). Children and young people with SLCN may experience difficulties with making inferences and with emotional awareness which hinders reading social cues and may be another contributing factor to social difficulties

(Bakopoulou and Dockrell, 2016). The difficulties with social relationships may increase during adolescence owing to the increasing amounts of dialogue used and the nuances within the dialogue, such as sarcasm, local jargon and so on (St. Clair *et al.*, 2011). Indeed, children and young people with SLCN have been observed to experience greater difficulties in the building of positive friendships (Bakopoulou and Dockrell, 2016). In our professional experience protective factors may mean that children and young people with SLCN are more able to develop friendships. An example of a protective factor is a shared interest between children and young people, such as involvement in sports activities.

Pro-social behaviours

Developing pro-social behaviours is important for school readiness and learning academic skills (Hartas, 2011). Difficulties with language comprehension may be an underlying factor for difficulties with social interactions (St. Clair *et al.*, 2011). While links have been made between difficulties in different aspects of language skills and some patterns of behaviour within some studies (St. Clair *et al.*, 2011), other studies suggest that there is a lack of clarity between the role of language and social-emotional skills (example studies: Yew and O'Kearney, 2013; Lindsay and Dockrell, 2012). This suggests the importance of considering language and communication skills within an analysis which includes other potential influences upon observed behaviours.

Externalised and internalised behaviours

Externalised behaviours is the term being used here to represent those behaviours considered challenging, such as tantrums, aggressive verbal or physical outbursts.

Internalised behaviours is the term being used here to represent aspects such as withdrawal, depression, anxiety, fearfulness, trying to please.

Research studies have noted reports from teachers and parents of both externalised and internalised behaviours within children and young people with SLCN (for example, Charman *et al.*, 2015; Clegg *et al.*, 2015; Lindsay and Dockrell, 2012). Language difficulties may hinder the development of a lexicon and expressive language skills related to discussing and managing emotions, which in turn inhibits the development of more mature strategies to manage emotions and behaviours (Yew and O'Kearney, 2015). Another factor impacting upon emotional development, proposed by Yew and O'Kearney (2015), is that language difficulties may sustain or exacerbate innate difficulties. As stated in the previous section, speech, language and communication skills may need to be considered within a range of other possible influences upon children and young people's behaviours (Clegg *at al.*, 2015).

Self-esteem and self-belief

Difficulties with speech, language and communication have been linked to poor progress in academic skills, which may negatively influence children and young people's self-esteem and self-belief (Yew and O'Kearney, 2015, 2013). This is important because positive self-esteem and self-belief may mitigate against adverse outcomes (Lindsay and Dockrell, 2012). The educational environment is a key element within this; this is because the provision which is implemented and the learner's experiences may negatively or positively influence self-belief (Lindsay and Dockrell, 2012).

The rationale for the importance of recognising needs related to speech, language and communication is that there is the potential for children and young people's responses to situations to be misinterpreted by adults and not responded to appropriately. Examples of this are:

- At times when children and young people do not follow instructions correctly, an assumption is made that this is noncompliant behaviour rather than owing to a potential misunderstanding by the children or young person.

- Frequent arguments with peers may be owing to not having the language skills to negotiate and problem solve.

- Circumstances in which an assumption is made that the learner is not providing a good explanation of an incident because they are being difficult or noncompliant, rather than realising that the learner does not have sufficient language skills to be able to provide a clear or reliable explanation.

In relation to longer-term outcomes, SLCN has been identified as a risk factor for negative outcomes in relation to education, employment and offending behaviour (Snow and Powell, 2012).

What would you need in order to use this approach?

A school ethos which recognises that a holistic approach to supporting their learners and a recognition of the importance of identifying the factors underlying behaviour is needed.

As already stated, speech, language and communication needs may be difficult to recognise. Inclusion of CPD activities which develop awareness of SLCN and strategies to support learners with SLCN within the school cycle of professional development for all staff is a vital starting point.

The web links in the following section are links to websites which have information about SLCN and free downloadable resources, including checklists which can be used as an initial stage in assessment to identify whether or not a child or young person has SLCN needs.

Formal specialist assessments are provided by Speech and Language Therapists. Information about speech and language therapy services may be accessed from the local national health authority website for your local area.

Further reading/resources/websites

ICAN: www.ican.org.uk/

The Communication Trust: www.thecommunicationtrust.org.uk

The Communication Trust have a freely downloadable checklist for speech language and communication skills which can be used by school staff: www.thecommunicationtrust.org.uk/media/7415/universally_speaking_5-11_checklist_final.pdf

IDP checklist for school staff – self-audit of understanding of speech, language and communication: www.google.co.uk/search?source=hp&ei=4yMyXKmIEY-5kwXx0pvABw&q=slcn+checklist&oq=s&gs_l=psy-ab.1.0.35i39l2j0i67l2j0l2j0i131j0j0i131j0.3538.3538..6507 . . . 0.0..0.157.222.1j1 . . . 0 . . . 1..gws-wiz . . . 0.BkCbAV3m5Xg#

Afaisic: www.afasic.org.uk/ free downloadable resources and information: www.afasic.org.uk/resources/free-downloads/recognising-a-problem-and-getting-help/

Centre for Criminal and Youth Justice (2014) Speech, Language and Communication Needs in Youth Justice (report): www.cycj.org.uk/wp-content/uploads/2014/06/Youth-justice-in-scotland-Communication-section-final1.pdf

Hayden, S. and Jordan, E. (2007) *Language for Learning*. London: Routledge.

Let's Talk about it. What teachers need to know about children's communication skills. Available at: www.thecommunicationtrust.org.uk/media/12285/let_s_talk_about_it_-_final.pdf

Bercow Ten Years ON: www.bercow10yearson.com/

References

Alexander, R. (ed.). (2010) *Children, Their World, Their Education: Final Report and Recommendations of the Cambridge Primary Review*. London: Routledge.

Allenby, C., Fearon-Wilson, J., Merrison, S. and Morling, E. (2015) *Supporting Children With Speech and Language Difficulties*. Second Edition. Abingdon: Routledge and Nasen and Hull City Council.

Anderson, S.A.S., Hawes, D.J. and Snow, P.C. (2016) 'Language Impairments among youth offenders: A systematic review'. *Children and Youth Services Review*, 65, pp. 195–203.

Bakopoulou, I. and Dockrell, J.E. (2016) 'The role of social cognition and prosocial behaviour in relation to the socio-emotional functioning of primary aged children with specific impairment'. *Research in Developmental Disabilities*, 45–50, pp. 354–370.

Bercow, J. (2008) *A Review of Services for Children and Young People (0–19) With Speech, Language and Communication Needs*. London: DCSF.

Part III

Bercow, J. (2018). Bercow: *Ten Years On: An Independent Review of Provision for Children and Young People With Speech, Language and Communication Needs in England*. Available at: www.bercow10yearson.com/ (accessed 20 March 2018).

Charman, T., Rickette, J., Dockerell, J.E., Lindsay, G. and Palikara, O. (2015) 'Emotional and behavioural problems in children with language impairments and children with autism spectrum disorders'. *International Journal of Language and Communication Disorders*, 50(1), pp. 84–93.

Clegg, J., Law, J., Rush, R., Peters, T.J. and Roulstone, S. (2015) 'The contribution of early language development to children's emotional and behavioural functioning at 6 years: An analysis of data from children in focus sample from the ALSPAC birth cohort'. *The Journal of Child Psychology and Psychiatry*, 56(1), pp. 67–75.

Dockrell, J.E., Lindsay, G., Roulstone, S. and Law, J. (2014) 'Supporting children with speech, language and communication needs: An overview of the results of the better communication research programme'. *International Journal of Language and Communication Disorders*, 49(5), pp. 543–557.

Hanbury, M. (2007) *Positive Behaviour Strategies to Support Children and Young People With Autism*. London: Paul Chapman Publishing.

Hartas, D. (2011) *Children's Language and Behavioural, Social and Emotional Difficulties and Prosocial Behaviour During Toddler Years and at School Entry*, downloaded from University of Warwick repository, 8th August 2016.

Hayden, S. and Jordan, E. (2015) *Language for Learning in the Primary School*. Second Edition. Abingdon: Routledge and Nasen.

Law, J. and Plunkett, C. (2009) 'The interaction between behaviour and speech and language difficulties: Does intervention for one affect outcomes in the other?'. Technical report. In *Research Evidence in Education Library*. London: EPPI-Centre, Social Science Research Unit, Institute of Education, University of London. Reference number: 1705.

Lindsay, G. and Dockrell. (2012) *The Relationship Between Speech, Language and Communication Needs (SLCN) and Behavioural, Emotional and Social Difficulties (BESD)*. Available at: www.gov.uk/government/uploads/system/uploads/attachment_data/file/219632/DFE-RR247-BCRP6.pdf (accessed 24 October 2015).

Long, R. (2007) *The Rob Long Omnibus Edition of Better Behaviour*. London: Routledge.

Long, R. (2014) *Behaviour for Learning*. Conference. GCC Advisory Teaching Service. Cinderford, 5th November.

Porter, L. (2007) *Behaviour in Schools: Theory and Practice for Teachers*. Second Edition. Maidenhead: Open University Press.

Snow, P. and Powell, M. (2012) 'Youth (in)justice: Oral language competence in early life and risk for engagement in anti – Social behaviour in adolescence'. *Trends and Issues in Crime and Criminal Justice*, 435, pp. 1–6.

St. Clair, M.C., Pickles, A., Durkin, K. and Conti-Ramsden, G. (2011) 'A longitudinal study of behavioural, emotional and social difficulties in individuals with a history of specific language impairment(SLI)'. *Journal of Communication Disorders*, 44(2), pp. 186–199.

Westwood, P. (2015) *Commonsense Methods for Children With Special Educational Needs Strategies for the Regular Classroom*. Seventh Edition. London: RoutledgeFalmer.

Yew, S.G.K. and O'Kearney, R. (2013) 'Emotional and behavioural outcomes later in childhood and adolescence for children with specific language impairments: Meta-analyses of controlled prospective studies'. *The Journal of Child Psychology and Psychiatry*, 54(5), pp. 516–524.

Yew, S.G.K. and O'Kearney, R. (2015) 'Early language impairments and developmental pathways of emotional problems across childhood'. *International Journal of Language and Communication Disorders*, 50(3), pp. 358–373.

Chapter three
SOCIAL COMMUNICATION SKILLS

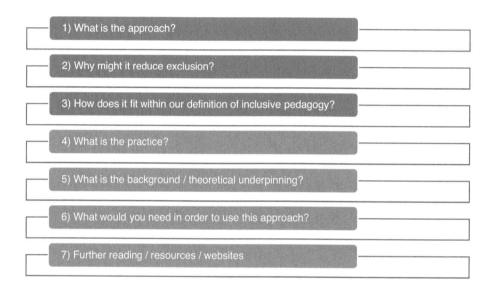

1) What is the approach?

2) Why might it reduce exclusion?

3) How does it fit within our definition of inclusive pedagogy?

4) What is the practice?

5) What is the background / theoretical underpinning?

6) What would you need in order to use this approach?

7) Further reading / resources / websites

What is the approach?

Social communication skills relate to competences in understanding and using language within social situations (Hayden and Jordan, 2012). Thus, these skills are key to support developing relationships with others, important for friendships and for working collaboratively. Social communication skills are also termed pragmatic language skills (Afasic, 2009) and include:

- Turn-taking in conversations

- Maintaining topics of conversations

- Being able to repair a conversation, for example identifying that our listener does not understand what we are saying and adjusting or amending our explanation to help them to understand

- Understanding and using nonverbal communication:

  - Eye contact

  - Facial expressions

  - Body language and gesture

  - Tone of voice

  - Personal space

These competences underpin social-emotional understanding, social relationships and expected social behaviours (Hayden and Jordan, 2012). We use the skills identified earlier to analyse and thus understand the communication of others and to enable us to adapt our communication to match the social situation (Afasic, 2009). These skills are also involved in academic aspects of school, for example we draw upon these skills in collaborative or shared learning tasks and in following the dialogue within class teaching.

Children and young people's social communication skills develop across all phases of schooling. Thus, practitioners from early years through primary and secondary phases need to reflect upon their learners' skills in this area.

Some children or young people experience difficulties with social communication skills and there may be differing factors which underlie their difficulties. The presenting behaviour we observe in school may include issues such as:

- Difficulties with conversations within class or during the social aspects of school life (such as break-time)

- Difficulties with making inferences and with understanding sarcasm, banter and idioms, which triggers inappropriate responses or behaviours

- Difficulties with interacting socially with others and being at risk of isolation

- Risk of negative interactions from others, such as being teased or bullied

- Difficulties with behaving in the ways expected for their age and the social situation

- Risk of negative impact upon their self-esteem

(Hayden and Jordan, 2012; Afasic, 2009)

Hence some children and young people may need to be explicitly taught the social communication skills that they are experiencing difficulties with.

Why might it reduce exclusion?

The difficulties experienced by children and young people who have deficits with social communication skills influence social behaviours and relationships. Difficulties with emotional understanding within themselves and others influence abilities with understanding and accepting that others may hold a different view than their own of situations.

Awareness of the difficulties in this area helps practitioners reflect upon the strategies, approaches and reasonable adjustments to work to mitigate against significant difficulties with behaviour, relationships and learning. This may help to reduce, or change, the behaviours which are of concern and thus the risk of exclusion.

How does it fit within our definition of inclusive pedagogy?

The exploration of the factors underlying behaviours which we observe as negatively impacting upon learning and relationships aligns with a holistic approach to the learner and the school context. Awareness and acceptance that there may be underlying causal factors to the presenting behaviours fits with an acknowledgement of learning and difference. This acceptance, together with the assessment of need and planning of strategies and/or interventions, to support the learner in overcoming barriers elicited by social communication difficulties fits with an inclusive approach. This work seeks to fulfil the principles of social justice and human rights through seeking to remove barriers hindering the access to the individual's right to education. Flexibility within planning for learning activities and the social aspects of school life encompasses creativity in adapting pedagogical approaches, routines and modes of task completion. This work also empowers learners through the development of skills to support them with better understanding of social situations and of the behaviour expected from them within such situations.

What is the practice?

The SEND CoP (DfE, 2015) sets out the graduated approach for meeting the needs of learners. This reminds us that planning for our learners should be informed from assessment to identify their strengths and difficulties. This provides a baseline which not only informs the identification of priorities for the next steps to be worked upon but also supports us with monitoring progress. As with many other skills, there is a plethora of published programmes which aim to support practitioners with developing social communication skills within their leaners. However, the learning activities and strategies we implement do need carefully planned learning outcomes, informed from identified needs, rather than working our way through a published programme in the hope that we will provide the skills the learner needs somewhere within that programme.

A social skills checklist can be helpful to support practitioners with analysing observations to identify children and young people's profile of strengths and difficulties with their social communication skills. The resources section (at the end of this chapter) contains links to free downloadable checklists and there are checklists books in the list in the following section by Hayden and Jordan.

Whole class pedagogical approaches

- Establish an ethos in which learners are encouraged to say when they did not understand or could not hear or follow the pace. Teaching specific strategies for ways in which this can be communicated (e.g. using cue cards, teaching scripts) will support learners with building the confidence to do this and how to do this appropriately. This will also support developing independence skills and empowering learners through the encouragement (and expectation) of learners to take ownership of identifying when they do and do not understand.

- Discuss social scenarios to explore why people say things and act (or do not act) in particular ways to build understanding. This can include discussing games and sports. In this way, implicit social rules can be made explicit for learners.

- Develop peer awareness of learning differences to encourage their understanding and support for others.

- Consider introducing some support or structure for unstructured times (e.g. break time). This might be in the form of clubs, responsibilities and/or supported areas for interacting with others.

- Provide visual support to help the learner's understanding of instructions and explanations and to provide prompts for expected social behaviours or scripts. This might include real objects, photos, pictures, symbols or text.

- Prepare students ahead of a change to the usual routine. A visual timetable will support organisation, learning the routine and with preparation for transitions and change.

- Provide positive, constructive and specific feedback on the learner's communication and its suitability for the situation.

- Model good conversation and interaction skills. It may be helpful to express thinking aloud to support explicit teaching of skills.

- Link with any individual or small group work – look for the skills being taught that are used in class or unstructured time and praise when specific skills being taught are used, and offer reminders and prompts if needed. This will support work to encourage the learner to generalise the skills being taught to other situations.

- Arrange a regular job or responsibility that the learner can take on. This will support developing self-esteem and self-belief. It will be important to consider the nature of the role being given, so that there are not too many demands initially upon social communication skills. Such demands can be increased over time as the learner's confidence and skills develop.

What is the background/theoretical underpinning?

Social communication skills (the term pragmatic language skills is also used) engage a range of language and communication competences which support our understanding and functional use of language to support appropriate social interaction with others (Bishop, 2014; Adams, 2002). Thus, the language and communication employed is well-matched to the context. Difficulties with social communication skills may be observed within the behaviours of children and young people who have a diagnosed condition, such as autism, and in those children and young people who do not have a formal diagnosis of a specific condition.

Frederickson and Cline (2015, p. 251) observe that 'pragmatic difficulties that lead to the inappropriate use or interpretation of language in different social contexts are strongly associated with behaviour problems across childhood'. This perspective is supported by Mackie and Law (2010) who reviewed several studies and noted frequent reports of co-existence of difficulties with language competences and with behaviour in children and young people. Mackie and Law (2010) reported that the language difficulties in children and young people who present with behaviour difficulties had often not been observed co-existing in children and young people.

Positive social relationships, such as friendships with peers, are important to support the development of positive self-esteem and self-confidence (Weare, 2000). Friends may be supportive to managing situations which the individual finds difficult. The ability to understand and use language and communication appropriately in social situations contributes to developing social relationships.

There are differing elements within the notion of relationships which are pertinent to the social and academic aspects of school and the wellbeing of our learners. This includes the interactions with others: the way one person responds to another, the skills which underpin building and maintaining positive relationships with others in social and learning activities, and the individual's learning about themselves, emotions and the development of self-esteem from interaction with others (Weare, 2000). 'Interpersonal intelligence' was the term used by Gardner (1993) to label the skills of social understanding and communication which support interactions with others. Weare (2000) highlights the role of the characteristics of empathy, respect and genuineness within social competences and engaging positively with others.

Listening is a vital component to social communication. The word listening in itself sounds simple, but the activity of listening is multifaceted, requiring the employment of a multitude of competences. These include such skills as:

• Maintaining eye contact

• Self-regulation of emotional responses to what is said to us

• Appropriate body language (e.g. stillness to show we are paying attention)

• Understanding the non-verbal cues of others to support our analysis of what is being communicated

Listening is included here because it is easy to assume that all children and young people know what is meant by good listening. However, this is a skill for which the component behaviours may need to be explicitly taught.

This highlights the value and importance of analysing our learners' understanding and competences in using social communication skills. School staff can then use this information to inform the planning of provision.

What would you need in order to use this approach?

The leadership of a school or setting needs to be proactive in promoting a whole school ethos, attitudes and practice in which a holistic, rather than a binary approach, to behaviour is adopted. This means that any presenting behaviour is analysed in order to work to identify underlying causation and triggers. Language and communication skills should be one factor included within this analysis. Including social communication skills within professional development for all staff and induction of new staff will play a key role in developing this practice.

It may be helpful to have a proforma or pack which teachers and TAs can use to support analysing behaviour which includes questions or checklists related to speech, language and communication. This would support directing or encouraging staff to consider this within both their assessment of a learner's needs and their planning of pedagogical approaches.

Further reading/resources/websites

Hayden, S. and Jordan, E. (2012) *Language for Learning in the Secondary School*. Second Edition. Abingdon: Routledge and Nasen.

Hayden, S. and Jordan, E. (2015) *Language for Learning in the Primary School*. Second Edition. Abingdon: Routledge and Nasen.

Both these books have information, checklists, strategies and resources within them.

The Communication Trust: The Communication Trust is a coalition of over 50 not-for-profit organisations, supporting those who work with children and young people with SLCN . Their website has information and resources available to download: www.thecommunicationtrust.org.uk/

The Communication Trust have a freely downloadable checklist for speech language and communication skills which can be used by school staff – some of the questions relate to pragmatic/social communication skills: www.thecommunicationtrust.org.uk/media/7415/universally_speaking_5-11_checklist_final.pdf

Social communication skills pragmatics checklist – downloadable from: http://successforkidswithhearingloss.com/wp-content/uploads/2012/01/PRAGMATICS-CHECKLIST.pdf

Training materials for teachers of learners with severe, profound and complex learning difficulties. Complex Learning Materials www.complexneeds.org.uk/ has CPD resources for a range of needs including the Pragmatics profile Manual available from: http://complexneeds.org.uk/modules/Module-2.4-Assessment-monitoring-and-evaluation/All/downloads/m08p080c/the_pragmatics_profile.pdf

Afasic: Charity representing children and young people with speech, language and communication needs. Their website has information and resources available: www.afasic.org.uk/

Afasic (2009) Including young people with speech, language and communication difficulties in Secondary Schools: www.afasic.org.uk

Inclusion Development programme (DfE and nasen) available from: www.idponline.org.uk/ has freely available suite of materials to support CPD for a range of SEN needs including speech, language and communication.

There are commercially produced materials available from LDA, Speechmark and Black Sheep press. These include visual prompts and cue cards and intervention programmes.

Social use of language programme – NFER.

References

Adams, C. (2002) 'Practitioner review: The assessment of language pragmatics'. *Journal of Child Psychology and Psychiatry, and Allied Disciplines*, 43(8), pp. 973–987.

Afasic. (2009) *Including Young People With Speech, Language and Communication Difficulties in Secondary Schools*. Available at: www.afasic.org.uk.

Bercow, J. (2008) *A Review of Services for Children and Young People (0-19) with Speech, Language and Communication Needs*. London: DCSF.

Bishop, D.V. (2014) 'Pragmatic language impairment: A correlate of SLI, a distinct subgroup, or part of the autistic continuum?'. In D.V.M. Bishop and L.B. Leonard (eds.), *Speech and Language Impairments in Children*. Hove: Psychology Press, pp. 113–128. Available at: www.researchgate.net/profile/Dorothy_Bishop/publication/215626835_Speech_and_Language_Impairments_in_Children_Causes_Characteristics_Intervention_and_Outcome/links/00b7d5155d35da5b46000000.pdf (accessed 27 February 2019).

Department for Education. (2015) *Special Educational Needs and Disability Code of Practice: 0 to 25 years. Statutory Guidance for Organisations Which Work With and Support Children and Young People Who Have Special Educational Needs or Disabilities*. DFE-00205-2013. London: DfES. Available athttps://www. gov.uk/government/publications/send-code-of-practice-0-to-25 (accessed: 14 February 2015).

Frederickson, N. and Cline, T. (2015) *Special Educational Needs and Diversity*. Third Edition. Maidenhead: McGraw Hill/Open University Press.

Gardner, H. (1993) *Creating Minds: An Anatomy of Creativity Seen Through the Lives of Freud, Einstein, Picasso, Stravinsky, Eliot, Graham, and Gandhi*. New York: BasicBooks.

Hayden, S. and Jordan, E. (2012) *Language for Learning in the Secondary School: Secondary School*. Abingdon: Routledge.

Mackie, L. and Law, J. (2010) 'Pragmatic language and the child with emotional/behavioural difficulties (EBD): A pilot study exploring the interaction between behaviour and communication disability'. *International Journal of Language and Communication Disorders*, 45(4), pp. 397–410. https://doi. org/10.3109/13682820903105137.

Weare, K. (2000) *Promoting Mental, Emotional and Social Health: A Whole School Approach*. Abingdon: Routledge.

Chapter four
EMOTIONAL LITERACY

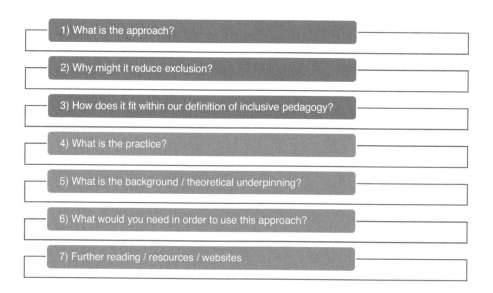

1) What is the approach?

2) Why might it reduce exclusion?

3) How does it fit within our definition of inclusive pedagogy?

4) What is the practice?

5) What is the background / theoretical underpinning?

6) What would you need in order to use this approach?

7) Further reading / resources / websites

What is the approach?

Emotional literacy relates to being able to discern emotions and having the abilities to aptly understand, manage and communicate feelings (Sloan *et al.*, 2017; Camerelli *et al.*, 2011; Hills, 2016; Ripley and Simpson, 2007). The focus of an emotional literacy curriculum is upon developing children and young people's awareness of their emotions and developing strategies to manage the behaviours arising from those feelings; this may support resilience and thus support psychological and physical health (Kay, 2018; Heydenberk and Heydenberk, 2007). The rationale for emotional literacy is that an increased understanding of emotions, and competences with strategies to manage behaviours and communicate feelings, may help children and young people's approaches to problem-solving and thus be supportive of pro-social behaviours needed for social and learning activities (Kay, 2018; Camerelli *et al.*, 2011; Ripley and Simpson, 2007).

Why might it reduce exclusion?

Social-emotional skills may not naturally develop (Ho, Carter and Stephenson, 2010). This means that some children and young people need explicit teaching to support them to develop competences with managing their impulsivity and for making successful relationships (Kay, 2018). Within school (and indeed outside of school) challenges will present themselves impacting upon children and young people's emotions. This may trigger challenging behaviours. Emotional literacy can support increasing children and young people's emotional lexicon which may help them to communicate their feelings and recount a situation more clearly and assertively. Children and young people who are able to manage the communication of their emotions, and the associated behaviours, may achieve greater success in their handling of differing situations. Hence, the teaching of emotional literacy may support reducing the incidents of challenging behaviours and thus reduce the risk of exclusion. Those who advocate the teaching of emotional literacy make the argument that social-emotional competences may be framed as a set of proficiencies and thus, considered in this light, schools are pertinent environments for teaching these skills (Kay, 2018; Nixon, 2016; Camerelli et al., 2011).

How does it fit within our definition of inclusive pedagogy?

Teaching children and young people knowledge, skills and understanding related to emotions, specifically:

- Emotional awareness

- How feelings can impact upon behaviours

- Strategies which can help them self-manage their behaviours

provides them with the tools to positively influence their access to the academic and social aspects of school life.

Emotional literacy works to support children and young people with understanding their emotions and managing their behaviours. This work thus seeks to empower children and young people by emancipating them from engaging in recurring patterns of negative behaviours and enabling them to consider potential options of behaviours and their consequences and thus make more positive choices. Working to develop these skills acknowledges learning and difference and seeks to better equip them to access education which is a fundamental human right. This approach reflects a creative approach to curriculum which values holistic approaches to meeting learners' diverse needs. From the dimension of humanism, emotional literacy facilitates children and young people to develop skills essential to building successful relationships essential to their academic, social and emotional development.

Employing evidence-informed approaches to the teaching of emotional literacy supports practitioners with reflection upon the elements that underlie the learner's presenting behaviours. It also informs the practitioner's plans of how the learner may be best supported to develop the skills, knowledge and competences to help them build positive relationships and access education. This aligns with the dimension of praxis within the theoretical framework for inclusion (presented on p.68).

What is the practice?

There are many variations of emotional literacy programmes available. As stated previously, emotional literacy focuses upon teaching emotional awareness and understanding and strategies to manage behaviours. The knowledge, understanding and skills taught through an emotional literacy programme may be taught individually or within a small group. The programme does need to be tailored to the learners' needs, rather than delivering a published programme inflexibly without relating to the specific difficulties or needs experienced by the learner. The starting point needs to be assessment of strengths and areas of difficulty to inform planning; this approach sits within the graduated approach required by the SEND CoP (DfE, 2015). Planning the emotional literacy programme using the information gained from assessment identifies the key components needed to support children and young people with understanding their emotions and self-management of their behaviours, rather than employing a programme inflexibly (Kay, 2018). Thus, it may be that the most pertinent parts of one programme are used or activities are drawn from a range of programmes.

In order to enable the learner to master these skills, and thus generalise them to a range of circumstances, the specific knowledge, skills and understanding being focused upon needs to be reinforced across the curriculum. This means that goals and strategies need to be planned and agreed and implemented by all involved with the learner. In addition, regular clear communication is essential to share the work done and the learner's responses, to agree goals and to support strategies to be implemented consistently by all adults working with the child. This suggests that working to develop children and young people's social and emotional awareness, as with other diverse needs, is a concern for the whole school, rather than just a concern for the learner's class or subject teacher (Weare, 2004).

What is the background/theoretical underpinning?

Developing children and young people's emotional literacy assists with work to encourage transforming or modifying established patterns of behaviour (Daunic et al., 2013; Corrie, 2003). This may be considered as a means of empowering children and young people to understand and manage their emotions to support their ability to handle social situations (Camerelli et al., 2011). This work may promote resilience (Lindenfield, 2000) which will help children and young people cope with adversities (Erwin, 1993). We acknowledge that this perspective which promotes emotional literacy, challenges those traditional views of education which place emphasis on academic skills. In addition, teachers may express the concerns regarding managing the demands of an academic curriculum and adding an emotional literacy programme into an already crowded timetable (Elias, Hunter and Kress, 2001). This view is supported by Brooker (2005) who suggests that many teachers feel inhibited from giving precedence to teaching social skills owing to great pressure from expectations to fulfil the demands of statutory regulations and the standards agenda. Research studies exploring personal, social and emotional health education (PSHE) have identified that school leaders' perceptions of the purpose of education influence the status given to PSHE. These studies suggest that when school leaders identified an explicit relationship between social-emotional competences and learning (and hence standards), then a higher status was conferred to PSHE within the curriculum (Willis, Clague and Coldwell, 2012; Formby and Wolstenholme, 2012; Goleman, 1996).

What would you need in order to use this approach?

In order to implement emotional literacy, the leadership team and the rest of the school team need to agree that emotional literacy is an approach they will all implement. This will need space within the professional development cycle to develop a secure understanding of the principles and implementation of emotional literacy for all staff. There also needs to be a commitment made for the time needed to plan the intervention programme, and for regular communication to share progress of the learner and success of strategies being implemented.

Further reading/resources/websites

Adams, J. (2006) *Emotional Literacy: 45 Lessons to Develop Emotional Competence.* Corsham: Hopscotch.

Goleman, D. (2014) *Daniel Goleman: We Should Be Teaching Emotional Literacy in Schools*: www.mindful. org/daniel-goleman-we-should-be-teaching-emotional-literacy-in-schools/

Kay, L. (2018) 'Searching for Dumbledore: A reflection upon the outcomes of a tailored emotional literacy programme on three key stage 2 children', *Support for Learning*, 33(2).

Social and Emotional Aspects of Learning (SEAL) (DfES, 2005): https://webarchive.nationalarchives. gov.uk/20110812101121/http://nsonline.org.uk/node/87009

Weare, K. (2004) *Developing the Emotionally Literate School.* London: SAGE.

References

Brooker, L. (2005) 'Getting it right: Supporting children's personal, social and emotional development in the primary years'. In A. Burrell and J. Riley (eds.), *Promoting Children's Well-Being in the Primary Years*. Stafford: Network Educational Press.

Camerelli, S., Curuana, A., Falzon, R. and Muscat, M. (2011) 'The promotion of emotional literacy through personal and social development: The maltese experience'. *Pastoral Care in Education*, 30(1), pp. 19–37.

Corrie, C. (2003) *Becoming Emotionally Intelligent*. Stafford: Network Educational Press.

Daunic, A., Corbett, N., Smith, S., Barnes, T., Santiago-Poventud, L., Chalfant, P., Pitts, D. and Gleaton, J. (2013) 'Brief report: Integrating social-emotional learning with literacy instruction: An intervention for children at risk for emotional and behavioural disorders'. *Behavioural Disorders*, 39(1), pp. 43–51.

Department for Education. (2015) *Special Educational Needs and Disability Code of Practice: 0 to 25 Years. Statutory Guidance for Organisations Which Work With and Support Children and Young People Who Have Special Educational Needs or Disabilities.DFE-00205–2013*. London: DfES. Available at: www.gov. uk/government/publications/send-code-of-practice-0-to-25 (accessed 14 February 2015).

Elias, M., Hunter, L. and Kress, J. (2001) 'Emotional Intelligence and Education'. In J. Ciarrochi, J. Forgas and J. Mayer (eds.), *Emotional Intelligence in Everyday Life: A Scientific Enquiry*. Hove: Psychology Press.

Erwin, P. (1993) *Friendship and Peer Relations in Children*. Chichester: John Wiley.

Formby, E. and Wolstenholme, C. (2012) '"If there's going to be a subject that you don't have to do . . ." Findings from a mapping study of PSHE education in English secondary schools'. *Pastoral Care in Education*, 30(1), pp. 5–18.

Goleman, D. (1996) *Emotional Intelligence: Why It Can Matter More Than IQ*. London: Bloomsbury Publishing.

Heydenberk, W. and Heydenberk, R. (2007) 'More than manners: Conflict resolution in primary level classrooms'. *Early Childhood Education Journal*, 35(2), pp. 120–125.

Hills, R. (2016) 'An evaluation of the emotional literacy support assistant (ELSA) project from the perspectives of primary school children'. *Educational and Child Psychology*, 33(4), pp. 50–65.

Ho, B.P.V., Carter, M. and Stephenson, J. (2010) 'Anger management using a cognitive-behavioural approach for children with special educational needs: A literature review and meta-analysis'. *International Journal of Disability, Development and Education*, 57(3), pp. 245–265.

Kay, L. (2018) 'Searching for dumbledore: A reflection upon the outcomes of a tailored emotional literacy programme on three key stage 2 children'. *Support for Learning*, 33(2), pp. 122–141.

Lindenfield, G. (2000) *Managing Anger Simple Steps to Dealing With Frustration and Threat*. London: Thorsons.

Lindsay, G., Dockrell, J. E. and Strand, S. (2007) 'Longitudinal patterns of behaviour problems in children with specific speech and language difficulties: Child and Contextual factors'. *British Journal of Educational Psychology*, 77, pp. 811–828.

Nixon, M. (2016) 'Knowing me knowing you: Enhancing emotional literacy through visual arts'. *International Journal of Education Through Art*, 12(2), pp. 181–193.

Ripley, K. and Simpson, E. (2007) *First Steps to Emotional Literacy*. London: David Fulton.

Sloan, S., Gildea, A., Miller, S., Poulton, L., Egar, C. and Thurston, A. (2017) 'Evaluation of Zippy's friends for improving social-emotional and academic outcomes in six to seven year olds: Protocol for a cluster randomised trial and process evaluation'. *International Journal of Research*, 82, pp. 200–209.

Weare, K. (2004) *Developing the Emotionally Literate School*. London: SAGE.

Willis, B., Clague, L. and Coldwell, M. (2012) 'Effective PSHE education: Values, purposes and future directions'. *Pastoral Care in Education*, 31(2), pp. 99–111.

Chapter five

THINKING ABOUT THE SENSORY ENVIRONMENT

| 1) What is the approach? |
| 2) Why might it reduce exclusion? |
| 3) How does it fit within our definition of inclusive pedagogy? |
| 4) What is the practice? |
| 5) What is the background / theoretical underpinning? |
| 6) What would you need in order to use this approach? |
| 7) Further reading / resources / websites |

What is the approach?

We are receiving and processing sensory information at all times. This is an automatic process and helps us to feel safe and comfortable; the processing and organising of the sensory information enables us to make decisions about how to respond to our environment (Yack, Sutton and Aquilla, 2002). Our brains process sensory information received from different sources in the environment:

- Sight/Visual

- Hearing/Auditory

- Touch/Touch

- Taste/Gustatory

- Smell/Olfactory

- Proprioception (awareness of the position and movement of your body)

- Vestibular (sense of balance)

- Interoception (signals internal sensations in our bodies, e.g. hunger, feeling full, heart beating fast)

Some learners experience difficulties with sensory sensitivity and may be hypersensitive or hyposensitive to sensory information from the environment they are in. A person who is hypersensitive is highly sensitive to the sensory stimuli, whereas a person who is hyposensitive has a decreased sensitivity to the sensory stimuli. The examples in Table 12.1 illuminate this.

It should be noted that this reaction to sensory stimuli is automatic and not a deliberate intentional action (Miller *et al.*, 2007). The spontaneous reactions to the sensory information may trigger anxiety and we may observe changes in presenting behaviours, such as difficulties with maintaining attention and focus, visible distress or discomfort, fear or a jumpy startled reaction, not being responsive to pain (Yack, Sutton and Aquilla, 2002). This is not an exhaustive list and just provides some examples to illustrate. Some reactions may include impulsive behaviours which are considered to be disruptive or challenging, such as angry or aggressive outbursts or the child or young person may become passive (Miller *et al.*, 2007). This may also negatively influence social interaction (Miller *et al.*, 2007).

Table 12.1

Sensory stimuli	Behaviours which may be observed	
	Hypersensitivity	Hyposensitive
Sound	Distress in response to specific pitch or volume of sound	Likes to listen to particular sounds close to their ear
Touch	Experience discomfort from particular texture of fabric or even a gentle touch	High threshold for pain, e.g. not distressed when they fall over/have an injection
Taste	Preference for bland food (food which is not bland is too strong)	Preference for strong tastes, such as spicy food
Smell	Find smells overpowering, e.g. mild perfume, shampoo	Not take notice of extreme smell (may include their own body odour)
Visual	Be distracted by visual information, such as patterns, movement	Difficulties with activities like throwing and catching owing to poor depth perception
Vestibular	Dislike of lifts, escalators	Rocking or leaning against other people, furniture or wall as they are trying to seek awareness of where their body is in space
Proprioceptor	Turn whole body around to look at an object	Stand too close to others (poor awareness of personal space)

There is a need therefore for school staff to be aware of sensory differences in processing information and a willingness to consider sensory differences when analysing observed behaviours. The following sections of this chapter explore how school staff may investigate this issue and how they may address the behaviours triggered from sensitivities to sensory information.

Why might it reduce exclusion?

Awareness of sensory sensitivities by school staff may help in understanding the potential of hypersensitivity or hyposensitivity underlying the behaviours we observe. Auditing the sensory environment and identifying triggers for children and young people to inform making adjustments may help reduce behaviours which may be considered as reasons to exclude.

How does it fit within our definition of inclusive pedagogy?

Recognition that some learners experience difficulties or differences with sensory processing acknowledges learning and difference or diversity. The awareness and acceptance that the hypersensitivity or hyposensitivity in response to sensory stimuli is not within the deliberate control of the learner recognises that there are underlying causes or triggers of behaviour. Responding to this by proactively planning adaptations to the environment or strategies to help children and young people manage their difficulties, rather than merely expecting children and young people to automatically comply to expected behaviours, has alignment with inclusive practice. The exploration to identify the difficulties or differences being experienced by the learner and potential resolutions engages everyone involved in the creative approach to planning those resolutions. This work to make adaptations which will positively influence the learner's access to academic and social aspects of school life is empowering in that children and young people are able to make proactive use of strategies to help them better manage the situational stimuli and have a better understanding of themselves and their needs. This approach also aligns with social justice and human rights beliefs that everyone has a right to education.

What is the practice?

Occupational therapists have specialist expertise in sensory integration with assessment and planning appropriate interventions or strategies to support children and young people experiencing difficulties with sensory sensitivities.

Careful observation of children and young people and their behaviours and responses to their environment underpins identification of particular or potential difficulties. The resources section of this chapter contains links to downloadable sensory checklists and environmental audit to support analysis of observations and the environment.

The following vignettes provide some examples to illustrate this.

Fred (upper KS2) was sensitive to light. His teacher was very concerned about the difficulties Fred had with attention and focus and hyperactivity. These behaviours appeared to negatively impact upon his academic work and progress in class. The classroom had strip lights which were controlled by a single switch and thus it was not possible to switch off the light close to his desk. Turning off all of the lights made the classroom too dark for the rest of the class. The teacher and Fred tried out different seating positions in the classroom but unfortunately they were not able to find a place which was better for Fred. The delivery of resources in a very large cardboard box gave the idea to cut out a side of the box and hang it from the ceiling to obscure the light closest to Fred's place. The teacher was highly surprised with the immediate improvement in the length of Fred's focus and attention and reduction of the hyperactivity.

Lisa (KS3) was highly sensitive to noise and experienced anxiety in the busy school corridors and in lessons which had noisy or lively activities (e.g. music). In response to the anxiety, Lisa would scream loudly and at length – it took a long while to calm Lisa.

Strategies used to support Lisa:

- Early exit card from lessons to enable Lisa to walk through corridors when they were not busy

- Safe quiet space for times when Lisa was feeling overwhelmed

- Planning ahead for activities which may prove difficult for Lisa – involving Lisa in identifying strategies to help or provision of alternative activities if solution could not be identified

Gerald (lower KS2) was highly sensitive to smell. This sensitivity triggered hyperactivity (large movements and loud verbal outbursts which school staff described as 'bouncing off the ceiling').

One example of how this affected school activities was the daily assembly. Everyday assembly was at 11.30 a.m.

The school kitchen was attached to the hall and thus the smells from the dinner being prepared sometimes pervaded the assembly ambience. On days when there was a pungent smell, Gerald's behaviour in assembly was extremely disruptive. The school set in place an action whereby the TA went into the hall a few minutes ahead of assembly to do a 'sniff test'. If a pungent aroma was detected, an individual or small group activity was put into place for Gerald with the direct support of the teacher or TA. Over time, Gerald appeared to become less sensitive to smells and was able to manage assembly and other activities which may have a pungent aroma involved.

What is the background/theoretical underpinning?

The notion of sensory integration is attributed to Dr Ayres, an occupational therapist (Zimmer *et al.*, 2012; Yack, Sutton and Aquilla, 2002). Ayres set out (within the theory of sensory integration) typical and atypical sensory integration and this work has informed intervention programmes and strategies to support those who experience difficulties (Yack, Sutton and Aquilla, 2002). There has been further research within this field since Ayres' original work to continue to develop understanding and intervention, although some authors contend that the research has limitations.

Five interrelating factors are identified within the process of sensory integration: sensory registration, orientation, interpretation, organisation of a response and its execution (Yack, Sutton and Aquilla, 2002). These five factors encompass awareness of sensory input, inhibiting and attending to different inputs and responding to the sensory information (Yack, Sutton and Aquilla, 2002). This process of integration is essential to enable us to make sense of the stimuli we receive and then plan and act appropriately in response (Miller *et al.*, 2007; Iarocci and McDonald, 2006).

Sensory sensitivities, or differences in responses to sensory input, have been identified in children and young people with some neurodevelopmental conditions, e.g. Autism, ADHD and developmental coordination disorder.

The vestibular system is used to make sense of information related to movement and gravity and enable us to keep our balance and produce movement which is well-coordinated (Miller *et al.*, 2007). Yack, Sutton and Aquilla (2002, p. 45) contend that this system is also involved in calming and regulation of behaviour and identify close links between the vestibular and auditory systems. Example of behaviours which may be observed in children and young people who experience difficulty with vestibular input include: being fearful of changes in their centre of gravity or heights, avoidance of activities which will trigger these changes or experiences, such as PE activities or boat rides; they may also appear to be always moving and experience difficulties with maintaining stillness, such as rocking (Yack, Sutton and Aquilla, 2002).

What would you need in order to use this approach?

The Autism Education Trust has freely downloadable sensory checklists and audits (see the next section) – these documents can be helpful to support school staff in identifying potential issues within the environment and potential areas of difficulty for children and young people. This should always be discussed with the parents and carers and with children and young people. The next section has links to further information and reading.

As previously stated, occupational therapists have expertise and specialist knowledge and it may be helpful to contact your local OT service to find out about any professional development opportunities, referrals or advice.

Further reading/resources/websites

- Sensory Integration Therapy (Ulster University): www.sensoryintegration.org.uk/
- Sensory Integration Therapy (Royal Free London NHS Foundation Trust: www.royalfree.nhs.uk/services/services-a-z/occupational-therapy-services-for-children-and-young-people/specialist-services/sensory-integration-therapy/
- Yack, E., Sutton, S. and Aquilla, P. (2002) *Building Bridges Through Sensory Integration*. Arlington: Future Horizons.
- Do You Know me poster: http://s3-eu-west-1.amazonaws.com/files.royalfree.nhs.uk/Service/Occ_therapy_-_paeds/Do_you_know_me_poster.pdf
- Sensory processing Disorder Foundation: www.spdstar.org/
- Autism Education Trust Sensory Audit for Schools and Classrooms: www.aettraininghubs.org.uk/wp-content/uploads/2012/05/37.1-Sensory-audit-tool-for-environments.pdf
- Autism Education Trust Sensory Checklist: www.aettraininghubs.org.uk/wp-content/uploads/2012/05/37.2-Sensory-assessment-checklist.pdf
- Autism Toolbox: sensory issues: www.autismtoolbox.co.uk/resources/Topic-resources/Sensory-issues/

References

Iarocci, G. and McDonald, J. (2006) 'Sensory integration and the perceptual experience of persons with Autism'. *Journal of Autism and Developmental Disorders*, 36(1), pp. 77–90. https://doi.org/10.1007/s10803-005-0044-3.

Miller, L.J., Anzalone, M.E., Lane, S.J., Cermak, S.A. and Osten, E.T. (2007) 'Concept evolution in sensory integration: A proposed nosology for diagnosis'. *The American Journal of Occupational Therapy*, 61(2), pp. 135–140. Available at: https://pdfs.semanticscholar.org/7ed5/d3e7abf8f78b5d26feaba5b1925511c9eb14.pdf (accessed 2 January 2019).

Yack, E., Sutton, S. and Aquilla, P. (2002) *Building Bridges Through Sensory Integration*. Arlington: Future Horizons.

Zimmer, M., Desch, L., Rosen, L.D., Bailey, M.L., Becker, D., Culbert, T.P., McClafferty, H., Sahler, O.J.Z., Vohra, S., Liptak, G.S. and Adams, R.C. (2012) 'Sensory integration therapies for children with developmental and behavioral disorders'. *Pediatrics*, 129(6), pp. 1186–1189. Available at: http://pediatrics.aappublications.org/content/129/6/1186.full (accessed 2 January 2019).

Chapter Six
TRANSITION

1) What is the approach?
2) Why might it reduce exclusion?
3) How does it fit within our definition of inclusive pedagogy?
4) What is the practice?
5) What is the background / theoretical underpinning?
6) What would you need in order to use this approach?
7) Further reading / resources / websites

What is the approach?

Many children respond to inner emotional conflicts by behaving in ways that may be inappropriate or destructive.

(Long, 2007, p. 54)

Transitions permeate the whole of school life, from small transitions between activities throughout the day to more major transitions, which include moving schools. Transitions elicit anxiety for some learners, which may range from a mild or moderate level to what may be framed colloquially as 'flooding them'. This anxiety is often communicated through behaviours rather than verbal means, especially with younger children or those with speech, language and communication needs. It should also be acknowledged that some children and young people mask their anxiety and the resultant manifestation of the anxiety they have been holding onto emerges at a later time, perhaps when they go home from school or when they can no longer internalise their anxiety. The underlying cause of the anxiety in relation to transition may arise from a variety of reasons such as:

- A neurodevelopmental condition, such as autism

- Social emotional mental health needs

- Language and communication needs – if the learner experiences difficulties understanding language they may find change difficult to manage owing to the change in the routine or activity they understand to something they are not sure of

The manifestations of anxiety may present as:

- Verbal or physical angry outbursts.

- Refusal to follow instructions.

- Withdrawal, which may appear as quiet acceptance.

- Visible distress.

- Withdrawal from the environment, e.g. leaving the learning space or curling up under the table

- Internalised anxiety may be difficult to identify – there may be some nuanced signals observed by those who know the learner well and who have become attuned to indicators of mood and emotional responses; however, in our professional experience children and young people may appear calm on the surface and display no visible signs.

- Learners may use coping strategies such as copying other pupils, this may only become apparent if they choose to emulate the wrong role model and the resultant response from others may trigger other behaviours in this list.

Why might it reduce exclusions?

The behaviours which may manifest in response to the anxiety elicited by the transition may be challenging for adults to manage and be considered disruptive to the learning environment (see list in previous section). Sometimes behaviours are not recognised as a form of communication and the strategies used to manage the behaviour lead to an escalation of the behaviours. The child or young person may thus be excluded from the classroom to another space within the school, not to provide an opportunity for calming (and then return to class) but as a punishment for the behaviours perceived to be disruptive. This exclusion may also extend to an exclusion from the school.

How does it fit within our definition of inclusion?

Imagine being in a place where you do not speak the language, there are no visual signs or prompts to aid you in understanding and someone is trying to direct you away from where you are (a space or activity you have become comfortable with) to somewhere else – you do not understand what is being communicated or why. In this situation, it is understandable that the individual concerned may feel anxious or fearful. This may trigger some of the survival responses of fight, flight and fright.

Now imagine, that same situation but there are actions which support you to prepare for the change in place or activity. These might encompass visual aids, including gestures, signing and picture prompts and some preparation ahead of when you will actually be required to move.

Consider the difference between those two scenarios and how this may influence your understanding, emotional and physical responses.

In the second scenario, consideration has been given to the individual's needs and how they may best be supported to manage the transition that is going to be asked of them. The planning of strategies and approaches for transitions fits within our theoretical framework for inclusion in that:

- It acknowledges learning differences and how these might best be supported to facilitate success.

- It acknowledges the rights of the individual to be respected and access to education.

- Learners are given agency to succeed in their environment and thus empowered to achieve (including them in planning strategies which work well for them will further support this).

- Providing flexible approaches to support learning forms part of responding creatively to learners' differing needs and valuing the diversity within our learning community.

- It responds to a humanistic approach of acting ethically and with concern for others.

- Planning for transitions using evidence-based approaches to improve learning for all embodies developing practice (Praxis).

What are the principles and approaches in planning for transition?

At the heart of supporting transition is the recognition of need for clear communication which supports understanding of what the individual is required to do and reassures them, thus reducing anxiety. This means that practitioners need to consider these factors within their planning:

- The learner's language and communication competences.

- Key information about the learner's needs (e.g. any diagnosis such as autism); this supports understanding of why the learner experiences difficulties with managing change.

- Does the learner display any non-verbal or verbal cues which indicate signs of anxiety?

- Are there any sensory sensitivities which may underlie any difficulties with transitions?

- Does the learner respond best to warning a longer or shorter period ahead of a change or transition?

- Communication between key adults: identify who needs to be involved and how communication will be managed.

The knowledge held by the adults involved with the child or young person (e.g. parents and carers, school staff) needs to be shared to construct a shared understanding of the factors in the list and the child's responses to change and transitions.

Supporting frequent/small transitions

This section is focused upon the many changes which occur throughout the school day. Examples of this include a visitor to class or school, changes to the usual routine such as change in time of assembly or specific lessons, school trips, supply teacher covering the class, special activity days or weeks and fire drills. In addition, the school day comprises many transitions, such as moving between the classroom and another area (e.g. to the hall for assembly or PE or to the playground for play) or from one activity to another (e.g. carpet to table, finishing one activity to move to the next, tidy up time).

What is the practice?

Key to planning for transitions is using the knowledge of the child, analysis of behaviours and reflecting upon what changes and transitions are happening which are likely to trigger anxiety and confusion for the child. In our professional experience, this is unique to each child. We have worked with children and young people who cope well with changes such as having supply teachers teach their class or school trips, but if their favourite blue pencil is not in the pencil pot then they experience great difficulties in coping with using a different pencil. Other children and young people have needed to be given warnings ahead of every small transition throughout their day.

It is important that the strategies employed are used consistently by all adults as varying how transitions are managed will add to the learner's confusion.

At times of anxiety, processing of verbal language may be difficult, thus use of visual approaches is extremely helpful, even when visuals may have been reduced for other situations owing to the learner's increased competence with speech, language and communication.

Communication between home and school is also vital to enable parents and carers to support their child with being prepared for some changes to the usual routine, such as a supply teacher or school trip.

What is the background/theoretical underpinning?

Planning to support transitions seeks to use strategies which provide clarity, and aid understanding, to the learner about the change in activity, the actions they are expected to engage in and how they may access support (Morling and O'Connell, 2015). In this way, as explained in the previous sections, the work is aimed at reducing anxiety and facilitating their ability to manage the change or move from one activity to another.

What would you need in order to use this approach?

It may be helpful to note that some of these strategies will be supportive to learners who do not experience difficulties with managing change, such as those learners who experience difficulties with organisation, planning and memory.

Pre-warning – warnings ahead of transitions and changes may be provided in verbal, verbal and visual form or visual format. This may be as simple as ' in 5 minutes we are all going to stop writing and', 'the bell for the end of the lesson will ring in two minutes'. This will be managed in a mode which is individualised to the learner.

Visual timetables, whether in text or pictorial format, offer preparation for what will be happening next. A symbol (e.g. star/question mark) can be used to indicate when a change to the routine will happen.

Visual schedule sets out in text or text and picture symbols the activities the learner is expected to complete within a specific activity/lesson/time period.

Visual prompts can be helpful as reminders of specific behaviours or actions the learner is required to do, e.g. lining up, moving to the carpet to sit, listening or specific tasks during a tidy up. These can be presented as text and symbol/picture or a 'job list' type format as appropriate to the learner's developmental stage.

Timers may be helpful to provide a visual prompt for the child or young person. An example of this is a sand-timer being used to show how long until an activity must finish and when the next activity must start.

Social stories (Gray, 1998) may be helpful to help the child or young person understand the expected social behaviours for particular situations. Social stories set out a clear description of a social situation, the behaviours expected in that situation and offer affirmation for the learner for following those behaviours. This approach offers a visual technique which can be tailored to the learner's strengths and difficulties – this may be text only or pictures and text. The text is helpful as it keeps everyone consistent with the description and explanations being given to the learner. Social stories may also offer reassurance to the learner in regard to the particular situation. A social story may thus be used to support a new activity such as a school trip by providing details of what will happen throughout the trip and how the learners will be expected to act. This strategy may also be used to support changing problematic behaviours which occur at times of transition, such as tidy time, lining up, end of playtime, etc.

Supporting sensory sensitivities: Pupils may present with behaviours which may be problematic to the context at transition times owing to sensitivities or differences with sensory processing. An example of this is a learner who experiences sensitivity to loud noises or noises or particular pitches or to busy situations. Such sensitivities may underlie behaviours such as angry physical or verbal outbursts, extreme distress or withdrawal from the situation. Thus a busy secondary school corridor, primary school cloakroom in the pre- or post-playtime period or tidy up time in an Early Years classroom may trigger behaviours described here. The following examples from practices (names changed to maintain anonymity and confidentiality) have been used to illustrate how planning strategies may help everyone to manage these circumstances.

Harry

Harry (aged 3) became very lively during tidy up times in his pre-school class. He would run between the doors at each end of the classroom, at high speed and shouting. This resulted in anyone or anything in his way being bulldozed out of the way, which was a health and safety concern for both Harry and the other children. This was managed through a staged approach.

Stage 1

Harry loved stories, so was taken to a quiet corner just ahead of the start of tidy time. He and one of the practitioners sat with their back to everyone (to reduce visual distraction for Harry) and while everyone else tidied up, Harry enjoyed stories and joined the class just as they sat down together for the next activity.

Stage 2

Harry was pre-warned of tidy time (visual timetable and prompts supported this) and then supported by the practitioner to put away a small number of items before going to have a story quietly together as in Stage 1.

Stage 2

Harry had a slightly delayed start to tidy time and then tidied up his activity supported by an adult (when it was less busy as some children had already moved to the carpet) but always joined the other children in time to start the next activity. Alternatively, Harry tidied up first and then had a story book to look at on the carpet until everyone in class was on the carpet. The choice was dependent upon the contextual factors such as Harry's interest in the activity or his mood.

Stage 3

Over time, Harry became able to cope with tidy time and was able to join in with this activity, provided he was pre-warned and reminded of what to do. These prompts were provided through pictorial prompt cards and some signing.

Isobel

Isobel (aged 12) was observed by staff in her secondary school to walk through the corridors with her back dragging along the wall and appeared to be almost clinging to the walls. Sometimes, Isobel became very distressed sobbing very loudly.

Isobel was provided with an early exit card from lessons which she could show to the class teacher to remind them that Isobel needed to leave the class 5 minutes early to walk to her next lesson, while the corridors were quiet. Teachers were also reminded by the SENCO and Head of Year to ensure that homework had been set and explained before this time so that Isobel did not miss out on vital information.

Peter

Peter (age 7) experienced great difficulties with managing changes to the usual routine which triggered some challenging aggressive and non-compliant behaviours. His TA designed postcards which had the star symbol used on the class timetable to indicate change on one side – on the other was written a note to Peter and his Mum to alert or remind them of a change (e.g. Miss Brown has to go to a meeting on Friday so Mr Timms is coming to teach the class). Alongside this a series of social stories had been written for particular situations, such as a supply teacher teaching the class and for trips which could be adapted as needed and reprinted. Photos of the supply teacher or trip destination would be sent home if possible to support the preparation for the change.

For times when changes were last minute, such as teacher illness or fire drills, if possible a text was sent to the parents, but always a familiar adult met Peter on arrival to discuss what was happening and provide reassurance.

Calm or happy book – It may be helpful for some children and young people if the adults take photographs of them at a time they have coped well with a different activity. These photos can be stored in a book with annotations and brought out to share with the child or young person to discuss and offer affirmation that they can and do manage situations they think will be difficult. This can build confidence and resilience.

Calming activity – It may be helpful for the learner to have something which supports them with managing stress and calming themselves, such as stress balls to squeeze. This will need to be identified with the learner as what works will be individual to them.

Communication between home and school – This may be managed in a variety of ways which should best fit the school, parent or carer and child. Some ideas for this:

- Emails/texts to remind of changes such as school trips or alert to fact that a supply teacher or different member of staff will be teaching the class (e.g. at times when usual teacher is ill)
- Postcards with the symbol used to indicate change on one side and a brief explanation to the parent or carer on the other (for changes known ahead such as trips, visitors)
- Conversations or notes in the home-school diary

Supporting major transitions

This section is focused on transition from one school to another. Examples of this are an Early Years child starting primary school or Year 6 learner moving to Secondary School. The learner may be moving to another school owing to a family or managed move or to a specialist setting from mainstream. The strategies identified within this section may also be helpful to support the learner with moving to their new class at the end of each academic year.

What is the approach for planning for transition?

The planning for supporting a learner with SEN with moving from one setting to another needs to start early. It is important that this planning is collaborative work between the schools, parents and carers and the child or young person. There may be other professionals involved with the learner who can contribute to the planning and preparation too.

The planning will include sharing information about the child or young person:

- Strengths, interests and needs
- Social interaction/friendships
- Strategies and approaches which work positively to support the learner (or do not which can be helpful to know too)

The support for transition may also include planning of visits to, or outreach activities from, the new setting. Key staff from the new setting should also be invited to meetings such as ECH Plan review meetings. This planning should include thinking about academic, organisational and social aspects of school life and needs two-way communication between both schools and highlights strengths in addition to thinking about planning to meet needs (Roffey, 2011).

Once the learner has transferred to the new school it is important that transition remains a focus; thus, staff need to check at regular intervals to ensure that the learner is settling well.

What is the background/theoretical underpinning?

Many learners may worry about transition, particularly about big transitions such as moving to secondary school from primary(Rae, 2014); whilst many learners may settle well into their new school, children and young people with SEN may be at greater risk of experiencing difficulties with transitions (Bunn, Davis and Speed, 2017; Hughes, Banks and Terras, 2013). There is an interplay of factors which influence this, including emotional, biological, cognitive, cultural and practical issues (Doyle, McGuckin and Shevlin, 2017). Transition brings positive and negative aspects of change for the child or young person to manage (Rae, 2014; Coffey, 2013). Rae (2014) identifies that part of this is loss, which the child or young person needs to be reconciled to. The experiences of the change impact upon 'the balance between risk and resilience factors' which is part of a range of influencing factors upon mental health (Rae, 2014, p. 3). This highlights the importance of sharing information from the school or setting the learner is moving from to the new school, so that staff at the new school can reflect upon the elements which negatively influence risk and positively influence resilience in their planning for the learner (Rae, 2014).

It is important to acknowledge that there are children and young people with SEN who do settle and cope with the adjustment (Rae, 2014).

The strategies used to support children and young people with managing transitions work to support building understanding of what is happening, why it is happening and what is expected of everyone in that situation (Morling and O'Connell, 2015). This is because transition engages the child or young person in change, which elicits anxiety and may trigger challenging behaviours (Briggs, 2016). The anxiety may be related to worries about building new relationships and making friends, the potential for negative social experiences (such as bullying), the amount and level of work and factors related to new routines such as change in the length of the school day (Hughes, Banks and Terras, 2013). This is supported by Evangelou et al. (2008, p. 4) who analysed transitions from primary to secondary school and identified factors which are involved within transition and against which judgements can be made about whether the transition experience has been effective: 'social adjustment, institutional adjustment and curriculum interest'. These factors relate to activities which support the learner with:

• Building relationships and friendships

• Learning and understanding the new routine

• Understanding the expectations of the work and curriculum from the new school
(Coffey, 2013; Evangelou et al., 2008)

It is always important to remember the voice of the child or young person within planning for transition (Bunn, Davis and Speed, 2017). Briggs (2016, p. 153) argues that the child or young person's level of confidence will be higher 'when working through the transition *with* others rather than *by* others being propelled into a new situation'. Parents and carers also need to be involved within this work (Doyle, McGuckin and Shevlin, 2017). Every child and young person is unique and while there will be some similar characteristics, their profile of concerns, difficulties, strengths and the strategies which work positively for them will differ (Hughes, Banks and Terras, 2013). This adds support to the need to include children and young people and their parents and carers in the discussions, to support identification of important information and in planning strategies to support the transition. It also highlights that planning for transition should aim to address the key factors of relationships, routines and organisation, and curriculum ensuring that strategies employed work to align with the learner's profile of language, academic, emotional and social skills (Doyle, McGuckin and Shevlin, 2017; Hughes, Banks and Terras, 2013).

What would you need in order to use this approach?

Planning of meetings – this should start as early as possible, for example inviting Secondary School staff to attend Year 5 review meetings. Sharing copies of the child's profile documentation with the new school staff will help them to start thinking and planning ahead for when the learner joins the role. Schools need to work closely together in order to support learners with moving to their new school (Tutt, 2011).

Orientation – visits to the new setting will be helpful with familiarising the child or young people with the building and site, people and with key routines. This may be considered in phases which could be selected as appropriate for the individual:

Table 13.1 Orientation activities to support transition to new school/setting or class

Phase 1	Visits to the new class or setting when it is a quieter time, e.g. after the end of the school day or during assembly with a familiar adult (you could consider including a friend too).
Phase 2	Visit with an adult to take photographs for a social story or information book/ poster – it may be helpful for the learner to be involved in selecting areas to photograph which they feel will help them feel secure about their new school/ class.
Phase 3	Make a social story or information book/poster about the new setting or class. The mode of this will be dependent upon the developmental level of the learner and they may be involved in the making of this. This should be shared with the child or young person to support discussions to prepare them for their new setting/class. It may be helpful to focus on what will be the same or similar in addition to what will be different, as this will provide some reassurance.
Phase 4	Visits to talk to key adults and/or join in or observe some activities. These can be chosen and planned, tailored to meet the needs of the learner.
Phase 5	Joining in with the usual schedule of visits – the previous phases aim to prepare the learner to manage these visits.

Key information book/Poster or social story – see phases 2 and 3 in Table 13.1.

Further reading/resources/websites

NASEN Transition Booklet, *A Quick Guide to Supporting the Needs of Pupils and Their Families When Moving Between Educational Settings*: www.google.co.uk/url?sa=t&rct=j&q=&esrc=s&source=web&cd=3&cad=rja&uact=8&ved=2ahUKEwiBy62Rn_feAhVljqQKHUjZC3QQFjACegQIBxAC&url=http%3A%2F%2Fwww.nasen.org.uk%2Futilities%2Fdownload.E57C5F2E-CFE0-4B75-BA50C7BF00085DBE.html&usg=AOvVaw3Rq1oCJ9qnFVGYMEPR52jg

Rae, T. (2014) *Supporting Successful Transition From Primary to Secondary School: A Programme for Teachers*. Abingdon, Oxon: Routledge.

Moving on: a guide for pupils with special educational needs moving on to secondary school a booklet from the Foundation for People with Learning Difficulties (Part of Mental Health Foundation) free to download from: www.mentalhealth.org.uk/learning-disabilities/publications/moving-on-tips-for-pupils-with-special-educational-needs

Early Years transition – SEN and disability in the early years: A toolkit from Council for Disabled Children: www.google.co.uk/url?sa=t&rct=j&q=&esrc=s&source=web&cd=7&cad=rja&uact=8&ved=2ahUKEwj9uJOroffeAhUxsaQKHTlxCp8QFjAGegQIBBAC&url=https%3A%2F%2Fwww.foundationyears.org.uk%2Ffiles%2F2015%2F06%2FSection-10-Transitions.pdf&usg=AOvVaw34OqLq_v3gi8LrFJPb8Spk

Social stories

Information from the National Autistic Society: www.autism.org.uk/about/strategies/social-stories-comic-strips.aspx

Carol Gray website: https://carolgraysocialstories.com/social-stories/what-is-it/

References

Briggs, S. (2016) *Meeting Special Educational Needs in Secondary: Inclusion and How to Do It*. Second Edition. Abingdon: Routledge.

Bunn, H., Davis, D. and Speed, E. (2017) 'High school transition – An intervention that empowers children with special educational needs and improves school practice'. *Support for Learning*, 32(3), pp. 231–244. Available at: https://doi-org.glos.idm.oclc.org/10.1111/1467-9604.12167.

Coffey, A. (2013) 'Relationships: The key to successful transition from primary to secondary school?'. *Improving Schools*, 16, pp. 261–271. https://doi.org/10.1177/1365480213505181. Available at: https://s3.amazonaws.com/academia.edu.documents/34301640/Improving_Schools.pdf?AWSAccessKeyId=AKIAIWOWYYGZ2Y53UL3A&Expires=1552510970&Signature=NMPVlAMGpxeXphjv0Y6FakAy13g%3D&response-content-disposition=inline%3B%20filename%3DRelationships_The_key_to_successful_tran.pdf (accessed 10 March 2019).

Doyle, A., McGuckin, C. and Shevlin, M. (2017) '"Close the door on your way out": Parent perspectives on supported transition planning for young people with special educational needs and disabilities in Ireland'. *Journal of Research in Special Educational Needs*, 17(4), pp. 274–281. https://doi.org/10.1111/1471-3802.12385.

Evangelou, M., Taggart, B., Sylva, K., Melhuish, E., Sammons, P. and Siraj-Blatchford, I. (2018) *What Makes a Successful Transition From Primary to Secondary School*? Findings from the Effective Pre-school, Primary and Secondary Education 3–14 (EPPSE) project. DCSF-RB019. ISBN 978 1 84775 085 3. Available at: www.dcsf.gov.uk/research/ (accessed 12 December 2018).

Gray, C.A. (1998) 'Social stories and comic strip conversations with students with asperger syndrome and high-functioning autism'. In E. Schopler, G.B. Mesibov and L.J. Kunce (eds.), *Asperger Syndrome or High-Functioning Autism?. Current Issues in Autism.* Boston: Springer, pp. 167–198. Available at: https://link.springer.com/chapter/10.1007/978-1-4615-5369-4_9.

Hughes, L.A., Banks, P. and Terras, M.M. (2013) 'Secondary school transition for children with special educational needs: A literature review'. *Support for Learning*, 28(1), pp. 24–34. https://doi-org.glos.idm.oclc.org/10.1111/1467-9604.12012.

Long, R. (2007) *The Rob Long Omnibus Edition of Better Behaviour*. Abingdon: Routledge.

Morling, E. and O'Connell, C. (2015) *Supporting Children With Autistic Spectrum Disorders*. Second Edition. Abingdon: Routledge and Nasen.

Rae, T. (2014) *Supporting Successful Transition From Primary to Secondary School: A Programme for Teachers*. Abingdon, Oxon: Routledge.

Roffey, S. (2011) *Changing Behaviour in Schools: Promoting Positive Relationships and Wellbeing*. London: SAGE.

Tutt, R. (2011) *Partnership Working to Support Special Educational Needs and Disabilities*. London: SAGE.

Chapter Seven
NURTURE GROUPS

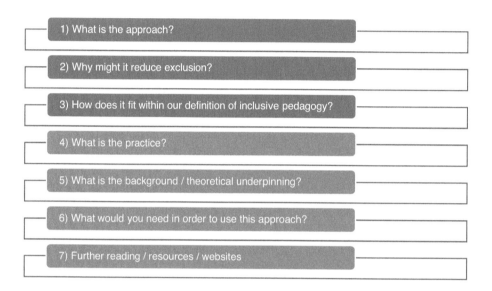

1) What is the approach?

2) Why might it reduce exclusion?

3) How does it fit within our definition of inclusive pedagogy?

4) What is the practice?

5) What is the background / theoretical underpinning?

6) What would you need in order to use this approach?

7) Further reading / resources / websites

What is the approach?

A nurture group is an intervention which aims to develop the social, emotional and mental health competencies of learners.

A nurture group aims to model and encourage secure relationships for learners by creating structures and positive attachments through routines, structure and staff responsiveness to the learners' emotions, needs and developmental stages (Birch, 2016, p. 40).

A traditional nurture group provides a small group of learners, usually six–eight (Bishop, 2008), with a dedicated learning space staffed by two adults and attended daily. The curriculum is focused on psycho-social development (Hughes and Schlösser, 2014) alongside more formal or academic activities.

Why might it reduce exclusion?

Nurture groups provide the opportunity for learners who struggle to participate in mainstream classes to experience relationships and learning activities which are developmentally more appropriate to their needs. Through providing positive, trusting relationships and opportunities to explore boundaries, challenges and their own potential, learners learn the skills and attitudes needed to become ready to re-join mainstream learning situations.

This provision removes or mediates some of the potential stressors and triggers for learners with social, emotional and mental health challenges which may exist in mainstream classes. As a result, the behaviours they present can be managed and worked with and routes towards exclusion can be avoided.

A recent article identified nurture groups in Glasgow as a provision with a substantial role in successfully reducing exclusions and maintaining vulnerable young people in education (March and Kearney, 2017).

How does it fit within our definition of inclusive pedagogy?

Nurture groups recognise that there are different needs for learners and provide adapted learning spaces and curricula. This approach is grounded within an understanding of difference and seeks to recognise and work with the different needs of learners by adapting provision and expected outcomes. This practice is heavily influenced by a humanist approach, which has at its core the notion of the value and empowering nature of empathy in the nurture group practitioner's practice.

> Empathy, that ability to begin to see the world through the eyes of the child's experience is an important component in any approach's success. Empathy provides the adult with the question that needs to be asked continuously . . . 'Why do I think this child behaved in this way and what does it mean for the approach I use?' It provides the basis upon which the pupil can begin to feel valued and understood.
>
> (Visser, 2002)

What is the practice?

There is a clear model for nurture group practice, however there is evidence of a range of variations to this practice (Cooper and Whitebread, 2007). The seminal authors on nurture groups describe them as a class in a school where two adults work with 8–12 children or young people to provide a carefully structured curriculum experience (Bennathan and Boxall, 1996) to develop their emotional preparedness for learning and their social skills (Davies *et al.*, 2019). The original model of nurture groups was conceived as a group or class which children attended on a full-time basis for a full academic year, whilst still maintaining registration and links with their mainstream class. This model was also conceived for the primary school age range. Many variants of this model work on a more part-time basis over differing periods. In the last fifteen years the development of nurture groups in secondary school settings has also developed. What is maintained across the majority of models is the focus on an emotional curriculum, based on attachment theory, where the classroom is set up to resemble aspects of a family home, with opportunities for developmental play and times set aside for less common classroom activities, such as sharing food. Development is assessed using the Boxall Profile (Bennathan and Boxall, 1984), now available as an online tool from NurtureUK. The Boxall Profile is a diagnostic tool which provides a framework through which practitioners can profile a learner's social and emotional development and identify areas for focus.

What is the background/theoretical underpinning?

'The underlying assumption of the Nurture Group . . . is that children who have faired badly through the learning processes of early childhood need extra support and appropriate experiences' (Wearmouth, 2019, p. 172). This approach is based on attachment theory (Bowlby, 1982; Ainsworth *et al.*, 2015), which links future relationships and interactions to early relationships between child and caregiver. The nurture group approach was first developed in the 1970s as a specific approach to support children in mainstream schools who were at risk of exclusion (Bennathan and Boxall, 1996). A recent survey indicated that there are 2114 schools in the UK with nurture groups (Nurture Group Network, 2015).

The nurture group approach is underpinned by the six principles of nurture:

- Learning is understood developmentally

- The classroom offers a safe base

- The importance of nurture for the development of wellbeing

- Language is a vital means of communication

- All behaviour is communication

- The importance of transition in the lives of children and young people

(Lucas, Insley and Buckland, 2006)

What would you need in order to use this approach?

The guidance from Nurture Group Network (2017) suggests that in order to set up a nurture group you need 'a budget, a suitable room and two permanent staff to act as NG practitioners'. Most nurture groups cost less than £10,000 to establish. There are ongoing staffing implications for settings which have a nurture group provision and research evidence points to the need for a whole school understanding of the nurturing approach in order for the provision to be successful (NurtureUK, 2018).

Recommended resources

There is a wealth of information available about nurture groups from NurtureUK (formerly the Nurture Group Network) at www.nurtureuk.org

Bennathan, M., & Boxall, M. (2000) *Effective Intervention in Primary Schools: Nurture Groups*. London: David Fulton Publishers Ltd.

Bishop, S. (2008) *Running a Nurture Group*. London: Sage Publications Ltd.

Bowlby, J. (1982) 'Attachment and loss: Retrospect and prospect'. *American Journal of Orthopsychiatry*, 52(4), pp. 664–678.

Rose, J. (2010) *How Nurture Protects*. London: Responsive Studios.

Sloan, S., Winter, K., Lynn, F., Gildea, A. and Connolly, P. (2016) *The Impact and Cost Effectiveness of Nurture Groups in Primary Schools in Northern Ireland*. Belfast: Centre for Evidence and Social Innovation, Queen's University Belfast.

References

Ainsworth, M.D., Blehar, M.C., Waters, E. and Walls, S.N. (2015) *Patterns of Attachment: A Psychological Study of the Strange Situation*. New York: Psychology Press.

Bennathan, M. and Boxall, M. (1984) *The Boxall Profile: A Guide to Effective Intervention in the Education of Pupils With Emotional and Behavioural Difficulties*. London: Nurture Group Network.

Bennathan, M., & Boxall, M. (1996) *Effective Intervention in Primary Schools: Nurture Groups*. London: David Fulton Publishers Ltd.

Birch, E. (2016) '"You do what you need for your children, don't you?": An exploration of the current range of practice and priorities of nurture group staff in a local authority'. *Educational and Child Psychology*, 33(4), pp. 40–49.

Bishop, S. (2008) *Running a Nurture Group*. London: Sage Publications.

Cooper, P. and Whitebread, D. (2007) 'The effectiveness of nurture groups on student progress: Evidence from a national research study'. *Emotional & Behavioural Difficulties*, 12(3), pp. 171–190.

Davies, O., Billington, K., Middleton, T., Green, H. and Madden, E. (2019) *Executive Summary: A Survey of Nurture Groups and Nurturing Practice: A Snapshot Study Within the County of Gloucestershire*. Gloucester: Gloucestershire Educational Psychology Service.

Hughes, K.H. and Schlösser, A. (2014) 'The effectiveness of nurture groups: A systematic review'. *Emotional and Behavioural Difficulties*, 19(4), pp. 386–409.

Lucas, S., Insley, K. and Buckland, G. (2006) *Nurture Group Principles and Curriculum Guidelines: Helping Children to Achieve*. London: The Nurture Group Network.

March, S. and Kearney, M. (2017) 'A psychological service contribution to nurture: Glasgow's nurturing city'. *Emotional and Behavioural Difficulties*, 22(3), pp. 237–247.

Nurture Group Network. (2015). *Nurture Group Census*. Available at: www.nurtureuk.org/research-evidence/ngn-commissioned-research/nurture-group-census (accessed 14 June 2019).

Nurture Group Network. (2017) *Nurture Groups*. Available at: www.nurtureuk.org/sites/default/files/ngn_-_nurture_groups-2017-05web.pdf (accessed 14 October 2018).

NurtureUK. (2018) *Inclusion Support Solutions: A Child Centred Approach to School Improvement*. London: Nurture Group Network.

Visser, J. (2002) 'The David Wills lecture 2001: Eternal verities: The strongest links'. *Emotional and Behavioural Difficulties*, 7(2), pp. 68–84.

Wearmouth, J. (2019) *Special Educational Needs and Disability: The Basics*. Third Edition. Abingdon, Oxon: Routledge.

Chapter eight
THRIVE

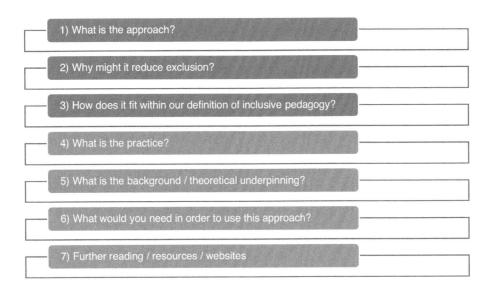

1) What is the approach?

2) Why might it reduce exclusion?

3) How does it fit within our definition of inclusive pedagogy?

4) What is the practice?

5) What is the background / theoretical underpinning?

6) What would you need in order to use this approach?

7) Further reading / resources / websites

What is the approach?

Thrive is an approach to supporting children which is promoted and held by a private company. As such information about this approach is not available in published books or journal articles.

The Thrive website (www.thriveapproach.com) states that the approach uses a combination of neuroscience, attachment theory and theories of child development to support the social and emotional development of children and young people. The Thrive approach places a heavy emphasis on play and creative learning opportunities and appears to be focused more generally towards the primary age range. The Thrive approach demands that the whole school adopts the practice. There are therefore, significant implications for training of staff across the school. The training has a key focus on developing practitioners' understanding of children and young people communicating through their behaviour. When a school buys in to the Thrive approach, in addition to training, the school will adopt an approach to using a specific online assessment tool, Thrive Online, to assess or screen all children and young people in each class. The Thrive Online tool will then support the school practitioners to plan a social and emotional curriculum for individual class members and will also suggest specific strategies and activities.

Why might it reduce exclusion?

The Thrive approach of understanding the behaviour of children and young people as a way of communicating can offer a key starting point in reducing exclusions, as this understanding may act as a buffer for practitioners. Their understanding may support them to mediate their reactions to extreme behaviours and question the view that young people may be simply choosing bad behaviour. The focus on social and emotional development, with specific strategies and activities planned for children and young people, which are successful, is also likely to minimise behaviours that may have led to exclusion. In a testimony on the Thrive approach website, the head teacher of a primary school states that use of the Thrive approach has led to a reduction in exclusions to zero over two years (www.thriveapproach. com/exclusions-thrive-approach/).

How does this fit with our definition of inclusive pedagogy?

The Thrive approach, with its use of attachment theory and focus on understanding that creative and play approaches can support the developmental needs of some children, links to inclusive approaches of understanding difference, adapting provision and being open to different outcomes for learners. The Thrive approach conceptualises creativity in a different way to that in the authors' conceptualisation of inclusion. The authors' view of creativity is not linked to the arts-based curriculum content, but the nature of learning outcomes being open. The Thrive approach's focus on play and arts-based activities does, however, link to open outcomes for learning and conceptualises these activities as learning events. This links to the conceptualisation of inclusive learning being concerned with difference, moving away from norm-referenced activities and outcomes.

What is the practice?

The Thrive approach provides support for school settings to put provision in place through a process of group profiling using the Thrive Online tool, leading to some individual pupil profiling. It then offers practitioners proformas and practical plans and ideas, which they can use to create class and group action plans. The online tools allow the setting to monitor progress of learners and to map this progress to other school data, such as attendance and achievement data.

What is the background/theoretical underpinning?

The Thrive approach uses evidence from neuroscience, theories of child development and principles of attachment theory to underpin the approaches taken. It uses arts-based approaches to support the development of learners' social and emotional competencies.

The Thrive website (www.thriveapproach.com/impact-of-the-thrive-approach/) cites an evaluation of the Thrive approach by McGuire Snieckus in 2018 which identifies the outcomes of Thrive as improving social symptoms, behaviour and attainment, however this evidence was not publicly available at the time of writing.

What would you need in order to use this approach?

The Thrive approach is only available to school settings which sign-up with the Devon-based company, which administers this approach. The Thrive approach also offers training for parent groups and foster carers. There is a financial cost to using the Thrive approach and when a setting subscribes to this approach, there is an understanding that the majority of school practitioners will be trained in this approach. As such, this implies a significant financial investment. The assessment approach as part of the Thrive approach is undertaken online and settings need to also subscribe to this.

Further reading/resources/websites

There is limited information about the Thrive approach available on their website, however the organisation offers a number of 'awareness raising' events, which are free to attend, so that practitioners can find out more about the approach.

The Thrive website – www.thriveapproach.com/the-thrive-approach/

Chapter nine
RESTORATIVE JUSTICE

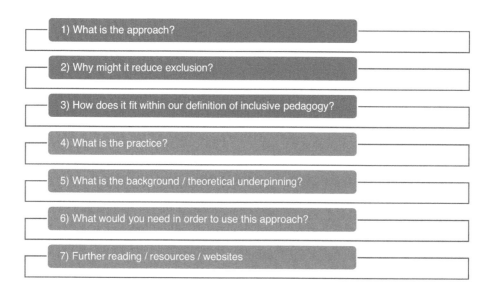

1) What is the approach?

2) Why might it reduce exclusion?

3) How does it fit within our definition of inclusive pedagogy?

4) What is the practice?

5) What is the background / theoretical underpinning?

6) What would you need in order to use this approach?

7) Further reading / resources / websites

What is the approach?

Restorative justice is a practice which originated in criminology as a new way of thinking in response to the outcomes of wrongdoing. This approach has recognised that a focus on harsh punishment or retribution does not view the event and those involved in a holistic way and therefore restricts the opportunities for healing (Zehr, 1990). The concept of restorative justice has been adapted for use in schools and renamed as Restorative Practice. The use of restorative justice approaches in schools has developed as a way of managing and developing learner behaviour.

Why might it reduce exclusion?

The restorative justice approach aims to resolve the conflict situation that often remains when the actions of one party have contravened rules and caused harm to another party. This approach builds on the view that punitive reactions to the wrongdoing of one party, in the form of punishment, can sometimes act as a dis-incentive to repeat wrongdoing, but that it does not create a solution to the harm that has been done by the wrongdoer. Furthermore, the wrongdoer, having breached rules and caused harm, will often have caused harm to themselves. They may also carry negative feelings as a result of their actions, such as guilt. In addition to the negative feelings, as a result of breaching the school rules, the wrongdoer will often feel alienated from the school. The restorative justice approach aims to build towards resolution of these issues, thereby intervening in the commonly identified downward spiral of further breaches of rules and harm-causing, which will often end in some form of exclusion. Research into the use of the restorative justice approach in Bristol schools identified significant reductions in exclusion rates (Skinns, Du Rose and Hough, 2009).

How does this fit within our definition of inclusive pedagogy?

The restorative justice approach begins from the recognition of difference and diversity. It recognises that this diversity can result in conflict when people come together and negotiate different attitudes and beliefs which are manifested in their behaviours. Rather than focusing on the need to coerce individuals to conform to a set of rules (norms), the restorative justice approach aims to develop an understanding of different views in search of resolution of the conflict. Through working together without imposing set outcomes for solutions, the approach facilitates creative solutions. It does this through the use of non-judgemental language and an explorative approach to the events. This approach, where difference is acknowledged and worked with, aligns to an inclusive approach. The prominence of positive solutions rather than adherence to a set of rules or approaches charts a creative route through issues. The agency of those involved, as negotiators in the process and the problem solving is an empowering approach which links closely to the authors' definition of inclusion having empowerment at its heart. The restorative justice approach has the fundamental underpinning of social justice at its core, recognising that whilst those involved may perceive there to be perpetrators and victims, there are two parties involved who share fundamental human rights. The approach is underpinned by a humanist belief that positive solutions are desired by all.

The restorative justice approach: what is the practice?

There are two significant strands to using a restorative justice approach within a school setting. The first is the use of a structured approach to resolving conflict situations, through the use of restorative conferences. The second strand is a whole-school approach to managing conflict, with implications for school rules and policies, approaches to conflict and the language used by practitioners.

The restorative conference

Where significant incidents of wrongdoing, disagreement or conflict have occurred a restorative conference is arranged. These conferences have clear structures and processes, all parties attend and they are facilitated by a trained member of staff. In order for restorative conferences to be successful there needs to be an understanding of the process and the rationale for and values behind restorative justice to be understood by practitioners and learners involved, as well as significant stakeholders, for example parents and carers.

A whole school approach

In order to implement a restorative justice approach, there needs to be an agreement amongst the school community that restoration is morally desirable, or the right thing to do (Zehr, 2002) and the adoption of the approach needs to happen at a whole school level in order to be successful (Hopkins, 2004). The development of a restorative practice approach in schools often begins with a conscious agreement to modify the language used by practitioners, moving the meanings away from judgement and blame, towards a restorative vocabulary of exploration and understanding. School policies and procedures, in particular those related to behaviour or discipline need to be changed in order to reflect the focus on understanding and restoration. As such restoration does not solely happen as a result of restorative conference sessions, but through incidental and everyday interactions and the enactment of the policies and procedures of the setting.

What is the background?

The restorative justice approach has developed following experiments which took place in the 1970s (Galaway and Hudson, 1974), with learning being drawn from a range of indigenous communities dating back many years (Walker, 2013). In these experiments, those who had committed crimes were brought together with those they had hurt, with a focus on healing the wounds that had been created. This was in the context of growing recognition that reactions of retribution, punishment and deterrence are often unsuccessful approaches. Retribution implies further harm and can be regarded as perpetuating approaches of wrongdoing. When the approach of punishment is taken, significant issues of power and the imposition of partial moral values are raised. Punishment removes the wrongdoer from the process and is a disempowering process (Barnett, 2013), with the likely impact that the wrongdoer becomes alienated from the community, potentially leading to further acts of wrongdoing. Deterrence is frequently costly and difficult to manage, whilst leaving the needs of those who committed the initial wrongdoing with unresolved issues. The restorative justice approach seeks to heal on three levels; healing the victims, the offenders and the community (Van Wormer and Walker, 2013). By moving away from solutions based on retribution and towards a restoration of positive relationships and considering learners not just as individuals but as part of a caring community (Wearmouth, Mckinney and Glynn, 2007) the restorative justice approach presents an inclusive approach to the need for dynamic and adaptive solutions to enable learning communities to manage human interactions and conflicting perspectives.

What would you need in order to use this approach?

In order to implement a restorative justice approach into a school setting the initial requirement is that the leadership and the school agree that it is an approach they can commit to. This will then require space for the development of a whole school understanding of the principles of restoration and restorative practice, both for staff and learners, as well as parents, carers and wider stakeholders.

There would be a need to review school policies and procedures to reflect the restorative justice approach.

Training would be required for staff members leading on the development of the approach and for those who would take the responsibility of facilitating restorative conferences.

A commitment would need to be made to provide the required space for conducting restorative conferences and the staff time to enable them to participate in the conferences.

It may also be worth considering undertaking the Restorative Service Quality Mark with the Restorative Justice Council.

Resources

IBARJ (nd) *Restorative Practices in Schools*. Available at: www.ibarj.org/schools.asp (accessed 6 December 2018).

International Institute of Restorative Practices. Available at: www.iirp.edu/

Lyubansky, M. (2016) 'New study reveals six benefits of school Restorative Justice'. *Psychology Today*. Available at: www.psychologytoday.com/gb/blog/between-the-lines/201605/new-study-reveals-six-benefits-school-restorative-justice (accessed 6 December 2018).

Pethean, S. (2016) *Restorative Approaches: School Information Pack*. SW Surry Specialist Teachers for Inclusive Practice. Available at: www.surreycc.gov.uk/__data/assets/pdf_file/0019/101827/Introduction-to-restorative-approaches-for-schools.pdf (accessed 6 December 2018).

Restorative Justice Council – Restorative Service Quality Mark. Available at: https://restorativejustice.org.uk/restorative-service-quality-mark

References

Barnett, R.E. (2013) 'Restitution: A new paradigm of criminal justice'. In K.S. Van Wormer and L. Walker (eds.), *Restorative Justice Today: Practical Applications*. Los Angeles: SAGE, pp. 47–56.

Galaway, B. and Hudson, J. (1974) 'Undoing the wrong: The Minnesota restitution center'. *Social Work*, 19(3), pp. 313–318.

Hopkins, B. (2004) *Just Schools: A Whole-school Approach to Restorative Justice*. London: Jessica Kingsley Publishers.

Skinns, L., Du Rose, N. and Hough, M. (2009) *An Evaluation of Bristol RAiS*. London: Institute for Criminal Policy Research, King's College London. Available at: http://most.ie/webreports/march2010/RAiS%20Bristol%20Full%20Evaluation.pdf (accessed 5 November 2018).

Van Wormer, K.S. and Walker, L. (eds.). (2013) *Restorative Justice Today: Practical Applications*. Los Angeles: SAGE.

Walker, L. (2013) 'Restorative justice: Definition and purpose'. In K.S. Van Wormer and L. Walker (eds.), *Restorative Justice Today: Practical Applications*. Los Angeles: SAGE, pp. 3–14.

Wearmouth, J., Mckinney, R. and Glynn, T. (2007) 'Restorative justice in schools: A New Zealand Example'. *Educational Research*, 49(1), pp. 37–49.

Zehr, H. (1990) *Changing Lenses: A New Focus for Crime*. Scottdale: Herald Press.

Zehr, H. (2002) *The Little Book of Restorative Justice*. Intercourse: Good Books.

Chapter ten
EMOTION COACHING

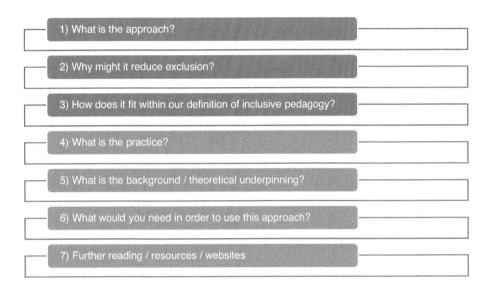

1) What is the approach?

2) Why might it reduce exclusion?

3) How does it fit within our definition of inclusive pedagogy?

4) What is the practice?

5) What is the background / theoretical underpinning?

6) What would you need in order to use this approach?

7) Further reading / resources / websites

What is the approach?

Emotion coaching is an approach for supporting children and young people to develop an understanding of emotions, of why the emotions they experience occur and of how they can manage emotions.

This approach was initially developed by Gottman, Katz and Hooven (1996, 1997), who identified five stages of emotion coaching:

1 Awareness of the adult's own emotions

2 Using emotion as opportunities for teaching and connectivity or intimacy with the child

3 Empathic listening and validation of the child's feelings

4 Supporting the child or young person to identify and label emotions

5 Supporting the child or young person to problem-solve

Key to this approach is building a positive and close relationship between the adult and the child or young person through sensitive awareness of their situation and needs, and also to teach particular knowledge and skills related to emotions.

Emotion coaching is an approach that is increasingly being provided as a tool for parents and carers to use, as a way of supporting and developing their relationships with their children. This use has developed following successful employment of the approach in work with foster and adoptive parents.

Why might it reduce exclusion?

The emotion coaching approach can have a positive impact on the reduction of school exclusion for three reasons. It is able to improve the relationships between the school practitioners and the child or young person, as connectivity development is a stage in this approach. With improved relationships a child or young person may be more likely to communicate with practitioners in a way which is less likely to lead to behaviours associated with exclusion. It should enable children and young people to understand their emotions and have more control over their emotions. As such they would be less likely to 'loose control' or behave in ways which are perceived as being unmanageable. An emotion coaching approach has been identified in research as reducing antisocial behaviours (Rose, Gilbert and Gus, 2015), which are frequently cited as reasons for school exclusions. The emotion coaching approach as a practice for practitioners also involves a change in pedagogical approach. This is described as 'connection before correction' (Golding, 2014). Through this change in approach practitioners may be less likely to seek to use measures such as exclusion, which are often used as 'corrective' strategies. Indeed, Rose, Gilbert and Smith (2013) found that through practising emotion coaching approaches practitioners felt more in control during incidents which occurred in schools.

How does it fit within our definition of inclusive pedagogy?

The emotion coaching approach uses the perspective of praxis, by beginning from research evidence linked to pedagogical practice, as well as attachment theory, theories of emotional development and neuroscience, with the aim of improving the outcomes for children and young people. It focuses on empowering the child or young person, through providing them with specific emotional literacy and intelligence-related skills and strategies in a social justice framework through a humanist approach, which places relations between individuals at the core of development. This approach works through beginning with a recognition of different developmental stages and aiming to understand the relation between the environment and experiences, and individual learning.

What is the practice?

The emotion coaching approach takes place within the five stages described in the section above.

The practitioner first examines their own attitudes and approach to their own emotions. They develop their understanding of the role that emotions play in all of our lives. They focus on observing and learning about the way in which children and young people express and communicate emotions. Their direct work with a child or young person begins with close attention to their emotions, through an empathic and accepting stance. They model and encourage talking about emotions, identifying opportunities for teaching. They continue with a respectful attention to the feelings of the child or young person ensuring understanding rather than criticism or judgement. The practitioner supports the child or young person to develop their emotional vocabulary and ability to identify and name emotions. This leads to the practitioner exploring solutions to problems with the child or young person, empowering them to make active choices.

What is the background/theoretical underpinning?

The emotion coaching approach links closely to work on emotional intelligence (Goleman, 1996) and emotional literacy (Bocchino, 1999) and develops an emphasis on the importance of the purpose and qualities of the relationship between the adult and the child or young person. This approach draws on attachment theory (Bowlby) and the understanding that nurturing emotional and psychological attunement can provide the emotional security for a child or young person to develop internal working models which enable them to successfully cope with challenges (Sroufe, 1997). It is further supported by developments in the understanding of neuroscience in relation to learning and motions (Cozolino, 2013). Research evidence points to a wide range of positive impacts for children and young people through the use of emotion coaching. In particular, improvement of emotional and behavioural wellbeing are cited as outcomes (Rose, Gilbert and Gus, 2015). Havighurst *et al.*'s (2013) research into using emotion coaching approaches with young children and their parents identifies a range of resulting positive changes. One of these is a reduction in teacher-reported behaviour problems.

What would you need in order to use this approach?

In order to implement an emotion coaching approach, there would be an initial need for training. Settings would need to consider the extent to which training would be spread across their staff group and whether only staff directly implementing the approach would need training or whether all staff which would work directly with the children or young people should be trained. When the choice of those to be trained has been made, there would need to be an undertaking by the practitioners of their willingness to change the nature of their relationship with the children and young people they work with. This would also involve a willingness in practitioners to examine their own approach to emotions and to challenge and adapt their reactions and thoughts around their emotions with the aim of developing their emotional interactions with children and young people. The setting would also need to make space in the curriculum for emotion coaching sessions to take place and also consider the implications for staffing and practice of changing the nature of the relationships in the setting.

Resources

A number of organisations offer training in emotion coaching, including local authority educational psychologist services and university CPD departments. Further training opportunities are frequently linked with services associated with looked after children, adoption and fostering. The private training company, Kate Cairns Associates, is one company which offers training in emotion coaching with a clear values-base to their service.

The presence of Emotionally Literate Support Assistants (ELSAs) is an approach to develop the skills of support staff in schools to support the wellbeing of children and young people. Some of the ELSA approaches are closely linked to emotion coaching. Further information about ELSA training is available from some local authority educational psychology services and there is also a national ELSA Network, whose website is www.elsanetwork.org

Further reading

Faber, A. and Mazlish, E. (2001) *How to Talk So Kids Will Listen & Listen So Kids Will Talk*. UK: Piccadilly Press Surrey.

Ginott, A. and Goddard, W. (2003) *Between Parent & Child (Dr. Haim Ginott)*. Three Rivers Press New York.

Siegel, D.J. (2014) *Brainstorm: The Power and Purpose of the Teenage Brain*. London: Scribe Publications.

Siegel, D.J. and Bryon, T.P. (2011) *The Whole-Brain Child*. London: Constable & Robinson Ltd.

Emotion Coaching UK – An organisation which provides practitioner training. Available at: www.emotioncoachinguk.com

A case study of a secondary school's use of Emotion Coaching is available at: https://drive.google.com/file/d/0B3LPE2BkjbjrTzFIUm85VFNkS1E/view

References

Bocchino, R. (1999) *Emotional Literacy: To Be a Different Kind of Smart*. Thousand Oaks: SAGE.

Cozolino, L.J. (2013) *The Social Neuroscience of Education: Optimizing Attachment and Learning in the Classroom*. First Edition. New York: W.W. Norton & Company (Norton Books in Education).

Golding, K.S. (2014) *Nurturing Attachments: Training Resource – Running Parenting Groups for Adoptive Parents and Foster or Kinship Carers*. London: Jessica Kingsley Publishers.

Goleman, D. (1996) *Emotional Intelligence: Why It Can Matter More Than IQ*. London: Bloomsbury.

Gottman, J.M., Katz, L.F. and Hooven, C. (1996) 'Parental meta-emotion philosophy and the emotional life of families: Theoretical models and preliminary data'. *Journal of Family Psychology*, 10(3), pp. 243–268.

Gottman, J.M., Katz, L.F. and Hooven, C. (1997) *Metaemotion: How Families Communicate Emotionally*. Mahwah: Lawrence Erlbaum Associates.

Havighurst, S.S., Wilson, K.R., Harley, A.E., Kehoe, C., Efron, D. and Prior, M.R. (2013) '"Tuning into kids": Reducing young children's behavior problems using an emotion coaching parenting program'. *Child Psychiatry & Human Development*, 44(2), pp. 247–264.

Rose, J., Gilbert, L. and Gus, L. (2015) 'Emotion coaching: A universal strategy for supporting and promoting sustainable emotional and behavioural well-being'. *Educational and Child Psychology*, 32(1), pp. 31–41.

Rose, J., Gilbert, L. and Smith, H. (2013) 'Affective teaching and the affective dimensions of learning'. *A Student's Guide to Education Studies*, pp. 178–188.

Sroufe, L.A. (1997) *Emotional Development: The Organisation of Emotional Life in the Early Years*. Cambridge: Cambridge University Press.

Chapter eleven
THERAPEUTIC APPROACHES

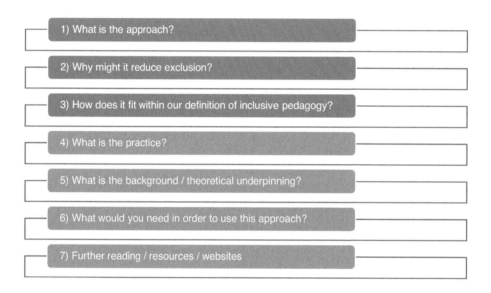

1) What is the approach?

2) Why might it reduce exclusion?

3) How does it fit within our definition of inclusive pedagogy?

4) What is the practice?

5) What is the background / theoretical underpinning?

6) What would you need in order to use this approach?

7) Further reading / resources / websites

What is the approach?

There are a range of practices within a therapeutic approach to support the needs of individual children and young people in school settings. There is a common factor among many of the therapeutic approaches, in that they do not have a goal or solution as the focus of the intervention. Instead the approach can focus on the need of the child or young person to explore issues they identify within a safe space, with an empathetic and non-judgemental therapist. Other therapeutic approaches may be more 'goal-focused', making use of therapeutic approaches to support a child or young person to reach a particular point. It is also important to acknowledge that a number of approaches which are discussed within other parts of this book may employ skills which have been learnt from therapeutic interventions. Indeed, the humanist perspective, which is discussed throughout this book, was developed by Carl Rogers, who was a therapist.

It is important for practitioners to understand that therapeutic approaches can be used to inform practice without actually using a specific therapeutic intervention. Through taking a person-centred approach and strengthening the focus on the relation between a child or young person and the practitioner, everyday practice may be infused with a therapeutic underpinning. Some perspectives upon therapeutic approaches consider that the simple nature of a positive relationship between the two individuals involved in the therapeutic event has a significant positive impact, as much as 30 per cent of the reason for the success (Hubble, Duncan and Miller, 2002).

Some examples of therapeutic approaches include:

Counselling, Play Therapy, Drama Therapy, Art Therapy, Sand Tray Therapy, Therapeutic Story Writing, and Mindfulness. Other therapeutic approaches are also used, some of which have developed from the approaches outlined earlier, to become specific therapeutic programmes, where information and training is linked to a specific organisation. One example of this is the Drawing & Talking approach.

It is important to remember that therapeutic interventions are not always the solution for social or emotional challenges that children and young people experience. In the case of mental health difficulties, whilst therapeutic interventions can ameliorate the situation for some, it should not be viewed as the medicine for mental health difficulties.

(Marzillier and Hall, 2009)

Why might it reduce exclusion

Therapeutic interventions can provide an outlet for the child or young person through offering the opportunity to explore difficult thoughts and emotions. This outlet can offer an alternative to coping with difficulties and communicating them through challenging behaviours, which can be given as a reason for exclusion. A therapeutic approach can also offer the opportunity to acknowledge issues, which the child or young person might be experiencing, within a safe and positive environment. In a busy classroom there is often not the opportunity or time for this to happen. Through acknowledgment and identification of issues, the child or young person can have the experience of being deeply heard (Rogers, 1967). This outlet for the expression of difficult issues and the opportunity for there to be the experience of a connection and understanding, in a relational sense, can also provide an alternative outlet that is less likely to lead to exclusion. The activities which form part of many of the therapeutic approaches can also offer the children and young people safe ways to express difficult issues as an alternative to challenging behaviours.

How does it fit within our definition of inclusive pedagogy?

Therapeutic interventions offer the opportunity for children and young people with different needs to explore the issues and challenges they face within a safe environment and through new and different methods. This approach is inclusive in that it acknowledges difference, both in terms of the needs of the learner, and also in recognising the benefit of different approaches. In taking a non-directive and more person-centred approach to provision, this approach has close synergies with humanism, as well as with the empowering approach of having no set outcomes or success criteria linked to the intervention approach, thereby linking to a more creative approach. Therapeutic approaches relate closely to a social justice and human rights perspective through providing the child and young person an empowering way of expressing their needs, thoughts and feelings.

A range of therapeutic approaches will be considered systematically in the following sections.

Mindfulness

What is the practice?

Mindfulness is different to many therapeutic interventions in that it is an approach or practical skill (Bostic *et al.*, 2015) which is taught and learnt, and that the actual approach can be a solitary event and a therapeutic other is not needed by the child or young person. The skills of mindfulness can be viewed as being closely aligned to meditation skills.

A commonly used approach to practising mindfulness is to sit and close your eyes, and begin to focus on your breathing and the sensations this leads to in the body. When doing this, extraneous thoughts are likely to enter your mind and distract you from this focus. The mindfulness skills you practice will allow you to note these thoughts and let them pass, rather than reacting to them, returning to your focus.

What is the background/theoretical underpinning?

The aim of using mindfulness skills is to enable the user to escape from difficult thoughts and experience the positiveness of being present in the moment. Through using this approach, the pressures and difficult events which encroach into one's life, whilst evoking strong emotions, need not have a negative impact. Instead, through mindful activities, the child or young person can understand that the emotions they are feeling are transitory and do not need to define the actions they take (Williams and Penman, 2013). According to Bostic *et al.* (2015) using mindfulness in response to stress provides the individual with resilience.

The benefits of mindfulness are claimed to be wide ranging with research pointing to benefits including pain management, reduction of the negative impacts of stress and depression, when used in both clinical settings and non-clinical groups (Baer, 2003; Greeson, 2009). More recently research has pointed to the successful use of mindfulness approaches to support the everyday wellbeing of children and young people (Burke, 2010).

What would you need in order to use this approach?

In order to use mindfulness approaches in your setting, very little is needed. Practitioners who understand and use mindfulness approaches themselves would be beneficial as models for others and training in mindfulness for young people would support practitioners. No particular materials or resources are needed for this approach, however regular space within the school timetable, to practice and develop mindfulness skills are recommended.

Resources

https://mindfulnessinschools.org/

Counselling

What is the practice?

Counselling could be described as a talking or listening therapy. It entails a particular way of talking and supporting someone to explore their thoughts and emotions within a safe space. The use of counselling in school settings has grown alongside the increasing understanding of the mental health and wellbeing challenges that are faced by children and young people.

Counselling usually consists of a series of regular, usually weekly, time-limited sessions where the counsellor meets with the child or young person on a one-to-one basis or as part of a group. The sessions take place in a confidential space where the child or young person is supported by the counsellor to talk about their thoughts and feelings whilst the counsellor attends, listens and supports them to explore these issues.

What is the background/theoretical underpinning?

The counselling approach grew from developments in psychology from the beginning of the 1900s, through the development of psychoanalysis and a person-centred approach, in contrast to practice based upon behaviourist notions of human development. Carl Rogers (1939) began the theoretical development related to the practice of counselling, communicating that a good counsellor would have psychological knowledge, be objective, understand the self and respect the individual. King (1999) suggests that the practice of counselling is focused on listening and responding skills. Counselling, or 'non-directive supportive therapy', is recommended by the National Institute for Health and Care Excellence (NICE) as a treatment for mild depression in children and young people, and many school-based counsellors can be considered to offer this type of therapy.

A key provider of counselling within schools across the UK, Place2Be, claims that 87 per cent of children identified improvements as a result of receiving counselling support (Place2Be, 2019). Lee, Tiley and White (2009) state that both teachers and parents identified the impact of Place2Be counselling to be improved social and emotional behaviour in children. More recent research into the impact of counselling in schools by Daniunaite, Cooper and Forster (2015) was more conservative in its findings, identifying improvement in just over 50 per cent of children and young people and identifying different levels of impact dependent on the starting point of those receiving counselling.

By nature of its approach, the effect of counselling is difficult to evidence through empirical research. Rogers (1967) rejected the scientific approach to evidencing person-centred work because of the focus of this relationship-based practice being focused on each person's unique experience and perception. However, research shared by Place2Be identifies that for every £1 spend on counselling in schools, there is a resultant benefit of £6.20 (Pro Bono Economics, 2017).

What would you need in order to use this approach?

Education practitioners often make use of counselling skills in their practice, and there are a number of books available to support teachers and other practitioners in the development of their counselling skills (King, 1999; Hornby, Hall and Hall, 2003). The authors recognise the value in the use of counselling skill, but recommend that in order to successfully support children and young people through a counselling approach the therapeutic individual should hold a recognised formal qualification in counselling (BACP/ Welsh Assembly Govt, 2011, p. 135). As such, in order to implement counselling in a school setting, the leadership will need to make the decision to allocate funding in order to employ appropriately qualified professionals (Lines, 2006). Furthermore, the process needs to be sustainable for a significant period of time, as it may take time for the children and young people to develop their understanding of the process before those with the greatest need will become open to engaging in the counselling process. Where counselling sessions are offered to children and young people in school, there needs to be a space available to be used, which is confidential and not open to interruptions. Space also needs to be available to children and young people to attend counselling sessions. Where children and young people are able to self-refer to a counsellor in a school setting, the school leadership needs to consider how parental or carer permission is sought, and whether it is done in anticipation for all of the children and young people. Understanding of the aims and outcomes of counselling needs to be developed for all of the school community in order that the expectations of counselling and the reactions to counselling are appropriate and realistic.

Further reading/resources/websites

British Association for Counselling and Psychotherapy www.bacp.co.uk

The Place2Be are a national charity which undertakes a wide range of work to support children and
young people's mental health and wellbeing. They are able to link trained counsellors with schools
and support counselling interventions in schools. www.place2be.org.uk

Creative therapeutic interventions

What is the practice?

There are a number of therapeutic interventions which use creative or arts-based activities
as the focus for sessions between the therapeutic lead and the child or young person. Such
interventions include play therapy, drama therapy, music therapy and art therapy. It can often
happen that a therapeutic lead will use activities from more than one of these approaches.
The therapeutic lead will be a trained psychotherapist, which means that they are trained in
using the relationship they create with the child or young person to understand and support
their psychological needs. The creative therapist will achieve this through using creative
activities to explore and communicate their thoughts, feelings and emotions. This therapeutic
approach can be practised on a one-to-one basis or one therapist can work with a group.

What is the background/theoretical underpinning?

This approach uses creative activity as a way for the child or young person to both
communicate their thoughts, feeling and emotions and also explore them. Through
participating in the activities or observing the child or young person, the therapist can use
their understanding to assess or diagnose the issues and needs communicated through
the creative activities. The creative activities can also offer the child or young person the
opportunity to work through difficult thoughts, feelings and emotions, by using the activity as
a safe metaphor, thereby enabling them to manage their reactions more successfully.

Creative therapeutic approaches are broadly located as person-centred approaches which
derive from the humanist practitioner Carl Rogers (1967) who placed the client at the centre
of the counsellor–client relationship.

Drama therapy is the approach where 'the content of drama activities, the process of creating
enactments and the relationships formed . . . within a therapeutic framework' (Jones, 2007,
p. 8) are combined to effect positive change.

Hickmore (2000, p. 110) identifies that children and young people can experience extremely
complex emotions in relation to their lives and that art and play therapies, 'enable this
jumbled, overwhelming mix to be disentangled, separated and then considered in bit by bit

manageable chunks'. In a meta-analysis of previous research into play therapy Bratton *et al.* (2005), whilst acknowledging the limitations of scientific research approaches in the field, conclude that evidence points to the positive impact of play therapy approaches, particularly for children with behaviour problems and social challenges.

What would you need in order to use this approach?

It is recommended that creative therapeutic interventions are only undertaken by trained psychotherapists. As such, if a school wanted to introduce one of these therapeutic interventions, they would need to allow a budget for the cost of an external professional. Consideration would also need to be given to the space which would be needed in the school day to facilitate the sessions and the consent of the child or young person's parents or carers would need to be given.

Resources

www.bacp.co.uk/
Association for Play Therapy www.a4pt.org
The British Association of Art Therapists www.baat.org
The British Association of Dramatherapists https://badth.org.uk/
Roundabout – A dramatherapy charity www.roundaboutdramatherapy.org.uk/
Mind – the mental health charity www.mind,org.uk

Therapeutic storywriting and sand play

What is the practice?

These two approaches bear close resemblance to some of the creative therapeutic interventions, as they borrow activities and approaches from them. These two approaches are examples of therapeutic interventions which can be led by school practitioners rather than trained psychotherapists. Both of these approaches offer a structured approach, through resources provided by the practitioner for the child or young person to explore and express their thoughts, feelings and emotions. The activities of writing or creating scenes in sand trays offer the child or young person this opportunity and the practitioner a way of interacting and supporting the child or young person to address issues raised. By keeping their thoughts, feelings and emotions within the activity, the child or young person can feel safer to explore.

What is the background/theoretical underpinning?

These approaches provide similar opportunities to creative therapeutic interventions, however, without a trained therapist. As such, the practitioner would not be expected to offer any psychological diagnosis and the extent to which they can support the psychological needs and development of the child or young person will be limited. The focus is orientated towards providing the child or young person the space and opportunity to explore themselves.

What would you need in order to use this approach?

The first step in implementing these therapeutic interventions is the identification of the practitioners who would be most suited to lead the approach and to then provide them with appropriate training. Many local authority educational psychology services offer training to schools on such approaches. You would need to consider the timetable for the sessions and how this would fit into the regular curriculum. Clear guidelines for the practitioner would need to be established around sensitive areas including communication with parents and carers, safeguarding and professional boundaries.

Resources

A further approach which school practitioners may find useful is 'drawing and talking'. This is an approach which uses drawing as a way to develop talk and to help the practitioner support the child or young person to access difficult thoughts and emotions. Training for school practitioners is available through the drawing and talking training consultancy. www.drawingandtalking.com/

Coaching

What is the practice?

Coaching can be seen as a therapeutic intervention in that it is focused on the needs of the individual and seeks to support them to develop self-understanding and awareness and thereby implement positive change. It is also based around the relationship developed within the coaching process and is based upon communication, which in the case of coaching is through conversation. Coaching can be seen as a process which has the aim of improving performance or behaviour, through the use of another person who acts as a coach. The role of the coach is not to instruct but rather to support the learner through a process of self-correction or learning through the use of their own resources. Coaching can take place within defined sessions or it can be a more general approach to learning adopted by the person leading the learning. There are a range of models and approaches which can be used within a coaching context, however the fundamental tool of the success of the coaching approach is the relationship between the coach and the child or young person and the skills of the coach that lead them in discovering the resources and approaches to develop their learning.

What is the theoretical underpinning?

The coaching approach is similar to other therapeutic approaches as it assumes a person-centred approach. The key approach is the activation and development of the skills of self-correction or self-generation (Flaherty, 2005) through engaging and empowering the child or young person in the process of change. Coaching is a process where the relationship is led by the coach, through a conversation-based process, where the strengths and skills of the child or young person are identified and built upon. The focus of the coaching activities can be problem-centred or goal-oriented and this focus is something which can be mutually decided upon. Through coaching approaches, the child or young person learns about themselves (Brockbank and McGill, 2006), and the outcomes are likely to lead to improved self-management skills and self-efficacy and congruence with the self (Campbell and Knoetze, 2010).

What would you need in order to use this approach?

As stated earlier, a coaching approach to learning can be handled through distinct sessions or key principles and techniques can be infused through the everyday teaching approaches employed in schools. Where distinct session are to be used, there are implications for staffing, time for the children or young people to engage in coaching sessions and the need for an identified private room. You may want to consider employing a coach with specific training to work with children and young people, which will have financial implications for the setting.

Where coaching approaches are to be developed as an addition to teachers' toolkits and infused into their approach, there will be a need for training and the space to develop and fine-tune the coaching skills. This will have financial implications and opportunities to be coached in using a coaching approach. Settings would need to carefully consider the timescale for the introduction of the use of coaching skills, to ensure confident and able staff.

Further reading/resources/websites

There are an abundance of resources which focus on coaching skills and PE with children and young people. The principles from a focus on PE can be valuable for those considering coaching approaches more widely. The UK coaching website is a wide-ranging resource focused on sports coaching, this is at www.ukcoaching.org There are a wide range of free downloadable resources which are the outcome of a Erasmus+ project to develop a European Coaching Children Curriculum. These are available from www.icoachkids.eu/european-coaching-children-curriculum.html

A range of academic institutions offer courses in using coaching approaches with children and young people and these are individually available online.

The Association for Coaching is an international charity which has the aim of promoting best practice in coaching. Their website is www.associationforcoaching.com

Beagley, M. (2009) *Every Picture Tells a Story*. Special First February 2009. Available at: www.learning-works.org.uk/spe_282930-pdf (accessed 11 December 2018).

References

BACP/Welsh Assembly Government. (2011) *School-based Counselling Operating Toolkit*. Available at: www.bacp.co.uk/media/2057/bacp-school-based-counselling-toolkit-welsh-english.pdf (accessed 11 December 2018).

Baer, R.A. (2003) 'Mindfulness Training as a Clinical Intervention: A conceptual and empirical review' *Clinical Psychology*, (10)2, pp.125–143.

Bostic, J.Q., Nevarez, M.D., Potter, M.P., Prince, J.B., Benningfield, M.M. and Aguirre, B.A. (2015) 'Being present at school: Implementing mindfulness in schools'. *Child and Adolescent Psychiatric Clinics of North America*, 24(2), pp. 245–259.

Bratton, S.C., Ray, D., Rhine, T. and Jones, L. (2005) 'The efficacy of play therapy with children: A meta-analytic review of treatment outcomes'. *Professional Psychology: Research and Practice*, 36(4), pp. 376–390.

Brockbank, A. and McGill, I. (2006) *Facilitating Reflective Learning Through Mentoring & Coaching*. London: Kogan Page.

Burke, C.A. (2010) 'Mindfulness-based approaches with children and adolescents: A preliminary review of current research in an emergent field'. *Journal of Child and Family Studies*, 19(2), pp. 133–144.

Campbell, M.M. and Knoetze, J.J. (2010) 'Repetitive symbolic play as a therapeutic process in child-centered play therapy'. *International Journal of Play Therapy*, 19(4), pp. 222–234.

Daniunaite, A., Cooper, M. and Forster, T. (2015) 'Counselling in UK primary schools: Outcomes and predictors of change'. *Counselling and Psychotherapy Research*, 15(4), pp. 251–261.

Flaherty, J. (2005) *Coaching: Evoking Excellence in Others*. Oxford: Elsevier Butterworth-Heinemann.

Greeson, J.M. (2009) 'Mindfulness research update: 2008'. *Complementary Health Practice Review*, 14(1), pp. 10–18.

Hickmore, H. (2000) 'Using art and play in assessment and intervention for troubled children'. In N. Barwick (ed.), *Clinical Counselling in Schools*. London: Routledge, pp. 108–123 (Clinical Counselling in Context).

Hornby, G., Hall, C. and Hall, E. (2003) *Counselling Pupils in Schools: Skills and Strategies for Teachers*. London: RoutledgeFalmer.

Hubble, M.A., Duncan, B.L. and Miller, S.D. (2002) *The Heart & Soul of Change: What Works in Therapy*. Washington, DC: American Psychological Association.

Jones, P. (2007) *Drama as Therapy: Theory, Practice, and Research*. Second Edition. London: Routledge.

King, G. (1999) *Counselling Skills for Teachers: Talking Matters*. Buckingham: Open University Press (Counselling Skills).

Lee, R.C., Tiley, C.E. and White, J.E. (2009) 'The Place2be: Measuring the effectiveness of a primary school-based therapeutic intervention in England and Scotland'. *Counselling and Psychotherapy Research*, 9(3), pp. 151–159.

Lines, D. (2006) *Brief Counselling in Schools: Working With Young People From 11 to 18*. London: SAGE.

Marzillier, J. and Hall, J. (2009) 'The challenge of the Layard initiative'. *The Psychologist*, 22(5), pp. 396–399.

Place2Be. (2019) *Children and Young People*. Available at: www.place2be.org.uk/impact-evidence/children-and-young-people.aspx (accessed 4 February 2019).

Part III

Pro Bono Economics. (2017) *Economic Evaluation of Place2Be's Counselling Service in Primary Schools.* Available at: www.probonoeconomics.com/sites/default/files/files/Economic%20Evaluation%20 of%20Place2Be%E2%80%99s%20Counselling%20Service%20in%20Primary%20Schools_0.pdf (accessed 5 February 2019).

Rogers, C. (1939) *The Clinical Treatment of the Problem Child.* New York: Houghton Mifflin.

Rogers, C. (1967) *On Becoming a Person: A Therapist's View of Psychotherapy.* London: Constable.

Williams, M. and Penman, D. (2013) *Mindfulness: A Practical Guide to Finding Peace in a Frantic World.* London: Piatkus.

Chapter twelve
STAFF WELLBEING

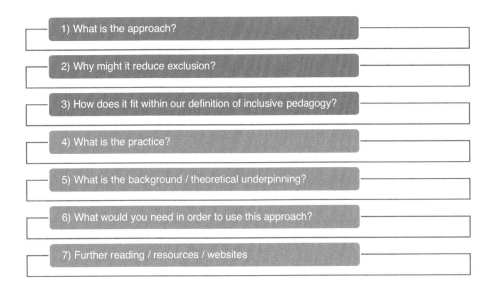

1) What is the approach?

2) Why might it reduce exclusion?

3) How does it fit within our definition of inclusive pedagogy?

4) What is the practice?

5) What is the background / theoretical underpinning?

6) What would you need in order to use this approach?

7) Further reading / resources / websites

What is the approach?

Practitioners and school leaders can look at the topic of staff wellbeing from two different perspectives. The first perspective is that if staff wellbeing is positive then the school is likely to be in a better position to provide for the needs of children and young people in the setting. This perspective is perhaps key to the emphasis of this book and also to the primary concerns of practitioners who share a belief in the values of inclusive education and focus on the needs of the learners they work with. The second perspective may also be an important consideration for those who believe in reframing the education systems we work within. This second perspective views a school or other learning institution as a community and that there is a responsibility to apply inclusive practice to all members of the community, including the staff, rather than exclusively for the learners.

Whichever of the two perspectives are placed as the primary reason for developing practice to enhance practitioner wellbeing, the approaches available are the same. There are key aspects of practitioners' professional lives which can be impacted positively to support their wellbeing. These aspects, adapted and enhanced from the Education Support Partnership (2017) are:

- Workload

- Having a clear professional role

- Experiencing success in their professional role

- Agency – the extent to which the practitioner can influence how they carry out their role

- Support in their institution

- Relationships

- Change and how it is managed in their institution

The approach to improving the wellbeing of practitioners is to assess or audit these aspects of practitioners' professional experiences and then identify actions which can be taken to improve them. In addition, there are other areas outside of the school setting which can also influence practitioner wellbeing, including personal relationships, health and exercise, and the impact of the challenges which everyday life presents. Some of these external influences may be positively influenced by moves within schools to improve work/life balance, whilst at times these factors can be areas that are outside of the influence of actions taken by school settings. These may be areas which could be supported by schools, but individual practitioners would need to work on themselves. For example, there are well-documented links between exercise and mental wellbeing (Fox, 1999) and whilst schools may decide to offer the opportunity for on-site exercise classes, it is the individual's own decision to take up additional exercise which would lead this development.

Why might it reduce exclusion?

Where practitioners have poor wellbeing it is likely that they will be stressed or their attention will be distracted from their professional role. They are likely to be irritable and have less patience with children and young people. Consequently, if practitioners' wellbeing is improved, they will be likely to be more focused on their role and have more patience when dealing with children and young people who present challenging behaviours which may lead to exclusion. Underpinning this all is the importance of the relationships between practitioners and children and young people, and a key aspect of positive relationships is positive wellbeing.

How does this fit with our definition of inclusive pedagogy?

The two perspectives discussed in the previous sections are not mutually exclusive, in fact they can complement each other. In terms of inclusion of children and young people, we have already addressed the potential for positive outcomes when practitioners have positive wellbeing, in that they will be likely to have more capacity to be reflective, and their ability to be more patient will enable the space for diversity to be expressed and creative outcomes to be explored.

Where the perspective of widening the inclusive approach to encompass all of the school community is adopted, there are more significant links to inclusive pedagogy. There are implications for a collective approach to education, where the distinctions between learner and teacher are reduced and approaches to co-learning and empowerment through more equitable power relations is developed. Where the practitioners are providing the opportunities for their own wellbeing, there are links to empowerment, social justice, creativity and humanism. If an inclusive approach encompasses all people in the school community, the children and young people will be likely to experience practitioners modelling this practice amongst each other and consequently providing enhanced opportunities for the pupils to learn through an inclusive approach.

What is the practice?

Improvements in practitioner wellbeing can be brought about by both individual and collective actions on the part of the practitioner or through actions taken by school leaders by school-wide actions. The motivations for these improvements can be varied, as discussed earlier, and there are a range of approaches which can be taken.

The first step is to recognise the importance of wellbeing and where practitioner wellbeing is placed within the complex systems and relationships that form a school community. Through an inclusion lens, this leads to developing a culture which values all those within the community and, therefore, the recognition of the importance of the wellbeing of the practitioners.

For an individual, having recognised the importance of their own wellbeing, they will then be more able to engage in discussions about their wellbeing and assert their needs. Where a positive and open culture has been developed, the individual practitioner is empowered to take these actions.

As may be clear through this section, it is difficult for an individual to improve their wellbeing where the setting is not supportive of this. As such, we would argue that the promotion of practitioner wellbeing needs to be supported through whole school approaches which encompass the practitioners within the community (Mentally Healthy Schools, 2019).

In order to take a whole school approach to develop the wellbeing of practitioners, it is key to understand the current situation and how the wellbeing of practitioners is being impacted. Reviewing the current situation can be facilitated when using a framework and then identifying aspects where improvements can be made. When done collectively this can be extremely beneficial in terms of empowering the members of the community and gaining shared insights, which may challenge the perspectives of school leaders. We have proposed a basic framework at the beginning of this chapter and a range of other frameworks are signposted within the resources we outline at the end of this chapter.

What is the background/theoretical underpinning?

Employee mental wellbeing has benefits in terms of increased commitment and job satisfaction, staff retention, reduced absences and improved performance (NICE, 2009). Having positive practitioner wellbeing is linked to positive learner outcomes (Briner and Dewberry, 2007; Roffey, 2012; Paterson and Grantham, 2016).

There is clear evidence of the need to improve the wellbeing of practitioners at both a national and European level, given the current available evidence. Teaching is amongst the occupations in the UK which are recognised as having the highest levels of stress and all employees within public service industries, including education, experience workplaces with the highest levels of stress. (Health and Safety Executive, 2018). High and increasing levels of teacher and practitioner stress are also recognised (Travers and Cooper, 2016; Education Support Partnership, 2017) and seen as factors contributing to burnout and retention difficulties. Teacher retention and recruitment is a significant and growing issue in the UK, with the overall numbers of teachers falling behind the growing numbers of pupils and pupil numbers set to increase by 15 per cent between 2018 and 2025 (Foster, 2019, p. 4). Fifty-seven per cent of teachers surveyed in 2015 were considering leaving the professional as a result of work/life balance issues (NUT/YouGov, 2015). Some of these issues are amplified when considering practitioners who work with children and young people who are more likely to experience exclusion. 'Key Data on Education in Europe' highlights the issue of teacher burnout as a result of stress caused by the challenges of working with pupils with social problems, special educational needs and verbal and physically aggressive behaviours (EACEA/Eurostat, 2009, p. 168). Research points towards high levels of distress and burnout experienced by teachers working with learners with Special Educational Needs (Greenglass, Burke and Konarski, 1997; Billingsley, 2004) and those working with learners with social, emotional and mental health difficulties have the highest rate of burnout (Garwood, Van Loan and Werts, 2018).

Given the context of the challenges faced by practitioners in schools and in particular those working with children and young people at risk of exclusion, it is clear that practitioner wellbeing is an important issue. Schleicher (2018, p. 89) proposes that, 'for teaching and learning to be at its most effective, teachers should have high levels of well-being, self-efficacy, and confidence'.

Dogra and Leighton (2009) point to the importance of empowerment and enabling individuals to take responsibility for their wellbeing through offering environments where there is openness to talk about mental health. Furthermore, the empowering aspects having a shared belief, good relationships have been identified as significant supportive factors for practitioners working with children and young people with social, emotional and mental health difficulties (Middleton, 2018).

The key to developing practitioner wellbeing, alongside the wellbeing of the children and young people in the school, is the development of a caring community (Allan, 2003) where the rights of fellow human beings is the significant factor, thereby reducing judgement and increasing the recognition and value of diversity.

'Flourishing teachers create the foundations for learning to flourish' (Lovewell, 2013).

What would you need in order to use this approach?

Approaches to support and develop the wellbeing of practitioners can be developed in a number of ways. In order to begin to address staff wellbeing there needs to be a recognition of its importance. For individuals, this recognition can provide the motivation to take actions and access resources to help themselves as well as providing the strength and motivation to discuss this with colleagues and leaders, in order to prompt changes in their school. School leaders who recognise the importance of the need to enhance wellbeing for both learners and staff in order to have the best outcomes (Glazzard and Bostwick, 2018) will be in a position to implement changes to conditions and practice in order to have a positive impact on wellbeing. There may be funding implications for some approaches, in particular those which seek to reduce workload and those where time may be needed in order to develop relationships. There are other aspects where the willingness to create an open and safe environment for staff to discuss challenges, to develop agency and empowerment amongst practitioners, and to provide support and recognition of achievements, are not reliant on funding. Instead, motivation, awareness and improved communication can be identified as the key requirements for improving practitioner wellbeing.

Further reading/resources/websites

The Whole School SEND/nasen community of practice were due to publish a DfE commissioned induction pack for new SENCOs at the time of publication. This has a section about practitioner wellbeing which lists a range of resources practitioners can access to help them to address the issue of teacher and practitioner wellbeing. It should be freely available for those who are registered as part of the community.

This can be accessed at www.sendgateway.org.uk/whole-school-send/join-our-community-of-practice.html

'The Wellbeing Toolkit Part 2' written by Dr Tina Rae is a significant resource aimed at supporting the professional development of education practitioners working to support the wellbeing of children and young people. This has a number of sections which relate to practitioner wellbeing, including the impact of working with children and young people who are frequently present in exclusion statistics, and offers clear approaches which can positively impact upon practitioner wellbeing. This is available from NurtureUK at: www.nurtureuk.org/our-services/training/wellbeing-toolkit-2-professionals

The Educational Support Partnership is an educational charity which supports the mental health and wellbeing of education staff and organisations. They offer a free 24-hour telephone and text helpline for practitioners. FREE HELPLINE 08000 562 561 Text: 07909341229.

The Mentally Healthy Schools website is a resource which arose from the charity Heads Together and is supported by Place2Be, Young Minds and the Anna Freud Centre. It provides a range of information and links related to mental health and wellbeing in schools. It can be accessed at: www.mentallyhealthyschools.org.uk

References

Allan, J. (2003) 'Productive pedagogies and the challenge of inclusion'. *British Journal of Special Education*, 30(4), pp. 175–179.

Billingsley, B.S. (2004) 'Promoting teacher quality and retention in special education'. *Journal of Learning Disabilities*, 37(5), pp. 370–376.

Briner, R. and Dewberry, C. (2007) *Staff Well-Being Is Key to School Success*. London: Worklife Support Ltd/Hamilton House.

Dogra, N. and Leighton, S. (2009) *Nursing in Child and Adolescent Mental Health*. Maidenhead: Open University Press/McGraw-Hill Education.

EACEA/ Eurostat. (2009) *Key Data on Education in Europe 2009*. Available at: https://edudoc.ch/record/105413/files/03Key_data_2009_EN.pdf (accessed 11 March 2019).

Education Support Partnership. (2017) *Looking After Teacher Wellbeing*. Available at: www.educationsupportpartnership.org.uk/sites/default/files/looking_after_teacher_wellbeing.pdf (accessed 11 March 2019).

Foster, D. (2019) 'Teacher Recruitment and retention in England'. *House of Commons Briefing Paper 7222*, 12 February 2019.

Fox, K.R. (1999) 'The influence of physical activity on mental well-being'. *Public Health Nutrition*, 2(3a), pp. 411–418.

Garwood, J.D., Van Loan, C.L. and Werts, M.G. (2018) 'Mindset of paraprofessionals serving students with emotional and behavioral disorders'. *Intervention in School and Clinic*, 53(4), pp. 206–211.

Glazzard, J. and Bostwick, R. (2018) *Positive Mental Health: A Whole School Approach*. St. Albans: Critical Publishing.

Greenglass, E.R., Burke, R.J. and Konarski, R. (1997) 'The impact of social support on the development of burnout in teachers: Examination of a model'. *Work & Stress*, 11(3), pp. 267–278.

Health & Safety Executive. (2018) *Work Related Stress Depression or Anxiety Statistics in Great Britain, 2018*. Available at: www.hse.gov.uk/statistics/causdis/stress.pdf (accessed 11 March 2019).

Lovewell, K. (2013) *Teacher Development Trust Newsletter March 2013*. Available at: https://tdtrust.org/nten-easter-2013-newsletter (accessed 1 December 2013).

Mentally Healthy Schools. (2019) *Supporting Staff Wellbeing*. Available at: www.mentallyhealthyschools.org.uk/whole-school-approach/supporting-staff-wellbeing/ (accessed 11 March 2019).

Middleton, T. (2018) 'Working with children with social, emotional and mental health needs in a nurture group setting: The professional and personal impact'. *International Journal of Nurture in Education*, 4(1), pp. 22–32.

NICE. (2009) *Mental Wellbeing at Work*. Available at: www.nice.org.uk/guidance/ph22/chapter/1-Recommendations#why-employees-mental-wellbeing-is-important-to-organisations-productivity-and-performance (accessed 11 March 2019).

NUT/YouGov. (2015) *Teacher Survey October 2015*. Available at: www.teachers.org.uk/news-events/press-releases-england/nutyougov-teacher-survey-government-education-policy (accessed 11 March 2019).

Paterson, A. and Grantham, R. (2016) 'How to make teachers happy: An exploration of teacher wellbeing in the primary school context'. *Educational & Child Psychology*, 33(2), pp. 90–104.

Roffey, S. (2012) 'Pupil wellbeing – Teacher wellbeing: Two sides of the same coin?'. *Educational and Child Psychology*, 29(4), p. 8.

Schleicher, A. (2018) *Valuing Our Teachers and Raising Their Status: How Communities Can Help. International Summit on the Teaching Profession*. Paris: OECD Publishing. ISBN 978-92-64-29261-1.

Travers, C. and Cooper, C. (2016) *Teachers Under Pressure: Stress in the Teaching Profession*. London: Routledge.

PART IV

This section of the book presents practitioners with a framework to support their reflection about their own practice and the policies and procedures in their settings. Using the six dimensions of inclusion, we present a range of questions which are related to key areas of practice in settings. These questions are not meant to be used as an audit process, or a series of questions to be worked through and answered. For schools seeking to audit their practice through an inclusion lens, there are specific processes already available, such as the Inclusion Quality Mark's Evaluative Framework. The questions in this framework are provided as prompts to support reflective thinking which is targeted towards inclusive practice. These questions can be used by individuals or shared in groups, perhaps as prompts for staff meetings. We hope that this framework will provide practitioners with a way of proactively addressing issues related to inclusion and support them and their settings to reduce exclusion.

FRAMEWORK FOR REFLECTION

Dimension of Theoretical Framework for Inclusion	Learning and Difference	Social Justice and Human Rights	Empowerment	Creativity	Humanism	Praxis
Area of focus						
Defining inclusion/ inclusive practice for our school	What are our key values? What principles underpin our definition of inclusion? How do we define inclusive practice?	What are our key values? What principles underpin our definition of inclusion? How do we define inclusive practice? What do we currently do which excludes learners from learning, the environment or social elements of our school?	What are our key values? What principles underpin our definition of inclusion? How do we define inclusive practice? How do we communicate our definition of inclusion and inclusive practice? How do we encourage, support and enable our children and young people to build relationships?	What are our key values? What principles underpin our definition of inclusion? How do we define inclusive practice? Are our definitions of inclusion and inclusive practice open to development and change?	What are our key values? What principles underpin our definition of inclusion? How do we define inclusive practice? How do we define exclusion?	What are our key values? What sources of information have we drawn upon to inform our definition of inclusion?

(Continued)

[Continued]

Dimension of Theoretical Framework for Inclusion	Learning and Difference	Social Justice and Human Rights	Empowerment	Creativity	Humanism	Praxis
School Ethos	What is our belief about learning and ability – is it fixed or responsive to teaching? Who holds responsibility for children and young people with SEN? How do we develop a shared approach to supporting individual needs? How do we talk about our learners in dialogue with one another? What words and phrases do we use? What do our school rules and policies communicate about our attitude to difference? What does our school environment communicate about our attitude to difference? Does our staff body reflect a diverse collection of people?	What strategies do we use to proactively include all learners in the social aspects of school? What strategies do we use to proactively facilitate access to a broad and balanced curriculum? Do we focus on strengths as well as areas of difficulty in our learners?	How do we enable our learners to share their views, experiences and aspirations of the social and academic aspects of school life? How do we enable our pupils to share their views, experiences and experiences of life outside school? How frequently do we enable this to happen? Do we/How do we enable our population of learners to share in the decision-making for school? Do we include children and young people with SEN within any involvement in planning and decisions for school?	What do we celebrate as achievement? How do we demonstrate that we value the things we have identified to our learners? How do we communicate that alternative outcomes are possible and welcomed?	Do we have holistic or caring goals at the centre of our school vision and core purpose? Do we focus upon a medical model or a social model of disability? How do we resolve difficult decisions, when values sit in opposition to another?	What sources of information have we drawn upon to inform our: – School ethos – School vision – School development/ improvement planning

Dimension of Theoretical Framework for Inclusion	Learning and Difference	Social Justice and Human Rights	Empowerment	Creativity	Humanism	Praxis
The Learner	What do our individual learners identify as their own strengths and difficulties? How do we know what our learners think about their own skills and abilities? How often to do we talk to learners about how they perceive their strengths and difficulties? And about what their interests are? What are the learners' views of what is important in our setting?	How do our leaners talk about opportunities inside and outside of school? What do they perceive their opportunities to be? How do we know? Do learners perceive they have equal opportunities within: – the academic curriculum? – The social aspects of school (e.g. extra-curricular activities)? How are the school policies and procedures made accessible to the learners?	How do we tailor approaches for individual learners to share their views, experiences and aspirations of the social and academic aspects of school life? How do we tailor approaches for individual learners to share their views, experiences and experiences of life outside school? How do we tailor approaches for individual learners to share in the decision-making for their targets, goals and provision?	What do our learners value in their learning? How do we know? What are the aspirations of each of our learners? How do we know?	How do our learners view themselves and their interaction with others? Do our learners know how to make friends? Do our learners know strategies to help them sustain friendships? What helps our learners feel happy or secure at school? What actions do we take which demonstrate a humanist approach?	Do you create spaces within school meetings to engage in critical reflection and dialogue with learners: – Upon their learning? – Upon the learning environment? – Upon the social environment? – Their responsibilities within learning? – What works well for them/ what acts as barrier for them?

(Continued)

[Continued]

Dimension of Theoretical Framework for Inclusion	Learning and Difference	Social Justice and Human Rights	Empowerment	Creativity	Humanism	Praxis
The Wider Community *Includes parents & carers, partners, community*	How do we communicate our school vision to the wider community? Do we take account of learning and difference in the modes of our communication? How do the parents and carers of our school population perceive the school? How does the wider community perceive the school? How do we know? Are we proactive in finding out?	How do we perceive the responsibilities that parents and carers have to engage with our setting? What actions do we take to engage the wider community? How do we collect and act upon the views of the wider community? How are the school policies and procedures made accessible to the learners?	What factors do you think contribute to effective partnership working? What factors do you think hinder/provide barriers to effective partnership working? Think about an example of working in partnership with parents and carers and/or outside agencies from your own experience: – What elements or activities do you think supported the successes? – What elements or activities do you think hindered working effectively?	What are the expectations of the parents and carers? Are there any ways in which we could see this differently? What are our success criteria for parental engagement? How do we view engagement with wider family members of our pupils?	How do we draw upon the wider community to support holistic goals? How might we investigate opportunities to seek support from the wider community? How might we investigate opportunities to offer support to the wider community? How do we show that we value the members of the wider community?	What sources of information and expertise have we drawn upon to inform – How we listen to and communicate with parents and carers? – How we listen to and communicate with the wider community?

Dimension of Theoretical Framework for Inclusion	Learning and Difference	Social Justice and Human Rights	Empowerment	Creativity	Humanism	Praxis
School Leadership Governors/ Trustees, SENCOs	Who are the leaders in your school? What leadership approach is taken in our setting? Do the values of the senior leaders match those of the rest of the school community? What actions do you take to ensure focus upon learners with SEN is included with school arrangements for monitoring and appraisal? How do we as senior/middle leaders know the views of our – Staff team – Pupil population in relation to learning and difference? How do we demonstrate (or model) valuing learning and difference to others?	How does your school data in relation to excluded pupils or those at risk of exclusion compare with the national data? How do the senior leadership and middle leadership teams set and develop the expectation that learners with SEN are the class/ subject teachers' responsibility (i.e. not just the SENCOs)? How do we review the actions we plan to support our learners with: – Social relationships?	To what extent does the leadership team facilitate the empowerment of others: – Pupils? – School staff? – Parents and carers? How do senior leaders listen to: – Middle leadership? – Teachers? – TAs and other practitioners? – Parents & carers – Other support teams and staff?	Who are the leaders in your school? How do we build capacity to respond to and meet a range of diverse needs? How do we find ways to include CPD for SEN needs within all other CPD so that it is not perceived as a separate entity? How do leaders facilitate creative and proactive planning for transitions? How do leaders facilitate flexible modes of responding to factors within: – Physical environment?	How do you think the wider policy context influences the broader environment in which your own school or setting operates? How do the senior and middle leadership teams encourage teachers to engage with learners with SEN?	How do you think the wider policy context influences inclusion and exclusion in your own school or setting? Do you create spaces within school meetings to engage in critical reflection and dialogue of policy and practice?

(Continued)

(Continued)

Dimension of Theoretical Framework for Inclusion	Learning and Difference	Social Justice and Human Rights	Empowerment	Creativity	Humanism	Praxis
		– Physical and emotional wellbeing? – Self-reflection? – Opportunities to succeed? – Raising aspirations/ widening horizons?		– Sensory environment? – Social-emotional environment? which may constrain learner's opportunities. What are the learners' views about the school leadership? What are the parents' and carers' views about the school leadership?		

Dimension of Theoretical Framework for Inclusion	Learning and Difference	Social Justice and Human Rights	Empowerment	Creativity	Humanism	Praxis
Pedagogical approaches	How do you perceive ability and learning? Is this something which is fixed or is this responsive to teaching? Can ability and learning change? Do the teachers teach the learners in your class(es) with SEN or do you hand them over to other adults? How do you maintain oversight of what's being taught in withdrawal activities? What do you need to find out to inform your planning? Is there more you need to know? How might you identify what that is and where you might source the knowledge you feel you are missing from?	How do we adapt our pedagogy to: – Reduce barriers to learning? – Increase participation and access to learning? – Support diversity? (Booth and Ainscow, 2002).	Do you create spaces in your learning and teaching activities to engage in active listening to your pupils? How do you seek the views of your learners on their learning? What strategies to do you use to encourage learners to communicate with you about their learning?	How do we assess children and young people's knowledge, skills and understanding (summative evidence)? How do you require learners to record their learning? Do you offer flexible approaches? What strategies you could you utilise to offer flexible approaches to recording work? What strategies could you utilise to offer flexible approaches to assessment?	How do we build good working relationships with our pupils? How do we develop, facilitate and engage in dialogical relationships with our learners?	Have you assessed the different aspects of the environment to explore factors which constrain, accommodate or enhance learning: – Physical environment – Sensory environment – Social-emotional environment What sources of information have we drawn upon to inform decisions about pedagogy? Do you create spaces within school meetings to engage in critical reflection and dialogue of pedagogy?

(Continued)

Dimension of Theoretical Framework for Inclusion	Learning and Difference	Social Justice and Human Rights	Empowerment	Creativity	Humanism	Praxis
				What strategies you could you utilise to offer flexible approaches to: – Recording work? – Assessment? How are records of achievement and progress used to reflect creative outcomes?		Do you create spaces within school meetings to use practitioner-inquiry to critically explore practice?
Curriculum	Do we offer opportunities for learners to engage in dialogue about learning and difference to build awareness and understanding? Do our resources reflect diverse communities?	How do we ensure 'appropriate educational experiences' (Ekins, 2015, p. 5) for all of our learners? How do we articulate this in our policies and programme documentation? How do we include the values of equality and social respect within our curriculum?	Does the curriculum explicitly teach learners how they can use strategies to empower themselves? Does the curriculum offer include activities to raise aspirations and expectations?	Do we use creative/thinking outside box approaches to manage the curriculum offer so that we can include teaching about diversity? How might we do this? How do our learning outcomes and learning tasks promote creative outcomes?	How do we model and teach: – Social-emotional skills? – Making and sustaining relationships? – Working collaboratively?	What sources of information have we drawn upon to inform decisions about curriculum? Do you create spaces within school meetings to engage in critical reflection and dialogue about the curriculum offer? Do you create spaces within school meetings to use practitioner-inquiry to critically explore and develop the curriculum?

Dimension of Theoretical Framework for Inclusion	Learning and Difference	Social Justice and Human Rights	Empowerment	Creativity	Humanism	Praxis
Inclusion for the school team	Do we create spaces in which to reflect upon learning and difference and how we respond to this? Are diverse practitioners valued in our setting?	Do we create spaces in which to reflect upon diversity and how we respond to this? Are there ways in which staff members can raise issues about their experiences without concern for repercussions?	What opportunities are offered for staff members to become empowered? To what extent do the school team take up opportunities and empower themselves?	Do we use physical and human resources and time creatively to facilitate addressing SEN? How do systems allow for creative approaches to personal and professional development and other management needs?	Is there a culture where practitioners can safely discuss difficult issues? Do staff members care about each other? How is care for one another communicated?	Are all the school team offered equitable access to opportunities to increase their knowledge, experience and understanding? To what extent do the school team take up opportunities to increase their knowledge, experience and understanding?

Part IV

Reference

Ekins, A. (2015) *The Changing Face of Special Educational Needs. Impact and Implications for SENCOs, Teachers and Their Schools*. Abingdon: Routledge.

PART V

This final chapter considers other learners with diverse needs and then moves on to explore the importance of practitioner attitudes within inclusive approaches.

CONCLUSION

Inclusive practice

This book is part of the nasen-Spotlight series and therefore, in its discussion of inclusion, it maintains a focus on children and young people and the field of SEND. We recognise that school exclusion is not just a significant issue for children and young people identified as having SEN. In the research for this book, we have been drawn to the experience of exclusion of a number of other inclusion groups, some of whom are represented in national government statistics, such as those from black and minority ethnic backgrounds and those from low income families. For example, in 2016/17, pupils from the Traveller of Irish Heritage and Gypsy/Roma ethnic groups had the highest rates of both temporary ('fixed period') and permanent exclusions and black Caribbean pupils were permanently excluded at nearly three times the rate of white British pupils (DfE, 2018). There are, however, other inclusion groups for whom exclusion statistics are not routinely collected by the English government. These include: children and young people with mental health difficulties that are not recognised as being Special Educational Needs, looked after and adopted children and young people, children and young people who are refugees or recent immigrants, and children and young people who identify as LGBT+. It is also important to recognise that being identified with SEN does not mean that children and young people cannot also be part of other inclusion groups and that these characteristics can lead to dual or multiple risks of exclusion. It is therefore important to acknowledge the available information which links school exclusion to children and young people who are part of these inclusion groups.

Beyond the DfE statistics for children and young people who have identified SEN, Ford et al. (2018) state that there are no systematic studies which focus on school exclusion and children and young people with mental health difficulties and propose the view that there is a bidirectional relationship between school exclusion and psychiatric disorders. In other words, psychiatric disorders lead towards school exclusion and are also augmented by school exclusion.

Looked after children are twice as likely to be excluded from school (Gill, Quilter-Pinner and Swift, 2017). Adopted children and young people are four times as likely to be excluded from school, five times more likely to be permanently excluded, and sixteen times more likely to be excluded in Key Stage 1, than the general school population (Armstrong Brown and White, 2017). Armstrong Brown and White (2017) also report that 12 per cent of adopted children and young people and their carers who were surveyed had the experience of being advised by their school to change school in order to avoid exclusion and that just under a quarter had experienced informal illegal exclusion.

There is no clear picture nor guidance related to the needs and experiences of children and young people who are recent refugees or asylum seekers in relation to school exclusion (Sullivan and Simonson, 2016). In a more general analysis of the social and educational landscape for this inclusion group, Graham, Minhas and Paxton (2016) identify that there is a likelihood of them experiencing cumulative risk factors related to educational disadvantage. As the reader will be aware, educational disadvantage is closely linked with school exclusion. Furthermore, Fazel, Garcia and Stein (2016) have identified that this group have significant difficulties in accessing support with Mental Health needs.

There is very limited literature on LGBT+ experiences of school exclusion. In a review of recent available studies related to this inclusion group, the legacy of the era of Section 28 was still apparent. Section 28 was a part of the 1988 Local Government Act in England, which stated that local authorities and schools should not 'promote the teaching in any maintained school of the acceptability of homosexuality as a pretended family relationship' and had the impact of making the discussion of sexuality and gender in schools a source of anxiety and risk for practitioners. Section 28 was repealed in 2000 in Scotland and 2003 in the rest of the UK. This change in policy appeared to prompt a surge in writing about homonegative experiences in schools and the impact on inclusion (Rivers, 2000; D'Augelli, 2002; Rivers and Carragher, 2003) which has now reduced as a focus of research. Current academic studies around LGBT+ children and young people's school experience is focused heavily on bullying (Kull *et al.*, 2016; Russel *et al.*, 2016). Whilst we acknowledge that bullying in all forms is distasteful and undesirable, it could be considered that this is the wrong focus for studies which seek to promote inclusion. Bullying is a behaviour which is the manifestation or symptom of a deeper issue related to power and a negative attitude to difference. The valuing of difference, as a key tenet of inclusive education, may be a more urgent area of study related to LGBT+ children and young people, given that gender dysphoria continues to be viewed by some medical professionals as a mental health disorder and that children and young people with gender dysphoria are more likely to experience mental health challenges linked to the social stigma and isolation they experience (Ristori *et al.*, 2018). We look forward to the forthcoming publication of Dellenty, S. (2019) 'Celebrating Difference: A whole school approach to LGBT+inclusion' which we hope will provide practitioners with further resources to develop their inclusive practice.

An inclusive attitude

The latter chapters of this book have focused on providing approaches for practitioners in school to consider as ways of developing inclusive practice in their setting. The majority of these approaches are outward facing ones taken by practitioners, which make changes to the interactions which occur in the school setting. We have not directly considered curriculum design as a way of developing inclusive practice, as this is a wider topic and is addressed by other authors (for example, Nind, 2005; Harris and Luff, 2017 and the Routledge, 'Addressing SEND in the Curriculum' series). However, much thinking about curriculum focuses in the planned and delivered curriculum and the authors consider that further consideration may need to be given to the experienced curriculum and in particular the inclusivity of the context of the practitioners in the school. Whilst this is partially addressed in Part III, Chapter 12, which considers the importance of staff or practitioner wellbeing, a further important consideration is the demographic of the practitioners and the need to consider the diversity which is represented within the staff. If the make-up of the school staff reflects diversity through having members from diverse inclusion groups, this can be considered to explicitly model the valuing of diversity. For example, the consideration of demands for there to be a greater number of 'out' members of the LGBT+ community amongst school staff (Schools Out UK, 2017) is an important consideration for schools. Such considerations may need to be addressed within the context of a range of inclusion groups.

The authors also believe that it is important to acknowledge the challenges experienced by school practitioners within the current policy and funding context. The recent WorthLess campaign group of over 7000 school headteachers, a section of professionals not normally known for their political militancy, has highlighted the significant challenges schools are facing as a result of funding cuts. Total school spending per pupil has fallen by approximately 8 per cent between 2009–10 and 2017–18 (Institute for Fiscal Studies, 2018). Within this context the capacity for the development of inclusive approaches in school practice can be extremely challenging (European Agency for Special Needs and Inclusive Education, 2016).

A further challenge for practitioners who seek to develop more inclusive practice is the nature of the educational system itself. The history of our education system and the attitudes of ableism, competitiveness and the reduction in the importance of community are fore-fronted in Slee's (2018, p. 1) statement, 'Exclusion resides deep in the bones of education'.

Given the challenges of policy, funding and history, it is maybe not surprising that Haug (2016) states that the challenges of constructing an inclusive school system have not yet been overcome in any country. The context of the education system in England is one where the dominant climate and ethos can be seen to be at odds with an inclusive approach, with a normative outlook dominated by a standards agenda and an accountability framework (Middleton, 2019). This landscape is confused by contrasting agendas, policies and legislative aims, which build on positive moves towards inclusion or aspects of inclusive education. For example, there are positive intentions behind the SEND Code of Practice (DfE, 2015) to provide greater agency for children, young people and their families. However, whilst there may be positive or well-meaning intentions behind particular policy and legislative developments, in order for inclusive education systems to be enabled, a deep and fundamental change is needed in the education system encompassing financing, administration, design, teaching and monitoring (Cisternas Reyes cited in United Nation News, 2016).

This difficult landscape leaves the practitioner with a challenging choice. The practitioner seeking to develop inclusive educational practice can choose to follow the system's curricula, policies and guidance, focusing on the positive elements which align with inclusive education, and look forward to increasing developments which prompt the move onwards towards a more inclusive system. The alternative choice for the practitioner is to look towards themselves as agents of change within the system, being guided by their own ethos and beliefs. At times the results of this choice can be mirrored. For example, in Part III, Chapter 7 we propose nurture groups as an inclusive approach, whilst it can also be seen that Ofsted, who are key agents within the education system and are bound up with normative standards and competitiveness within the education system, also advocate the use of nurture groups as a way of reducing school exclusion (Ofsted, 2011).

We propose that, given the complex and sometimes contradictory nature of the education system, policies and regulations (Middleton, 2019), the practitioner needs to be led by their own ethos and values, making judgements based upon the approach which is right for their learners, within the context of their education community. We believe that education practitioners are able to lead the way in discovering and creating the inclusive spaces within the system, thereby developing inclusive education practices, from which society can learn and develop (Coles and Hancock, 2002). When the practitioner is engaged in thinking morally about the six dimensions of inclusion, as defined in Part II, Chapter 2, we believe that their passion and values and a desire for a 'more just and equal society' (UNESCO, 2009, p. 8) will be enhanced and they will be prepared to make the choice to develop the inclusive spaces in their practice and harness some of the approaches suggested in the previous chapters. In taking steps towards inclusive practices in their own work with children and young people, practitioners develop an approach or attitude. This attitude, informed by inclusive values and passion, draws on empathy, compassion, and a desire for learning. It impacts on the emotional or affective plane and supports the development of inclusive spaces. Fundamental to this inclusive attitude is the humanistic belief in the positiveness of others and the importance of relationships. It is these positive inclusive relationships which underpin the effectiveness of the approaches identified in this book and which are key to the success of inclusive education (Florian, Black-Hawkins and Rouse, 2017). In turn, this positive attitude to the value of others, enhanced rather than impaired by their diversity, is likely to improve their pedagogical practice with diverse learners. In a long-term project studying

SEN teaching in Canada, Jordan, Schwartz and McGhie-Richmond (2009) identified that teachers who attributed a blame for barriers to learning within the child or young person, focusing on their impairment or negative difference, had a significantly lower self-efficacy for teaching learners identified with SEN, than those who attributed blame outside the individual learner. Intertwined with this positive approach to the importance of diversity in learning within the inclusive attitude is the importance of the reflective or critical practitioner. When the practitioner welcomes diversity and empowerment of the learner, their own attitude of openness to new and creative practice will be enhanced, as they are more likely to see themselves as a learner alongside their own pupils and, in turn, be better placed to prompt and work with a changing educational approach (Claxton, 2001; Watkins and Donnelly, 2012).

Inclusive education is not a destination, but is a dynamic and evolving process (Booth and Ainscow, 2002), a journey towards the embodying of a set of values and beliefs which are enacted within individual contexts, encompassing changing communities and time which does not stand still. This book does not provide a recipe for practitioners to follow in order to adopt a model of 'good inclusive practice'. The aim of this book is to provide practitioners with an enhanced understanding of the context and theories relating to inclusion and school exclusion and provide a toolbox of approaches from which to select, try, adapt and evaluate as creative ways to promote learning for all through diverse experiences, learning from difference (Ainscow, 2005), and empowering learners to access their rights in a socially just way.

References

Ainscow, M. (2005) 'Developing inclusive education systems: What are the levers for change?'. *Journal of Educational Change*, 6(2), pp. 109–124.

Armstrong Brown, S. and White, R. (2017) *Adoption UK'S Schools & Exclusions Report November 2017*. Available at: www.adoptionuk.org/faqs/adoption-uks-schools-exclusions-report (accessed 7 March 2019).

Booth, T. and Ainscow, M. (2002) *Index for Inclusion: Developing Learning and Participation in Schools*. Revised Edition. Bristol: CSIE.

Claxton, G. (2001) *Wise Up: Learning to Live the Learning Life*. Stafford: Network Educational Press.

Coles, C. and Hancock, R. (2002) *The Inclusion Quality Mark*. Croydon: Public Sector Matters.

D'augelli, A.R. (2002) 'Mental health problems among lesbian, gay, and bisexual youths ages 14 to 21'. *Clinical Child Psychology and Psychiatry*, 7(3), pp. 433–456.

Dellenty, S. (2019 in publication) *Celebrating Difference: A Whole School Approach to LGBT+Inclusion*. London: Bloomsbury Publishers.

DfE. (2015) *Special Educational Needs and Disability Code of Practice: 0 to 25 Years: Statutory Guidance for Organisations Which Work With and Support Children and Young People Who Have Special Educational Needs or Disabilities*. DFE-00205–2013. London: DfES.

DfE. (2018) *Permanent and Fixed-period Exclusions in England: 2016 to 2017*. Available at: www. ethnicity-facts-figures.service.gov.uk/education-skills-and-training/absence-and-exclusions/pupil-exclusions/latest (accessed 9 March 2019).

European Agency for Special Needs and Inclusive Education. (2016) *Financing of Inclusive Education: Background Information Report*. Odense, Denmark: European Agency for Special Needs and Inclusive Education.

Fazel, M., Garcia, J. and Stein, A. (2016) 'The right location? Experiences of refugee adolescents seen by school-based mental health services'. *Clinical Child Psychology and Psychiatry*, 21(3), pp. 368–380.

Florian, L., Black-Hawkins, K. and Rouse, M. (2017) *Achievement and Inclusion in Schools*. Second Edition. London: Routledge.

Ford, T., Parker, C., Salim, J., Goodman, R., Logan, S. and Henley, W. (2018) 'The relationship between exclusion from school and mental health: A secondary analysis of the British child and adolescent mental health surveys 2004 and 2007'. *Psychological Medicine*, 48(4), pp. 629–641.

Gill, K., Quilter-Pinner, H. and Swift, D. (2017) *Making the Difference Breaking the Link Between School Exclusion and Social Exclusion*. Institute for Public Policy Research. Available at: www.ippr.org/publications/making-the-difference (accessed 9 March 2019).

Graham, H.R., Minhas, R.S. and Paxton, G. (2016) 'Learning problems in children of refugee background: A systematic review'. *Pediatrics*, 137(6), e20153994.

Harris, R. and Luff, I. (2017) *Addressing Special Educational Needs and Disability in the Curriculum*. Second Edition. Milton: Taylor and Francis (Addressing SEND in the Curriculum).

Haug, P. (2016) 'Understanding inclusive education: Ideals and reality'. *Scandinavian Journal of Disability Research*, 19(3), pp. 206–217.

Institute for Fiscal Studies. (2018) *2018 Annual Report on Education Spending in England*. Available at: www.ifs.org.uk/publications/13306 (accessed 10 March 2019).

Jordan, A., Schwartz, E. and McGhie-Richmond, D. (2009) 'Preparing teachers for inclusive classrooms'. *Teaching and Teacher Education*, 25, pp. 535–542.

Kull, R.M., Greytak, E.A., Kosciw, J.G. and Villenas, C. (2016) 'Effectiveness of school district antibullying policies in improving LGBT youths' school climate'. *Psychology of Sexual Orientation and Gender Diversity*, 3(4), p. 407.

Middleton, T. (2019) 'The Inclusive Teacher: Values and (com)passion in a wicked world'. *Practice*, In publication.

Nind, M. (2005) *Curriculum and Pedagogy in Inclusive Education: Values Into Practice*. London: RoutledgeFalmer.

Ofsted. (2011) *Supporting Children With Challenging Behaviour Through a Nurture Group Approach*. Manchester: Ofsted.

Ristori, J., Fisher, A.D., Castellini, G. and Maggi, M. (2018) 'Psychiatric aspects of gender dysphoria'. In E. Jannini and A. Siracusano (eds.), *Sexual Dysfunctions in Mentally Ill Patients: Trends in Andrology and Sexual Medicine*. Cambridge: Springer.

Rivers, I. (2000) 'Social exclusion, absenteeism and sexual minority youth'. *Support for Learning*, 15(1), pp. 13–18.

Rivers, I. and Carragher, D.J. (2003) 'Social-developmental factors affecting lesbian and gay youth: A review of cross-national research findings'. *Children & Society*, 17(5), pp. 374–385.

Russell, S.T., Day, J.K., Ioverno, S. and Toomey, R.B. (2016) 'Are school policies focused on sexual orientation and gender identity associated with less bullying? Teachers' perspectives'. *Journal of School Psychology*, 54, pp. 29–38.

Schools Out UK. (2017) *Home Page*. Available at: www.schools-out.org.uk/ (accessed 9 March 2019).

Slee, R. (2018) *Inclusive Education Isn't Dead, It Just Smells Funny*. Abingdon, Oxon: Routledge.

Sullivan, A.L. and Simonson, G.R. (2016) 'A systematic review of school-based social-emotional interventions for refugee and war-traumatized youth'. *Review of Educational Research*, 86(2), pp. 503–530.

UNESCO. (2009) *Policy Guidelines on Inclusion in Education*. Paris: UNESCO.

United Nation News. (2016) *Inclusive Education Vital for All, Including Persons With Disabilities*. Available at: https://news.un.org/en/story/2016/09/537952-inclusive-education-vital-all-including-persons-disabilities-un-rights-experts (accessed 8 March 2019).

Watkins, A. and Donnelly, V. (2012) 'Teacher education for inclusion in Europe – Challenges and opportunities'. In C. Forlin (ed.), *Future Directions for Inclusive Teacher Education: An International Perspective*. Abingdon: Routledge, pp. 192–202.

INDEX

Page numbers in italics indicate figures, in bold indicate tables.

Index

Index

"White Paper: Schools—achieving success" (2001) 6
whole class pedagogical approaches 18, 80, 131–132
whole school approach 169–170, 191, 212
working in partnership 95–96, 97–116, **202**; current context of support services 77; with external agencies 111–114; multi-agency working 111–112; with parents and carers 105–111; with pupils 101–104; team around the child 99, 106, 112; *see also* multi-agency; person-centred approaches; voice
World Bank 10–11

Youth Justice Board 55